Out of the Shadow

NUMBER NINE:
Foreign Relations and the Presidency
H. W. Brands, General Editor

Out of
the Shadow

*George H. W. Bush and
the End of the Cold War*

Christopher Maynard

TEXAS A&M UNIVERSITY PRESS
College Station

This paper meets the requirements of ANSI/NISO Z39.48–1992
(Permanence of Paper).
Binding materials have been chosen for durability.

Cover photo courtesy of the George Bush Presidential Library.

Library of Congress Cataloging-in-Publication Data

Maynard, Christopher, 1973–
    Out of the Shadow: George H.W. Bush and the end of the Cold War / Christopher
Maynard.—1st ed.
        p. cm.—(Foreign relations and the presidency ; no. 9)
        Includes bibliographical references and index.
        ISBN-13: 978-1-60344-039-4 (cloth : alk. paper)
        ISBN-10: 1-60344-039-9 (cloth : alk. paper)
        1. Bush, George, 1924–   2. Bush, George, 1924–   —Influence.   3. United
States—Foreign relations—1989-1993.   4. United States—Foreign relations—
Soviet Union.   5. Soviet Union—Foreign relations—United States.   6. Cold War.
7. National Security Council (U.S.)—History.   8. Germany—History—Unification,
1990.   9. Soviet Union—History—1985–1991.   10. Persian Gulf War, 1991.
I. Title.
E881.M29 2008
973.928092—dc22

                                                                    2007052620

For Carole

Contents

Preface

On the evening of November 9, 1989, thousands of East Germans and West Germans alike danced atop the Berlin Wall in celebration of the easing of border restrictions that had kept families apart for decades. Striking the wall with picks, shovels, or anything else they could find, men and women chipped at the wall, attempting to be a part of the moment. As the world watched the images on television, the electricity and jubilation of the moment seemed to jump off the screen. The Iron Curtain—so famously described by Winston Churchill more than forty-three years earlier—was crumbling; the Cold War was coming to an end.[1] In the White House that day, Pres. George Bush sat with National Security Advisor Brent Scowcroft in the study adjacent to the Oval Office and watched the live events on television. A short time later, Bush gave an impromptu press conference while seated at his desk. Speaking matter-of-factly and with little enthusiasm, Bush labeled the fall of the Berlin Wall as "a good development."[2] To the American public, Bush appeared distracted and disinterested. He seemed out of touch with the dramatic changes that they watched on television. At a time when he could have used a strong public performance to lead the nation in its celebration of the end of the Cold War, President Bush seemed to be asleep on the job. Unlike most observers, however, Bush knew that much diplomatic work still needed to be done before the Cold War could be concluded, and gloating about the fall of the Berlin Wall, as many of Bush's critics pressed him to do, would merely complicate matters. Certainly the images President Bush watched that day continue to be memorable to those who lived through this period of time when the Cold War was lurching to a final conclusion, but the Cold War did not end that November night: Germany was still divided, and Soviet troops still occupied Eastern Europe. President Bush would spend much of his administration working to resolve the still-tenuous situation.

The purpose of this book, which focuses solely on Bush administration policy dealing with the end of the Cold War, is to move toward a clearer understanding of that period in which the Cold War was resolved. It was during the Bush administration (1989–93) that the Berlin Wall fell, the Warsaw Pact dissolved, Germany was reunified, and the Soviet Union ceased to exist. A common misconception is that Bush's foreign policy achievements were merely an extension of Reagan's policies or, as some observers have suggested, clean-up diplomacy.[3] Bush did not, however, merely continue on the foreign policy path set by Reagan; he made a fundamental shift in foreign policy regarding the Soviet Union. This is not meant to argue that Bush ended the Cold War. No one leader can be credited with ending the Cold War; Ronald Reagan, Mikhail Gorbachev, George Bush, nor any other single leader had that much impact. Such an explanation distorts the end of the Cold War. It personalizes complex situations and processes and obscures the truth that the participants often had complicated motives and confused, often contradictory, objectives. But Reagan, Gorbachev, and Bush did influence when and how that end occurred with both foreign policy successes and mistakes. Members of those leaders' foreign-policymaking teams did not know what the outcome would be nor were they privy to archival information now available. They made their decisions and shaped policies with the same blinders that historians endured during the Cold War. Focusing on the outcome rather than the day-to-day process of foreign policymaking has led many Cold War historians and, indeed, the contemporary news media to stress the importance of *ideas* over *interests*. This has produced a distorted picture of the final years of the Cold War. According to this view, the participants were only important in regards to the ideas that they promoted. That is why Reagan and Gorbachev, who embraced strong ideological rhetoric, are seen as the major players and why Bush, who, in the words of his press secretary, "didn't give a damn about his public image," is seen as a non-factor.[4] This view discounts the type of practical diplomatic negotiations that led to the end of the division of Europe and neglects the fact that many decisions were made for purely political or economic reasons rather than because of ideology. This study is not meant to diminish the importance of ideology during this period but simply to underscore that ideology alone does not explain the end of the Cold War. As former president George Bush contends, "Clearly, the Cold War could not have been called dead as long as Eastern Europe was not free. Our approach was to encourage Gorbachev and the Soviet Union and to do all we could to facilitate the peaceful unification of Germany. Then, of course, when Kuwait was invaded by Iraq, there was a real opportunity to further constructive change by getting the Soviet Union to support us in the UN and, indeed, in the forthcoming battle to free Kuwait."[5]

Former National Security Advisor Brent Scowcroft agrees with President Bush: "The Reagan administration tends to think they ended the Cold War. I think the Cold War was not at all ended when Bush came into office.

Eastern Europe was still divided just like it was before. The Soviet army was still manning barricades and so on. No, it happened under President Bush, and it happened the way it did in considerable part because of his great skill at diplomacy about eliciting cooperation from people, both friends and opponents."[6]

Scowcroft is not arguing that Bush alone ended the Cold War. He is simply pointing to the fact that there was a great deal of uncertainty when President Bush took office that needed to be resolved before the Cold War could come to an end.[7] According to Scowcroft, the end of the Cold War was a process that benefited from both the presidency of Ronald Reagan and the presidency of George Bush: "What we needed was Reagan to restore American spirits and to have us stand up and stand up tall. But it took Bush to bring it [the Cold War] to an end."[8]

Marlin Fitzwater, who served as press secretary to both Reagan and Bush, agrees: "When Reagan came in . . . we were in the heat of the Cold War, and Reagan was *the* Cold Warrior. He knew how to fight communism. He had a strong ideology, a strong belief in America, and so he was a perfect president to take them on and say 'America's going to win this war.' And when President Bush came in, he had the international background and the diplomatic experience to then negotiate the new realities of an East-West relationship."[9]

In other words, both Reagan's grand symbolic gestures *and* Bush's foreign policy expertise were needed to end the Cold War. The Cold War was a process that only came to an end when there was a resolution of the ideological differences as well as the material interests of both sides. This study examines that process to determine how the Bush administration managed the end of the Cold War, helping it end not with a bang, but a peaceful whimper.[10]

Acknowledgments

I would like to thank all of the colleagues who read various versions of this book and provided constructive criticism. In particular, this work has been greatly enriched by David Culbert, whose overall direction of my graduate studies at Louisiana State University had a profound impact. H. W. Brands graciously read my manuscript, provided invaluable advice, and advocated the book on my behalf to Texas A&M University Press. He also chaired a panel that I was on at the 2004 annual meeting of the Society for Historians of American Foreign Relations. This panel provided excellent feedback for one section of my manuscript and helped me to solidify the direction that I took with the overall work.

Debbie Carter, Mary Finch, and John Laster of the George Bush Presidential Library were particularly helpful, and I owe them a debt of gratitude along with all those at the Bush Library who offered their assistance. I extend special thanks to the George Bush Library Foundation, who provided financial assistance for my research visits to College Station in the form of two Peter and Edith O'Donnell Grants. I am also grateful to Lisa Jones and other archivists at the Ronald Reagan Presidential Library for a pleasant and fruitful research experience. A faculty research grant from the University of North Alabama supplied the necessary funds for my research in California, and I would like to thank Vagn Hansen for his support and encouragement of faculty research.

This work was enriched by the contributions of many of the participants who served in the Reagan and Bush administrations. George H. W. Bush, Brent Scowcroft, James A. Baker III, Colin Powell, Marlin Fitzwater, and Jack F. Matlock Jr., gave so generously of their time for interviews for this study. John Robert Greene read an early draft of my manuscript and provided first-rate suggestions. He also kindly granted me access to interviews that he conducted for his fine study on the Bush presidency. Finally, I would like to thank my wife, Carole Medlin Maynard, who was instrumental in helping me finish this book.

Out of the Shadow

Chapter 1

The Primacy of the National Security Council

Beyond Containment in Europe

George Bush's capacity to be a successful world leader was not apparent to most when he took office in the spring of 1989. Although he entered the presidency being constantly compared and contrasted with his predecessor, Bush lacked Ronald Reagan's eloquence and adept use of the media. Consequently, he was lambasted by the press as Reagan's "lapdog" and labeled a "wimp." The press pushed Bush to be more Reaganesque, to establish themes to match policy goals and to use the bully pulpit to lead national debate, but Bush's continued refusal to make thematic addresses and create a "line of the day" for daily news cycles prompted journalists to characterize the Bush presidency as lacking an agenda. One difficulty that the Bush staff encountered in attempts to create a positive media image originated from the fact that Bush did not like being "handled." Unlike Reagan, who would meticulously memorize entire speeches written by his advisors, Bush rarely stayed faithful to a prepared text, preferring to use it as an outline from which he would ad lib. His improvisation provided ample room for mistakes as well as unfocused messages that did not make clear the administration's agenda. Too much access compounded the problem: Bush held more than 280 twenty-minute press conferences open to questions on any subject, which meant that he was more accessible to the media than any president before him, yet he has been viewed as failing miserably in his relations with the press, especially when compared to Reagan. The problem lay in how each man viewed the role of media. Bush felt that it was his obligation to meet with the press, a task to be endured, a task less important than governing, while Reagan relished the time he spent in front of audiences and the camera and utilized the media to promote a positive image of himself and his policies. Reagan's success with the media and Bush's failure have produced a misconception about the success and failure of each president's policies, especially foreign policy, where most Americans' opinions are based on information filtered through the media.

Part of Bush's problem with the media was of his own making. During his term as vice president, Bush refused to disagree publicly with President Reagan, even during the Iran-Contra affair, but this quiet loyalty did not allow Bush to establish a strong image that was distinct and independent of Reagan. His weak image intensified during the 1988 election when Bush billed himself as the candidate of continuity, as the vice president who had faithfully served an enormously popular president and who pledged to continue in Reagan's footsteps. Indeed Bush won the election of 1988 largely on the strength of Reagan's popularity, along with negative campaign ads attacking his inept Democratic opponent, Michael Dukakis. The campaign rhetoric, however, did more than just win Bush the election: it shaped how the public, and many historians, viewed these years. Thus, the period is usually referred to as simply the "Reagan-Bush years," indicating that Bush's term can best be explained as Reagan's third term. Although there is some validity to such attempts at periodization, too often scholars gloss over the differences between President Reagan's and President Bush's approach to foreign policy, particularly toward the Soviet Union. This is partly a result of the misconception that the Cold War was basically over by the end of the Reagan administration and that Bush merely signed agreements Reagan had already negotiated, an explanation that ignores the instability of the Soviet Union, as well as the potentially explosive situation in Central and Eastern Europe that still existed when Reagan left office.

Reagan's policy of peace through strength had all but guaranteed that the Cold War would come to an end because the Soviets simply no longer had the resources to match the military build-up of the United States. From its highpoint in the 1950s, the Soviet gross national product (GNP) had dropped steadily, with CIA estimates placing the annual average rates of growth of Soviet GNP at 4.8 percent in 1961–65, 3.0 percent in 1971–75, and 1.8 percent in 1981–85.[1] The Soviet GNP in 1980 simply could not compete with the GNP of the United States.[2] When Reagan unveiled the plan for his expensive Strategic Defense Initiative (SDI), the Soviets knew that their economy could not maintain the arms race for much longer. Even though

Reagan had promised to share SDI technology and even offered the Soviets "joint management of global defenses," the Soviet leadership was not prepared to place that much trust in their Cold War adversary.[3] According to Marlin Fitzwater, the summit meetings between Reagan and Gorbachev would always end with a Soviet plea to drop SDI, because the Soviet leadership knew that they could not afford to match it and reasoned that it was time to "get serious" with regards to nuclear arms reduction. President Bush "kept the pressure on" when he began meeting with Gorbachev and the focus did not change, with the Soviets still determined to convince the United States to abandon SDI.[4] Brent Scowcroft agrees with the fact that the Soviets simply could not afford to match SDI: "I think they were afraid of SDI . . . not so much because they thought it would work, but that if we went down that path, they would have to follow and it was too expensive for them. They didn't have the resources."[5]

If SDI had ever become operational, the Soviet defense budget would have had the added pressure of producing even more rockets and warheads. Perhaps even more troubling for the Soviets were the U.S. advancements in lasers, optics, supercomputers, guidance systems, and navigation.[6] Despite the Reagan administration's insistence that SDI represented "the first real opportunity to halt the arms race," one Russian spokesman warned of "a whole new arms race at a much higher technological level."[7] Ultimately, the Soviet Union could not afford to maintain the high level of defense spending that was bankrupting the country and, as Gorbachev was beginning to realize, in order to fund domestic economic reforms, the "gilded age" of Soviet military power needed to end. By the time Reagan left office, the question for U.S. policymakers had changed from how does democracy defeat communism to how does democracy help communism go away peacefully.

It was left to the Bush administration to manage the end of the Cold War so that it ended with a whimper and not a bang.[8] They were able to accomplish this in part by making a fundamental change in the foreign policy approach that had been used by the Reagan administration. During arms control negotiations, Reagan had placed the emphasis on numbers—reducing numbers by eliminating certain kinds of weapons, an approach that President Bush's national security advisor Brent Scowcroft disagreed with. Scowcroft had viewed President Reagan's rush toward disarmament as "a mighty dubious objective for grown-ups in this business" and believed that simply getting rid of certain kinds of weapons did not achieve the overall goal of arms control, which was to improve stability.[9] Instead, Scowcroft wanted to reduce the chances that in a crisis either side would resort to the use of nuclear weapons for fear of some vulnerability in the nuclear arsenal. Simply shifting the numbers would not necessarily lessen the possibility of nuclear threat. Negotiations between the United States and the Soviet Union historically had centered on arms control, but General Scowcroft intended to shift the focus to Eastern Europe. He wanted to take advantage of the ferment that was growing in Eastern Europe, especially in Poland, to force the Soviet army out of that area, or at least reduce their presence so that Eastern Europeans could develop in a progressive way. This meant putting arms control on the back burner until the situation in Eastern Europe unfolded, a move that would require a fundamental change in U.S. foreign policy toward the Soviet Union.[10] For the president who had promised to continue on the course set by his predecessor, this had the potential for drawing criticism, especially from the right-wing establishment who had always doubted Bush's credentials as a conservative. Rather than make an abrupt change, President Bush conducted a lengthy foreign policy review at the beginning of his term in office, a process that would allow him to make his own imprint on the nation's foreign policy and make sure that there had not been an overly aggressive effort made by the Reagan administration to conclude a deal with the Soviets before time ran out and they had to leave office.[11]

Hostile Takeover

Despite the public image of Bush continuing the Reagan presidency, it was clear in retrospect that Bush had very different policies in mind for his presidency. These differences became evident during the transition period, a transition that at times resembled one that normally occurs when one party transfers power to another. As Michael Beschloss and Strobe Talbott point out, Bush and his inner circle quickly established the fact that "a new man was in charge" by letting go of hundreds of Reagan appointees and reminding the new staff, as incoming Secretary of State James Baker told his aides, "this is *not* a friendly takeover."[12] On November 10, 1988, all presidential appointees were asked to submit their resignations "in order to give the President-elect Bush maximum flexibility in the staffing of his administration," and, on December 30, the call for resignations was expanded to all non-career SES and Schedule C appointees. All but those who were traditionally considered the career staff of the White House were informed that they would no longer be on the payroll after February 3, 1989.[13] The hostile takeover was not apparent in the composition of the cabinet, where seven Reagan holdovers continued either in the same position or in another capacity. While the public may have looked at these appointments as a sign that Bush would continue Reagan's policies, one historian notes that "those who judge (or judged) the Bush administration by the makeup of its cabinet know little about its relative power in the modern presidency. In short, it has none."[14] It is clear in retrospect that the real policy decisions would be made in the White House, and it was on the White House staff level that Bush made a significant break from the Reagan team, cleaning house and, in many cases, appointing outspoken critics of the Reagan administration's policies. This can most plainly be seen in Bush's appointment of Brent Scowcroft as national security advisor, and, since foreign policy concerns would dominate the Bush administration, it was here that the Bush team made its largest separation from the Reagan agenda.[15]

The National Security Council

The formulation of foreign policy in the Bush administration centered on the National Security Council, an inner circle of men that had the complete confidence of President Bush.[16] Bush's NSC was markedly different from the one that had existed during the Reagan presidency in that Reagan's foreign policy advisors were full of suspicion and mutual mistrust, in the words of James Baker, "a witches' brew of intrigue, elbows, egos, and separate agendas."[17] Baker claims not to "remember any extended period of time when someone in the National Security cluster wasn't at someone else's throat."[18] The fact that Ronald Reagan went through six national security advisors during the eight years that he was in office indicates that something was wrong, and Colin Powell, who served as Reagan's sixth national security advisor, described Reagan's National Security Council as "rudderless, drifting, demoralized."[19] That flaw started in Reagan's first year as president when, in an effort to end the rivalry that had existed between the NSC and the Department of State during the Carter administration, Ronald Reagan decided to downgrade the post of national security advisor. To facilitate this objective, National Security Advisor Richard Allen's office was placed under the supervision of Presidential Counselor Edwin Meese III, thus taking away the direct access to the president that the national security advisor position had enjoyed since 1959 when the NSC was created.[20] Reagan drove home the point in subsequent public statements by stressing that his secretary of state was his "primary advisor on foreign affairs, and in that capacity, he is the chief formulator and spokesman for foreign policy for this administration."[21] Reagan made clear that the State Department would handle foreign affairs decisions in his administration while the National Security Administration would merely be responsible for the "integration" of the policies proposed by the State Department. Further changes in the NSC were made at a February 25, 1981, meeting, which established three Senior Interdepartmental Groups (SIGs), chaired by the secretary of state, the secretary of defense, and the director of the Central Intelligence Agency, respectively. Each SIG would deal with specific issues through a series of assistant secretary-level Interdepartmental Groups (IGs). That same year Reagan went on to establish the Special Situation Group (SSG) and the National Security Planning Group (NSPG). It seemed that policy would be formulated anywhere but in formal meetings of the NSC, and Reagan's first national security advisor resigned within a year. The situation did not improve as the Reagan administration went on to form an additional twenty-two SIGs and fifty-five IGs, which allowed NSC officials such as Col. Oliver North to establish their own sub-domains. The role of the NSA became more prominent during the tenures of William Clark and Robert McFarlane, but too many people played activist roles in the management of daily U.S. foreign relations problems, with the lack of cooperation becoming evident to the public during the Iran-Contra affair and the subsequent appointment of the Tower Board that made recommendations for the reform of the NSC. During that investigation, Congress found that subordinates would sometimes ignore the wishes of the president and pursue their own policy schemes. Ironically, Bush would appoint to his National Security Council two men, John Tower and Brent Scowcroft, who had served on the Tower Board that investigated Reagan's NSC during the Iran-Contra affair. The Tower Board recommended that the size of the NSC staff be reduced, a legal counsel be appointed, and that the Crisis Pre-Planning Group be replaced with a Policy Review Committee. The NSC largely withdrew from its operational roles while the board's recommendations were implemented and maintained a low profile for the rest of Reagan's administration. National Security Advisor Frank Carlucci and his successor Colin Powell would use the time to implement many of the changes suggested by the Tower Board. As Colin Powell recalls, he and Carlucci "restored a sense of process and discipline to the National Security Council and its functioning" that "continued into and through the Bush administration."[22] By the start of the Bush administration, the changes in the NSC would once again allow it to play a constructive role in policymaking without fear of the improprieties experienced during the Iran-Contra affair, and it would be one of the lead members of the Tower Board that Bush would entrust to complete the changes in the NSC.

At the center of Bush's foreign-policymaking team was his national security advisor, Brent Scowcroft, a retired air force lieutenant general. Scowcroft had spent much of his time in the air force both studying and teaching international relations; his credentials included a Ph.D. from Columbia University, as well as teaching stints at West Point, the U.S. Air Force Academy, and the Naval War College. He had worked for the Department of Defense, served as deputy national security advisor under Henry Kissinger during the Nixon administration, and succeeded Kissinger as President Ford's national security advisor. After 1976, Scowcroft worked for Kissinger Associates as an international consultant, and, during the Reagan administration, Scowcroft served on various committees, including the Tower Board that was formed in 1986 to investigate the Iran-Contra affair. Although he had many close friends in the Reagan administration, including the vice president, Scowcroft had privately been one of the fiercest critics of Reagan's foreign and military policy. He felt that Reagan's initial hard-line approach was foolish and that his subsequent blind embrace of Gorbachev was naïve. Scowcroft especially objected to Reagan's policy on nuclear deterrence, terming Reagan's 1986 Reykjavik proposal to eliminate all ballistic missiles as "insane."[23] Bush's selection of Scowcroft sent a clear message to Washington insiders that he intended to change the direction of defense and foreign policy. Scowcroft's style also suited Bush's preference for staying out of the limelight and working quietly behind the scenes. Scowcroft's low-profile, self-effacing approach won Bush's complete trust, as did the fact that Scowcroft "worked the longest hours of anyone in the White House."[24] That was the type of loyal dedication that Bush prized above all other traits and was indicative of the close relationship the two men developed, going back to 1972. One of the first people that Bush asked to join his administration, Scowcroft had been considered to serve as the secretary of defense or possibly director of the CIA; however, Bush felt that Scowcroft's knowledge of foreign policy matters could best be utilized as national security advisor.[25] Bush's selection of Scowcroft would also "send a signal to my cabinet and to outside observers that the NSC's function was to be critical in the decision-making process."[26] It was clear that Bush intended to rely on the NSC, and Scowcroft, more than anyone else, would prove to be the chief architect of the foreign policy approach of the Bush administration. He answered directly to the president and always made sure that a third person was present to make a record of everything that was discussed and agreed upon, something that was not always the case with the Reagan administration. Ably assisting Scowcroft was his deputy, Robert Gates, a former deputy director of the CIA and Soviet specialist who, along with Scowcroft, were jokingly labeled the "Siamese twins of the White House" by State Department officials. As explained in the *New York Times,* the self-effacing Scowcroft and the near-invisible Gates

Figure 1. George Bush, Brent Scowcroft, and James Baker would prove to be the chief architects of Bush's foreign policy. *Courtesy of the George Bush Presidential Library*

provided an almost seamless working duo: "One runs at midnight and falls asleep in Cabinet meetings. The other jogs at dawn and stays up late reading intelligence on the Soviet Union. One jokes with the President and stays close to his side. The other squires the paperwork and keeps watch on other agencies from the Situation Room in the White House basement. In an Administration where secrecy and loyalty are prime virtues, Brent Scowcroft, the President's national security adviser, and Robert M. Gates, his deputy, are the most virtuous."[27] Even critics of the administration conceded that the NSC ran more smoothly under Scowcroft.

Scowcroft was joined on the National Security Council by Bush's campaign manager, James Baker, who had been offered the position of secretary of state two days prior to the 1988 election (fig. 1). Baker was one of Bush's oldest friends, going back to his pre-political days in Texas, where the two met in 1959 at a cookout when a mutual friend suggested that they become tennis partners at the Houston Country Club. The two men went on to win two club championships and form a lifelong friendship. After Baker's first wife died of cancer in 1970, it was Bush who was responsible for getting Baker interested in politics by involving him in his 1970 Senate campaign, and it was Bush in 1975 who helped get Baker his first public job when he persuaded President Ford to appoint Baker as under secretary of commerce. Baker had a large ego and could be abrasive if he felt that his time was being wasted; as Baker has admitted, he "did not suffer fools gladly."[28] Baker's critics have characterized him as a consummate pragmatist and tough politician. His years as a successful lawyer, however, allowed him to operate in a conciliatory manner when he wanted to gain an edge over someone. When he adopted this nonconfrontational technique, he could cleverly guide, or persuade, people to "choose" the option that he had intended all along. This type of strategy earned him the nickname "the Velvet Hammer" and allowed him to refrain from making too many enemies. It was a technique that he used while running Bush's campaigns and one that would serve him well when dealing with foreign leaders. All in all, Baker was tough, very competitive, a strong negotiator, and someone Bush could count on to state how he felt directly and forcefully, even when it was not the advice that Bush wanted to hear. Baker recalls that he often was the recipient of one of Bush's favorite jabs: "If you're so smart, why am I vice president [or president] and you're not?"[29] This usually indicated to Baker that Bush was cutting short their discussion because he did not like the advice he was offered. There were many times when the two men disagreed and became angry with one another, but neither man would voice his displeasure publicly. In the Bush administration, friendship and loyalty went hand in hand. That loyalty went with Baker as he assumed his new position at the State Department. In an interview with *Time* magazine following his appointment, Baker stressed that he intended to be "the president's man at the State Department, not the State Department's man at the White House."[30] Baker was determined to make it clear that President Bush made foreign policy, not the Foreign Service.

Dick Cheney became secretary of defense after John Tower's nomination was derailed by allegations of alcohol abuse. Cheney was a close friend of Scowcroft and shared his pragmatic, no-nonsense work ethic and lack of ego. His graduate degree in political science, stint as President Ford's White House chief of staff, and six terms in Congress were valuable assets. While chief of staff, Cheney routinely attended National Security Council meetings, and, at the time of his appointment, Cheney was serving as the senior Republican on the Budget Subcommittee of the Intelligence Committee, which authorized the activities of all intelligence programs. He had, therefore, a depth of understanding in very specific areas that come within the general jurisdiction of the Department of Defense and national security in general.[31] His greatest asset, however, was his friendship with key members of the Bush administration. According to Cheney, the close working relationship that Bush, Scowcroft, Baker, and Cheney had cultivated during the Ford administration ensured that the national security apparatus would function smoothly: "I think one of the strong features of the Bush National Security team was that we did all know each other, we'd worked [together] before, we trusted each other, you didn't have any of the kind of backbiting that is characterized in a lot of other administrations."[32]

Friction was handled privately, a process that was established early on in the administration as Baker was preparing for his first visit to Moscow in May 1989. Just prior to this trip, on April 29, Dick Cheney agreed to a CNN interview, during which he surmised that Gorbachev's push for perestroika would "ultimately fail." For the secretary of defense to be publicly predicting Gorbachev's failure would certainly have cast a shadow over Baker's trip to Moscow. Cheney called Baker and agreed with him that he had said something that was better left unsaid. Baker claims that it was the only major disagreement with Cheney involving turf during the entire administration.[33]

The role of the chairman of the Joint Chiefs of Staff had gone through major changes during the Reagan administration when the Defense Reorganization Act of 1986 provided the chairman of the JCS with real power.[34] Since its creation in 1949, the power of the chairman was limited to presenting the secretary of defense and the president with the watered-down consensus recommendations of the chiefs. As head of his own service, each chief had a separate agenda and a unique perspective of events, which meant that decision papers from the JCS tended to be guided by the least-common-denominator that "every chief would accept but few secretaries of defense or presidents found useful."[35] The 1986 act designated the chairman of the JCS as the "principal military advisor" who could give his own advice directly to the secretary of defense and the president. Adm. William J. Crowe Jr. was chairman when the 1986 reorganization went into effect, and Bush allowed Admiral Crowe to finish out his term until he retired at the end of September 1989. When it came time to decide on a replacement, Cheney advised Bush to consider Colin Powell, who had served as Reagan's national security advisor during the last year of his administration. Powell was one of the few people from the Reagan administration whom Bush had considered for the new team, offering him the job of deputy secretary of state or director of the CIA.[36] Powell had declined both offers, deciding to return to the army as commander in chief of Forces Command, a position responsible for all army field forces based in the United States and carrying a promotion to four-star general, the army's highest rank. Later in the year when Bush made him the offer to vault to the highest uniformed military post in the land as chairman of the JCS, it was too good to pass up. Both men were concerned with the fact that Powell was the most junior of the fifteen four-star generals who were legally eligible for the chairmanship, but, despite Bush's and Powell's reservations, Cheney was convinced that Powell's tenure as national security advisor as well as his military command credits had uniquely prepared him to operate between the Pentagon and the White House with ease. Assuming the position of chairman on October 1, 1989, Powell became the first chairman to begin his tenure with the added benefit of Goldwater-Nichols authority. Powell no longer had to "speak with the corporate voice" or need "the chiefs' vote on what [his] advice should be"; he could speak in his "own right as principal military advisor," a change that Powell found "was of enormous help."[37] But, as Powell recalls, just as important was the confidence that his superiors had in his ideas. The fact that Bush and Cheney found his ideas "useful and relevant to the challenges they had is really what made it work."[38] The relationship between Powell and Cheney in particular would become quite strong and add to the cohesion of the National Security Council.

One of the few holdovers from the Reagan administration was William Webster, who was asked to continue his role as the director of the Central Intelligence Agency (DCI). Despite having no background in intelligence or foreign policy, Webster had been offered the job as DCI upon the death of William Casey and in the aftermath of the Iran-Contra affair. Labeled by *Newsweek* as "Washington's most successful Mr. Fixit," the Missouri lawyer and former federal judge had served as director of the Federal Bureau of Investigation from 1978 to 1987, helping to reverse the agency's image that had been blighted by the legacy of J. Edgar Hoover. As the new DCI, Webster ended the off-the-books covert operations that had been routinely organized by Casey. Prior to Webster's new guidelines, as then deputy director Robert Gates recalls, covert operations "was a very informal kind of process, [but] now they actually sit down and debate the issue. They talk about it; they go through a long checklist of questions."[39] He also dramatically improved the CIA's relationship with Congress, something that had been virtually ignored by Casey. But Webster's main priority was to make a firm distinction between intelligence and policymaking, a line that Casey, as the first director of Central Intelligence to be named a member of the cabinet, had all but obliterated. Webster saw a problem with the director of Central Intelligence being part of the decision-making process because it "sent the wrong signal to people who are already suspicious that anything that came out of the agency would support the president's agenda if not the private agenda of the agency itself."[40] Refusing to be appointed to cabinet rank, Judge Webster defined his role as informing and implementing policy, not making it. He did not want to spin or edit or predetermine analytical conclusions on intelligence that the CIA was able to develop. Webster felt an obligation to "maintain trust" with the president and Congress and warned people in the agency not to "get cozy" with political figures.[41] He even went so far as to say that it was none of his business what policymakers did with his intelligence estimates, preferring to make the relationship between the director and president "professional and not a political relationship."[42] This matched President Bush's concept of the role of the DCI, a position Bush had held himself. It was clear that the DCI would provide the president with intelligence information but otherwise have no role in policymaking decisions.

As vice president, Dan Quayle also served on the NSC. His interest in arms control involved him in many of the discussions of the NSC; however, his input was usually only considered when it, at least loosely, fell in line with the direction in which Bush was already leaning. In an administration dominated by people with far more experience in foreign affairs, Quayle was primarily involved in domestic policy and congressional maneuvering. Even he admits that his contribution to foreign policymaking during the Bush administration was marginal.[43] He was, however, a faithful observer to the decision-making process. Each morning he attended the president's daily national security briefing with Scowcroft and CIA briefers, then stayed for Bush's meeting with the chief of staff to set the agenda for the rest of the day. Quayle continued to favor programs from the Reagan era such as SDI, and he continued the strong anti-Soviet rhetoric that was prevalent during Reagan's first term. While this endeared Quayle to the right wing of the Republican Party, it made Bush's more moderate advisors wary of Quayle's input and, consequently, further diminished his contribution to foreign policymaking during the Bush administration. His many hard-line speeches, however, did help mollify the right wing of the Republican Party, who never really trusted Bush, and gave Bush some political cover to institute his own, more moderate, foreign-policy decisions. Quayle's speeches also allowed the Bush administration to be critical of the Soviet Union and congressional Democrats without the criticism coming directly from the president, who could then distance himself from the comments using an often-repeated line: "I haven't seen what he said, so I can't tell you whether he speaks for me. I speak for myself. He speaks for himself."[44]

Two final people who should be mentioned are John Sununu and Marlin Fitzwater. Sununu had been appointed by Bush as White House chief of staff largely as a payback of a political debt because Sununu had been instrumental in the New Hampshire primary and had strong appeal with conservatives. One historian has noted that Sununu also helped balance Bush's managerial style: "Tough, blunt to a fault, Sununu provided the nasty edge to Bush's 'kindler, gentler' persona."[45] It is no surprise that Sununu's personality led him to be "reviled by virtually everyone in Bush's inner circle, and even held at arm's length by the president."[46] Regardless of their personal differences, the former governor of New Hampshire worked with the president on most important issues and did contribute at times to the foreign policy team; however, according to President Bush, Sununu was "involved mainly in domestic policy."[47] Sununu himself understood that the essential service that he provided the Bush administration was to "tighten up the conservative network" and "get support on issues, keep the conservative wing of the party in all the states comfortable and happy."[48] Although not officially a part of the NSC, Marlin Fitzwater attended the NSC meetings, sitting quietly to one side. He had decided early in his job as White House press secretary that he needed to attend National Security Council meetings and other foreign policy discussions in order to absorb the nuances of foreign policy and the rationale for policy changes. Reagan had allowed him this unusual level of access, and Bush, somewhat reluctantly, agreed to the continuation of this practice. During his six years with Reagan and Bush, he was never asked to leave a meeting, and his presence paid off with his improved ability to explain to the public the actions taken by the NSC.[49]

Together, these men represented a very capable NSC that Bush would rely on during the dramatic events leading to the end of the Cold War. That does not mean, however, that the NSC collectively made the decisions concerning foreign policy. Although Cheney, Powell, Sununu, Quayle, and Robert Gates would have significant influence over wartime policy during the Persian Gulf War as part of the so-called "Gang of Eight," Bush, Scowcroft, and Baker were clearly the inner circle. Even then, as Brent Scowcroft recalls, President Bush always made the final decision.[50] Perhaps because of his extensive background in foreign affairs, Bush enjoyed debating issues with his advisors, asking question after question, provoking people to defend their views (fig. 2). This helped him clarify the issues in his own mind and allowed him to make prudent, well-reasoned decisions. According to Scowcroft, Bush rarely made major decisions "without a lot of back and forth with his advisors in order to set things in his own mind."[51] This was a markedly different process than that which occurred during the Reagan administration. As Colin Powell, who served on both President Reagan's and President Bush's NSC, recalls, Reagan "relied more on his advisors to shape issues for him" while Bush "got a little more deeply involved in the shaping

Figure 2. Bush enjoyed debating issues with his advisors, a process markedly different than under President Reagan. *Clockwise around the room:* Bush, Scowcroft, Deputy National Security Advisor Robert Gates, John Sununu, Dick Cheney, and Baker. *Courtesy of the George Bush Presidential Library*

of the issues" and "wanted to hear more of the in and out, up and down and dialogues over the various issues than President Reagan."[52] In the final analysis the NSC during the Bush administration was better qualified, was more stable, had more clearly defined roles, and played a greater part in the decision-making process than it had under President Reagan.

The National Security Review of the Soviet Union (NSR-3)

With its foreign-policymaking team in place, the new administration was ready to assess the improvements in the U.S.-Soviet relationship that occurred during Reagan's second term. Unlike Reagan, who was often seen as detached from the process, Bush's knowledge and interest in foreign affairs placed him at the center of policymaking discussions. Out of this close-knit group emerged a consensus characterized by both skepticism of Gorbachev and criticism of Reagan's anti-nuclear weapons enthusiasm. That skepticism of Gorbachev was apparent in Baker's opening statements at the first cabinet meeting when he provided his analysis of the U.S.-Soviet relationship inherited from the Reagan administration: "Realism demands prudence.

We must be prudent, cautious, and realistic."[53] Baker's statement was an echo of one Bush had made at the beginning of his presidential campaign: "There are those who say that all's well, all's fine, everything's changed over there. And maybe they're right and maybe they're wrong and history will tell; and as we wait for history to render judgment, a prudent skepticism is in order."[54]

It was clear that the Bush administration was not ready to proclaim its foreign policy agenda without conducting a lengthy assessment, which finally got underway weeks after the inauguration. It quickly became clear to those conducting the foreign policy review that it was a waste of time and manpower due to the fact that many of the senior bureaucrats throughout the government were holdovers from the Reagan administration and, as one frustrated official exclaimed, "If we had any better ideas than the ones we had, we would have used them."[55] The process drifted on for over three months, prompting Gorbachev and Shevardnadze to privately begin to refer to the policy review as the *pauza*—the pause. Even Bush officials, such as Robert Gates, began to refer to it as "the pause," and outside observers began criticizing Bush for not seizing what they felt was a clear course of action inherited from Reagan.[56] Jack Matlock, the U.S. ambassador to the Soviet Union, angrily explained to colleagues at the State Department, "Our marching orders are clear: 'Don't just do something, *stand there!'*"[57] Matlock argues that the Bush administration was slow in recognizing that Gorbachev understood that the Cold War was coming to an end and was ready to make concessions. According to this view, the Bush administration was "not prepared to maintain the process that had gathered momentum in 1987 and 1988."[58] Matlock also sees practical considerations for the pause, believing it was intended by the Bush administration to reassure the right wing of the Republican Party, many of whom thought Reagan "had gone soft his last year or so," and to allow time for a complete overhaul of the government in terms of personnel because Bush had "purged almost everybody from the top ranks of the government."[59] Matlock, therefore, criticizes the foreign policy review as taking place largely for political reasons rather than necessitated by foreign policy concerns, which he felt warranted decisive action. James Baker argued that these critics were missing the main goal behind the lengthy foreign policy review, which was to put "a Bush imprint on the nation's foreign policy" and make sure that there had not been "an overly aggressive effort to conclude a deal . . . just before time ran out with the Soviets."[60] According to Baker, "nothing had been concluded"; Bush needed "to satisfy himself that Gorbachev was for real"; the Soviets "were still supplying weapons through Cuba to Nicaragua"; there was still "the Angola problem"; the administration still had "major arms control negotiations going on, and many of them were stuck"; there were still "a lot of problems." Those problems could not be addressed adequately by simply continuing Reagan's emphasis on reducing numbers of weapons; Bush needed to know if Gorbachev was actually prepared to fulfill his promises for fundamental change. Baker felt that Gorbachev's strategy depended on his ability to split the alliance in Western Europe by appealing to Western publics rather than Western governments, a strategy that would also elevate Gorbachev's own authority and stature within the Soviet Union. The only way to keep Gorbachev from gaining the advantage over the United States, according to Baker, was to "attack his strategy head-on and to craft initiatives that he would feel obliged to embrace."[61] After making such bold promises, Gorbachev could not easily say no to any positive initiatives from the West.

When the formal report from the strategic review on the Soviet Union (NSR-3) was presented to Bush on March 14, 1989, it was a big disappointment. As Brent Scowcroft recalls, "The chief problem with the policy reviews is that they didn't produce anything. They were sort of bureaucratic exercises, and it's not surprising that the bureaucracy thought everything was going well because they had designed the policy. So mostly we got back studies that said do more of the same. That was the principal problem, and as a result, we just fashioned policies ourselves within the NSC and then debated them in the NSC."[62]

The "big picture" document did not provide the kind of specific initiatives that were needed, and Bush simply was not satisfied with the approach suggested by the review that was quickly labeled "status quo plus." He and his team wanted policies that could cope with the radical change that was taking place in Eastern Europe. The Bush administration wanted "to signal the bureaucracy, the Congress, the media, and the public at large that it was time for a reassessment of old assumptions."[63] The review did not further that goal. As Baker explains:

Unfortunately, we made two mistakes in the way we set up the review. First . . . the review was run by Reagan administration holdovers. Since they were responsible for the development and articulation of the previous policy, these officials naturally had a personal and psychological investment in the status quo. It was pretty much like asking an architect to review his own work; he might change a door here or a window there, but it would be unlikely for him to question the basic foundations on which the structure stood. Needless to say, these officials found themselves incapable of truly thinking things anew. Second, instead of asking for ideas and suggestions from sources without a vested interest in established policy, we asked the bureaucracy itself to produce the papers. This resulted in least-common-denominator thinking, with every potentially controversial—that is, interesting—idea left out in the name of bureaucratic consensus. In the end, what we received was mush.[64]

Another disappointing aspect concerning the review was that it was ambivalent about whether or not Gorbachev could succeed in his efforts at reform. The report on the Soviet Union had suggested that Gorbachev had about a "50–50 chance" at overcoming his domestic problems and succeeding with his reforms and that, because of the uncertainty surrounding Gorbachev's ability to maintain power, U.S. policy should not be designed to either help or hurt Gorbachev. This was unacceptable to Bush. He needed to know that Gorbachev was a true reformer and that he could trust that Gorbachev would be successful. Bush needed to determine if perestroika was a breathing space *(peredyshka)* designed to overcome the stagnation and technological backwardness of the Brezhnev era and to revive the Soviet economy for further competition with democracy and capitalism into the twenty-first century, or if it was a fundamental shift *(perekhod)* in Soviet policy ushering in a new era of socialism.[65] The review offered no clear answers to these questions.

The End of "the Pause"

Instead of using the disappointing review, Scowcroft ordered the NSC to work "instead with a 'think piece' on Gorbachev's policies and intentions, drafted by an NSC team headed by Condoleezza Rice."[66] Rice's memo laid out a four-part approach that Scowcroft used as a blueprint to guide the development of an overall strategy.[67] First, the administration needed to work on the domestic side to strengthen the image of America's foreign policy as driven by clear objectives. Second, it needed to send a clear signal that relations with its allies was the top priority as a unified NATO would be the key to arms reduction talks. Third, the United States should undertake initiatives, particularly economic assistance, with Eastern Europe, a potential weak link in the solidarity of the Soviet bloc. Fourth, the United States should promote regional stability around the world.[68] Rice's memo eventually led to the end of the pause, but, in the meantime, the Bush administration continued to be criticized for its foreign policy review.

Marlin Fitzwater was acutely aware of the problems created by the lengthy foreign policy review at the beginning of Bush's term in office. Realizing the impatience of the news media and the pressures of a daily news cycle, Fitzwater knew that when the administration promised a policy review, the media would "expect to have it tomorrow or the next day."[69] The Bush administration did start to see attacks from the press, with one article in the *Washington Post* even reporting that Ronald Reagan was telling close friends that he had an "uneasy" feeling about Bush's "foreign-policy indecisiveness" and felt that Bush was squandering a "clear advantage in dealing with the Soviets" by not "plunging ahead with negotiations" and that Bush's hesitancy was allowing Gorbachev to regain the momentum in public opinion.[70] Reagan had been trying to avoid public criticism of Bush because he did not want to undermine him; however, it was clear that Reagan was starting to lose his patience with his successor. George Kennan, creator of the policy of containment, also criticized Bush. While testifying before the Senate Foreign Relations Committee, Kennan blamed Bush for failing to respond to Soviet initiatives. Margaret Thatcher sent Bush a message complaining that the policy review was taking too long.[71] When Gorbachev announced on April 7, 1989, that he was halting production of weapons-grade uranium and closing two plutonium plants, reporters pressed Bush for a response, prompting Bush to snap back, "We'll be ready to react when we feel like reacting."[72] Bush knew that he had to announce his new policy goals soon, and he also knew that the members of the press, as well as the public at large, were expecting some kind of climax to the policy review. After eight years of Reagan, people had come to expect grand speeches and dramatic press conferences. Certainly something as important as a fundamental shift in policy toward the Soviet Union would have required a prime time televised report to the nation in the Reagan era, but, typical of Bush's press style, his staff put together a series of four speeches that read more like position papers, and that would constitute the conclusion of the review: one speech each on Eastern Europe, Western Europe, the Soviet Union, and defense and arms control. None were nationally televised.

Commencement Season

Originally, all four of the speeches were to be given at university commencement ceremonies, but a historic agreement forced the speech on Eastern European policy to be moved up to April, well before the commencement season began. The opportunity to launch the new policy of encouraging reform in the governments of Eastern and Central Europe suddenly developed with the successful completion of ongoing talks between the Polish government and Solidarity, the first independent trade union behind the Iron Curtain. That agreement, signed on April 5, 1989, legalized Solidarity, created a new and powerful office of president along with a new 100-seat senate, and allowed for the opposition to compete for seats in the senate as well as for 161 of the 460 existing seats in the Sejm, or parliament.[73] The event required a U.S. response. The Polish Communist Party had maintained a forty-five-year monopoly of power, and now Poland was apparently moving outside of communist control and would be allowed autonomous political development. It was exactly the sort of reform that the Bush administration intended to promote all over Eastern Europe and provided an ideal opening for Bush's speech. White House planners chose Hamtramck, Michigan, as a good place to hold a speech on Eastern Europe, because the Detroit enclave had an unusually high concentration of blue-collar families with ties to Poland, as well as the rest of Eastern Europe. Only two problems existed: the new policy still had not been clarified, and the speech itself still needed to be written. Even after the long policy review, it had not been decided what kind of assistance the United States could afford to offer Eastern Europe. In the post-Reagan era, the huge federal deficit forced budgets to be extremely tight, and Bush had promised that new programs would not be approved unless funds could be diverted from other parts of the budget. Bush, however, knew that his plan required economic aid if it had any chance of working and instructed his planners to find the money somewhere. Perhaps the more difficult problem was deciding who would write the speech. The controversy, one of the few recurring disputes within the foreign policy apparatus of the administration, was between the NSC, who felt that they should be responsible for national security policy speeches, and the president's speechwriters, who felt that they should write all of the president's speeches. In the end, the two sides reached an uneasy compromise; however, as Brent Scowcroft recalls, "It remained a major irritant, with a negative impact on the quality of many of the President's foreign policy speeches throughout the administration."[74] The speech was finally given by President Bush on April 17 at Hamtramck City Hall:

My friends, liberty is an idea whose time has come in Eastern Europe.
. . . The West can now be bold in proposing a vision of the European future: We dream of the day when there will be no barriers to the free movement of the peoples, goods and ideas. We dream of the day when Eastern European peoples will be free to choose their system of government and to vote for the party of their choice in regular, free,

contested elections. And we dream of the day when Eastern European countries will be free to choose their own peaceful course in the world, including closer ties with Western Europe. And we envision an Eastern Europe in which the Soviet Union has renounced military intervention as an instrument of its policy—on any pretext. We share an unwavering conviction that one day, all the peoples of Europe will live in freedom. . . . Let us recall the words of the Poles who struggled for independence: "For your freedom and ours." Let us support the peaceful evolution of democracy in Poland. The cause of liberty knows no limits; the friends of freedom, no borders.[75]

As part of the speech, Bush promised new U.S. trade and credits to countries experiencing economic and political reforms, thus establishing a link between help from the West and significant political and economic liberalization. The Bush team hoped that by offering economic rewards, they could keep reform going in Eastern Europe and hoped to eventually extend the link between aid and reform to the Soviet Union itself. Unfortunately, the speech at Hamtramck also showed that the United States did not have the resources to provide the level of rewards that could genuinely stimulate the troubled economies of Eastern Europe. The administration, however, had finally taken a position on Eastern Europe. As Brent Scowcroft recalls, "It was only a beginning, but it was a crucial move to try to capitalize on the signs of thaw in the communist states of Europe and to steer events in productive directions, but at a speed Moscow could accept. It was a serious effort to address the central questions of the Cold War."[76] The speech was covered in full detail by the press in Europe and the Soviet Union, but at home Bush's first foreign policy address received little attention. Administration officials would later admit that part of the problem was of their own making. The White House did very little advance work with the press, and many of the Washington reporters simply refused to believe that Bush would make any important announcements at Hamtramck. As Marlin Fitzwater explains, Bush was just looking for "some way to put it out" and say to the American people, "Here's what my policies are going to be."[77] As a result, the first speech, which should have been a dramatic beginning to Bush's plan for foreign policy, was an easily forgettable event. Bush's preference for compartmentalization and behind-the-scenes discussions kept the U.S. public uninformed during the first months of his presidency. Now, his failure to learn the nuances of image management, something his predecessor had mastered, left much of the United States still unsure about the direction he wanted to pursue.

Figure 3. Bush's commencement speech at Texas A&M University on May 12, 1989, called for a fundamental transformation of the U.S.-Soviet relationship that would move "beyond containment." *Courtesy of the George Bush Presidential Library*

The second speech would be equally unmemorable. The president's commencement speech at Texas A&M University in College Station on May 12, 1989, announced his strategy for future policy toward the Soviet Union (fig. 3). Drawn primarily from a decision memorandum written by the NSC staff and based on an earlier memo written by Condoleezza Rice, the speech called for a fundamental transformation of the U.S.-Soviet relationship. It recognized that the Soviet Union was in the midst of change, but it challenged the Soviet Union to demonstrate with actions their commitment to Gorbachev's principles. Bush's policy, called "beyond containment," was explained in National Security Directive 23:

> The character of the changes taking place in the Soviet Union leads to the possibility that a new era may now be upon us. We may be able to move beyond containment to a U.S. policy that actively promotes the integration of the Soviet Union into the existing international system. . . . But a new relationship with the international system can not simply be declared by Moscow. Nor can it be granted by others. It must be earned through the demilitarization of Soviet foreign policy and reinforced by behavior. . . . We are in a period of transition and

uncertainty. We will not react to reforms and changes in the Soviet Union that have not yet taken place, nor will we respond to every Soviet initiative. We will be vigilant, recognizing that the Soviet Union is still governed by authoritarian methods and that its powerful armed forces remain a threat to our security and that of our allies. But the United States will challenge the Soviet Union step by step, issue by issue and institution by institution to behave in accordance with the higher standards that the Soviet leadership itself has enunciated. . . . The goal of restructuring the relationship of the Soviet Union to the international system is an ambitious task. The responsibility for creating the conditions to move beyond containment to integrate the Soviet Union into the family of nations lies first and foremost with Moscow. But the United States will do its part, together with our allies, to challenge and test Soviet intentions and, while maintaining our strength, to work to place Soviet relations with the West on a firmer, more cooperative course than has heretofore been possible.[78]

The speech given by President Bush mirrored the language of the NSC memorandum: "The Soviet Union says that it seeks to make peace with the world, and criticizes its own postwar policies. These are words that we can only applaud. But a new relationship cannot simply be declared by Moscow, or bestowed by others. It must be earned. It must be earned because promises are never enough."[79] Bush challenged the Soviets to reduce their conventional forces, abandon the Brezhnev Doctrine, and allow self-determination for all of Eastern and Central Europe, in the process removing the Iron Curtain. He urged diplomatic solutions to regional conflicts, respect for human rights, and for the Soviet Union to work with the United States to solve drug-trafficking and environmental dangers. Bush also resurrected Open Skies, a plan first introduced during the Eisenhower administration that allowed unarmed aircraft from the United States and the Soviet Union to fly over the territory of the other country, which would open military activities to regular scrutiny. Many considered Open Skies as proof that the Bush administration could not come up with anything new. After months of delay, the Bush administration simply dusted off a plan thirty years old and, unlike Eisenhower in the 1950s, Bush could rely on satellites to do the type of surveillance work that could be done by unrestricted flights over the Soviet Union. Certainly, the Open Skies proposal was outdated, and even a protective Brent Scowcroft admitted that the proposal "smacked of gimmickry."[80] Bush thought that the Open Skies proposal would show that his administration was acting boldly. He was wrong.

The speech on Western Europe was delivered at Boston University on May 21, 1989. Bush had just spent a weekend at his home in Kennebunkport, Maine, with French president François Mitterrand. Reagan and Mitterrand had never been close, in part because Reagan had been greatly troubled by Mitterrand's promise in 1981 to place communists in his government. Mitterrand felt that Reagan was too obsessed with communism and that he wrongly categorized all communists as aggressive Stalinists. Bush hoped that the relaxed setting in Maine would allow him to get to know Mitterrand on a personal basis, and unquestionably the salt air and waves pounding against the rocks provided a setting that was very different from the protocol and formalities of the Reagan years. It was Bush's style of personal diplomacy at its very best, and it helped establish a deep level of trust and personal rapport between the two presidents. So it was that Mitterrand accompanied Bush to Boston and followed Bush's speech with one of his own. Afterwards, the two leaders gave a joint press conference. In his address, Bush delivered a warning to those who would rush blindly into Gorbachev's proposals for Europe:

We must never forget that twice in this century, American blood has been shed over conflicts that began in Europe. And we share the fervent desire of Europeans to relegate war forever to the province of distant memory. But that is why the Atlantic Alliance is so central to our foreign policy. And that's why America remains committed to the Alliance and the strategy which has preserved freedom in Europe. We must never forget that to keep the peace in Europe is to keep the peace for America. NATO's policy of flexible response keeps the United States linked to Europe and lets any would-be aggressors know that they will be met with any level of force needed to repel their attack and frustrate their designs. And our short-range deterrent forces based in Europe, and kept up-to-date, demonstrate that America's vital interests are bound inextricably to Western Europe, and that is an attacker can never gamble on a test of strength with just our conventional forces. Though hope is now running high for a more peaceful continent, the history of this century teaches Americans and Europeans to remain prepared. As we search for a peace that is enduring, I'm grateful for the steps that Mr. Gorbachev is taking. If the Soviets advance solid and constructive plans for peace, then we should give credit where credit is due. And we're seeing sweeping changes in the Soviet Union that show promise of enduring, of becoming ingrained. At the same time, in an era of extraordinary change, we have an obligation to temper optimism—and I am optimistic—with prudence. . . . It is clear that Soviet "new thinking" has not yet totally overcome the old.[81]

Stressing that the Soviet Union still kept a formidable military machine in Europe, Bush pledged his determination to negotiate a less militarized Europe:

> I believe in a deliberate, step-by-step approach to East-West relations because recurring signs show that while change in the Soviet Union is dramatic, it's not yet complete. The Warsaw pact retains a nearly 12-to-one advantage over the Atlantic Alliance in short-range missile and rocket launchers capable of delivering nuclear weapons; and more than a two-to-one advantage in battle tanks. And for that reason, we will also maintain, in cooperation with our allies, ground and air forces in Europe as long as they are wanted and needed to preserve the peace in Europe. At the same time, my administration will place a high and continuing priority on negotiating a less militarized Europe, one with a secure conventional force balance at lower levels of forces. Our aspiration is a real peace—a peace of shared optimism, not a peace of armed camps.[82]

Bush made clear in his speech that a strong NATO became more important, not less, with the changes occurring within the Soviet Union. It certainly was not the time for the West to be overcome by complacency or division.

The fourth and final speech was delivered at the Coast Guard Academy commencement, May 24, 1989, and focused on defense strategy and arms control. Bush emphasized his commitment to maintaining an effective nuclear deterrent but promised to seek arms reductions that would allow stability with the lowest number of weapons that the administration felt was prudent. Any advance in arms control, however, would have to be prefaced by a Soviet move away from an offensive military strategy: "The USSR has said that it is willing to abandon its age-old reliance on offensive strategy. It's time to begin. This should mean a smaller force—one less reliant on tanks and artillery and personnel carriers that provide the Soviet's offensive striking power. A restructured Warsaw Pact—one that mirrors the defensive posture of NATO—would make Europe and the world more secure."[83] Thus, the series of speeches that had been designed to announce the conclusion of the administration's long foreign policy review came to a conclusion, and the "pause" was now officially over. The Bush administration would continue to clarify the new approach throughout the summer, relying on five basic talking points:

1. Cold War will come to an end when division of Europe is ended.
2. Beyond containment is not détente, which was premised in perpetual conflict.
3. Beyond containment means a fundamentally different relationship, one that seeks to integrate the Soviet Union into the world community.
4. Whether we are able to move beyond containment depends on the Soviet Union.
5. Soviet "new thinking" brought about by western strength and unity and Soviet economic problems.[84]

Brent Scowcroft summed up the new strategy that was unveiled with the four speeches: "It was cautious and prudent, an appropriate policy in a period of turbulence and rapid change, but it proved surprisingly durable and established a valuable framework for the conduct of policy. We were shifting policy from the old and narrow focus on strategic arms control to a wider dialogue designed to reduce the threat of war and bring real peace—including progress in Eastern Europe, CFE (conventional forces in Europe), and regional issues. All this was aimed at encouraging a 'reformed' Soviet Union, ready to play a trustworthy role in the community of nations—one far less threatening to the United States and its allies."[85]

The new strategy was a major departure and worked well within Bush's overall goal to establish his own mark on foreign policy distinct from his predecessor. Despite criticism over the length of the policy review, Bush had made significant changes in a short period of time. Addressing what former national security advisor Zbigniew Brzezinski had referred to as a "mid-life crisis" for the National Security Council during the Reagan years, Bush had restored the NSC to its former importance by issuing the first National Security Directive of his presidency, NSD 1, which reorganized the NSC.[86] Along with making fundamental changes in the NSC machinery, Bush appointed a trusted friend in Brent Scowcroft to be his national security advisor, thereby elevating the authority of the position. Bush, Scowcroft, and Baker would make all of the important foreign policy decisions. Bush's years of experience in foreign affairs necessitated a more hands-on approach that was markedly different than the complex system of SIGs and IGs that had been used by Reagan to delegate authority. The long policy review and the anti-climactic speeches that laid out the new policy helped provide a period of gradual transition that protected Bush from charges from the right wing of the Republican Party that Bush was not loyally following in Reagan's footsteps. By the summer of 1989, it was clear that the White House rather than the State Department would be in charge of foreign policy and that Bush, along with his close advisors, would bear the responsibility for reacting to the incredible changes that were happening in Central and Eastern Europe and within the Soviet Union itself. It would be up to this small group of men to manage the end of the Cold War and make sure that it ended peacefully.

Chapter 2

Bush and Gorbachev

The Road to Malta

It was sunny on December 7, 1988, as Mikhail Gorbachev rode the ferry to Governors Island in New York's harbor. He had just come from delivering an important speech at the United Nations announcing massive unilateral military cuts, the first Soviet leader to speak at the United Nations since Nikita Khrushchev in 1960. Now he was on his way to his fifth and final meeting with Ronald Reagan and his first meeting with George Bush since the president-elect's victory in November. As Reagan's national security advisor, Colin Powell, recalls, the meeting had been requested by Gorbachev as a way to "say goodbye Reagan-Gorbachev and also say hello to President Bush."[1] The Reagan administration had not expected any more meetings and, purposefully not calling it a summit, "made clear to the Soviets . . . that we were *not* looking for a substantive exchange."[2] The U.S. Coast Guard station on Governors Island was chosen as the sight for the luncheon, because security would be relatively simple to maintain and the Statue of Liberty could serve as a dramatic backdrop for what was expected to be little more than a historic opportunity for photographs. One last meeting "between old friends," however, masked Gorbachev's underlying motive, which was to size up the new president and receive assurances that there would be continuity in the relationship between the two countries after inauguration day on January 20, 1989. Even though the two men had met at the Chernenko funeral and again at the Washington summit, Gorbachev wanted to see for

Figure 4. The meeting at Governors Island on December 7, 1988, was the last official one between Reagan and Gorbachev. More importantly, it was the first between Gorbachev and President-elect Bush since his victory in November. *Courtesy of the George Bush Presidential Library*

himself if President Bush, now free to make his own decisions, would differ from Vice President Bush, who always supported Reagan's policies. According to Powell, the proposed meeting presented a difficult situation for Bush, who was nervous that "the Soviets might try to throw some proposal at us that [he] would have to deal with before [he] had even come into office."[3] Officially there as Ronald Reagan's vice president, Bush decided to finish out his job by refusing to bring James Baker, his nominee for secretary of state, lest it give the wrong signal to Gorbachev. When Reagan walked out to meet Gorbachev, Bush dutifully stayed inside until the two men had exchanged greetings and only then nonchalantly walked outside (fig. 4). Just prior to the luncheon, Reagan was asked by a reporter to respond to Gorbachev's announcement to reduce troops. His response: "I heartily approve." The reporter then turned to Bush, who awkwardly replied, "I support what the President said," making it clear that he was not ready to announce what his policy would be as president. After the media left, Reagan asked Bush if he had something to say, but Bush sidestepped the chance by stating that he "did not get to be president until January 20" and would need time "to review the issues."[4] Bush did state that he "wished to build on what President

Reagan had accomplished working with Gorbachev," to which Gorbachev responded that he hoped they would not simply build on what had been achieved, but "try to add to it."[5] Later, Bush quietly reassured Gorbachev that he looked forward to working with him "at the appropriate time."[6] The appropriate time, however, would be a while in coming as Bush and his foreign policy team had not yet decided how they were going to proceed. At least, they were not ready to announce their plan to the world because it would be markedly different from that of Ronald Reagan, and Bush's loyalty to his predecessor would make the transition from vice president to president a slow and difficult process.

Bush's change in foreign policy was orchestrated by his closest advisor, one of the Reagan administration's critics, Brent Scowcroft, who was convinced that the Cold War could only be brought to a conclusion if it ended where it had begun: in Central and Eastern Europe. More specifically, the Cold War had begun in Germany after World War II when the United States and the Soviet Union split Germany in two, creating spheres of influence that would pit the two sides against each other. In order for the confrontation to end, the German question would have to be tackled. As Scowcroft recalls, he wanted to focus on Eastern Europe: "There was ferment in Eastern Europe, especially in Poland. And I wanted to take advantage of that ferment to try and get the Soviet army out of Eastern Europe, or at least reduce their presence to allow the Eastern Europeans to develop in a progressive way."[7] This might seem like an obvious decision, but Reagan strongly disagreed. Reagan was obsessed with reducing nuclear weapons and more concerned with arms control discussions with Gorbachev than substantive proposals to reshape Central and Eastern Europe. As for the German question, Reagan's assistant secretary of state for European and Canadian affairs, Rozanne Ridgway, summed up the administration's position by arguing that the existing situation was stable and a source of peace and that renewed debate over the reunification of Germany would be premature and unwise.[8]

Despite the recommendations of the outgoing Reagan officials, many of whom worked on the Bush foreign policy review before leaving office, Scowcroft was committed to shifting American policy, suggesting that the goal of U.S. policy should be to "overcome the division of the continent through the acceptance of common democratic values."[9] The Bush administration, however, was careful not to make the same mistakes that had started the Cold War in the first place. Scowcroft, and particularly Baker, wanted to make sure that their initiatives would not give the impression that the United States and the Soviet Union were getting together to carve up Eastern Europe. They also did not want to bring about reckless change at a pace that might end in violence. According to Scowcroft, the United States did not stimulate ferment in Eastern Europe: "We had done that earlier in the '70s and indeed in the '50s when we helped stimulate the Hungarian revolt and so on. That turned out to be counter productive because when we turned people out in the streets, we weren't prepared to support them. So what we tried to do was encourage reform at a level that we thought would be below that that the Soviet Union would think they would have to crush it. So we wanted to keep it going but we didn't want it smashed, as was usually the case with revolt in Eastern Europe with all the leaders killed or put in prison. And that's what we tried to do and . . . because of our skill or because of luck it turned out that that was very effective in this case."[10] Bush made two European trips to further this goal, making the first to Western Europe in the spring of 1989, which coincided with the NATO summit that was scheduled to celebrate the fortieth anniversary of the alliance. The second was in the summer of 1989 and focused on Eastern Europe and ended with the G-7 economic summit in Paris. These two presidential trips, along with the speeches scheduled for the commencement season, gave the administration the opportunity to lay out its new policy initiatives and put pressure on other governments to respond. This was, in reality, a diplomatic offensive that finally allowed the new administration to break free from the Reagan-era policies and forge a new course, which—even though still somewhat fragmented—was more in line with Scowcroft's goal to capitalize on the ferment in Eastern Europe.

The NATO Summit

The NATO summit presented the Bush administration with some interesting challenges. Gorbachev had undertaken an intense public relations campaign, and his well publicized speeches about peace and democracy in Eastern Europe placed pressure on the West to respond. His message resonated with many European political leaders who questioned the need for defense spending at current NATO levels and who began to form the impression that, at a time when Gorbachev seemed to be moving beyond the Cold War, the United States was still "dourly debating tanks and missiles."[11] This, coupled with Gorbachev's dramatic arms control announcements in his speech to the United Nations in December, had placed the West on the political defensive. Both Baker and Scowcroft were determined to use the NATO summit to establish Bush as the sole leader of the alliance and gain the initiative. The two topics that needed to be addressed at the summit were the reduction of conventional (non-nuclear) forces in Europe (CFE) and the modernization and possible reduction of short-range nuclear forces (SNF). The general public tended to perceive these issues as boring, but Scowcroft knew that the Cold War would continue as long as the United States and the Soviet Union maintained opposing armed camps in Europe. The Bush administration needed to find a way to reduce the hundreds of thousands of Soviet troops, which they pinpointed as the true source of Europe's insecurity. This type of fundamental change had not been included in Gorbachev's flashier, yet less meaningful, arms control proposals. The way for the United States to effect change was to have an alliance in full agreement on the solutions and united behind President Bush, a goal that would require the Bush administration to immediately begin working on proposals to present at the NATO summit.

NATO needed modern nuclear forces to offset the conventional superiority of the Warsaw Pact. The SNF problem was made difficult because of West Germany, where Chancellor Helmut Kohl faced increasing public resistance, because short-range missiles, with a range of three hundred miles, would in all likelihood be directed at targets within Germany or Poland, a prospect that led to the sardonic German maxim: "The shorter the missile, the deader the German."[12] Understandably, a strong anti-nuclear movement in the Federal Republic began to call for the elimination of the current 88 SNF launchers (as opposed to around 1,400 for the Soviets!).[13] In 1987, NATO had agreed to delay the decision on modernization until a comprehensive plan could be formulated, scheduled to be finished by the 1989 summit. The United States, supported by most of the alliance, felt that the Warsaw Pact's superiority in conventional forces had to be addressed before major changes in NATO's nuclear weapons could be discussed. The Bush administration now faced increasing pressure to create both a CFE proposal and a SNF proposal before the NATO summit, a task Scowcroft calls "the first test of President Bush's alliance leadership."[14] In March 1989, NATO and the Warsaw Pact had agreed to a proposal presented by Baker of unequal CFE reductions to create an equal level of forces at about 5–10 percent below the current NATO levels. The proposal was criticized as insufficient, and Bush pushed for larger cuts. Less than two weeks before the summit, Bush sat down with his most trusted advisors to discuss a CFE initiative. Scowcroft and Baker pushed for bold cuts, Crowe and Cheney voiced objections, but President Bush had the deciding vote: "I want this [more radical proposal] done. Don't keep telling me why it can't be done. Tell me how it can be done."[15] The result was President Bush's Conventional Parity Initiative, which proposed a 20 percent cut in U.S. and Soviet troops in Europe and established a ceiling of approximately 275,000 each.

Figure 5. Baker and Bush at the NATO Summit in Brussels, May 29, 1989.
Courtesy of the George Bush Presidential Library

This would force the United States to withdraw and demobilize 30,000 troops and would require the Soviets to reduce their 600,000-strong Red Army in Eastern Europe by 325,000. In addition, President Bush proposed a reduction to parity of all tanks, armored troop carriers, artillery, and land-based combat aircraft and helicopters to a ceiling of 15 percent below the current NATO totals; weapons removed were to be destroyed. The president proposed that this reduction to parity be negotiated within six months to a year and that it be implemented by 1993 at the latest.[16] Bush knew that he would need the support of the major NATO leaders for his idea to work and sent Deputy Secretary of State Lawrence Eagleburger and Deputy National Security Advisor Robert Gates to Europe to win the support of Thatcher, Mitterrand, and Kohl.

The NATO summit took place May 29–30, 1989, in Brussels (fig. 5). President Bush presented his CFE proposal in the formal session, knowing full well that his public image in regards to foreign policy rested on the outcome of the summit. Margaret Thatcher praised Bush's initiative, claiming it would promote unity within the alliance, and Mitterrand offered his full support as well, labeling the CFE proposal as innovative and applauding Bush for displaying "imagination—indeed, intellectual audacity of the rarest kind."[17] Bush had scored the public victory that he had sorely needed as the alliance agreed that SNF negotiations leading to a partial reduction would begin, once implementation of conventional force reductions was underway. One London newspaper said that Bush had ridden "to the rescue like the proverbial U.S. cavalry, at the last possible moment."[18] Reporters in the United States would now have trouble accusing the Bush administration of lacking vision.

Bush next traveled to Germany to make one of the most important speeches of his presidency. In his address in the Rheingoldhalle in Mainz, Chancellor Kohl's home turf, Bush linked the end of the Cold War to an end of the division of Europe: "For 40 years, the seeds of democracy in Eastern Europe lay dormant, buried under the frozen tundra of the Cold War. And for 40 years, the world has waited for the Cold War to end. And decade after decade, time after time, the flowering human spirit withered from the chill of conflict and oppression. And again, the world waited. But the passion for freedom cannot be denied forever. The world has waited long enough. The time is right. Let Europe be whole and free."[19] He went on to issue an ultimatum:

> The Cold War began with the division of Europe. It can only end when Europe is whole. Today, it is this very concept of a divided Europe that is under siege. And that's why our hopes run especially high, because the division of Europe is under siege not by armies, but by the spread of ideas. . . . It comes from a single powerful idea— democracy. . . . As President, I will continue to do all I can to help open the closed societies of the East. We seek self-determination for all of Germany and all of Eastern Europe. . . . But democracy's journey East is not easy. . . . Barriers and barbed wire still fence in nations. . . . There cannot be a common European home until all within it are free to move from room to room. . . . The path of freedom leads to a larger home—a home where West meets East, a democratic home— the commonwealth of free nations.[20]

Bush made clear that the Cold War would not end until the division of Europe ended. His reference to the "commonwealth of free nations" was a deliberate response to Gorbachev's call for a "common European home." In essence it was a direct challenge to the proposals made by Gorbachev, arguing that even though *glasnost* was a Russian word, openness was a Western concept. To that end, Bush called for free elections and political pluralism in Eastern Europe, cooperation in addressing environmental problems in the East, and a less militarized Europe. Perhaps his most dramatic proposal, especially considering the venue for the speech, came when he noted that Hungary was tearing down its barbed wire fence along its border with Austria: "Just as the barriers are coming down in Hungary, so must they fall throughout all of Eastern Europe. Let Berlin be next! Let Berlin be next! Nowhere is the division between East and West seen more clearly than in Berlin. And there this brutal wall cuts neighbor from neighbor, brother from brother. And that wall stands as a monument to the failure of communism. It must come down."[21] Bush's statement lacked the drama and showmanship of Reagan's 1986 speech in Berlin, but the message was clear: the division of Berlin and Europe must end.

Tiananmen Square Massacre

Immediately following his return from Europe, Bush had to deal with a crisis in China that swept away many of the gains in Bush's public image. Just as 1989 was a historic year for Europe, it also was a historic year for China since it was the fortieth anniversary of the People's Republic. The year also marked the tenth anniversary of the reinstitution of formal diplomatic relations with the United States. No American was more keenly aware of this than George Bush, who had been selected by President Nixon as the first envoy to China. Emboldened by the reforms sweeping through Europe, protests arose pressuring the Chinese government to begin the same type of political and intellectual reforms that were occurring in the Soviet bloc. On June 4, 1989, armed units of the People's Liberation Army poured into Tiananmen Square in Beijing, brutally dispersing thousands of student demonstrators with bullets and tanks, leaving hundreds dead and thousands wounded.[22] The demonstrators had been gathering in the square since April 15 to mourn the death of Hu Yaobang, former general secretary of the Communist Party. Hu, who was removed from office in 1987 for excessive liberalism, was considered by many to be a sincere reformer. Hard-liners within the government reacted harshly to the demonstrators and sent police to breakup the demonstrations, beating students in the process. Soon, the mourning of Hu transformed to protests against the government, with calls for increased democratic freedoms, improvements in university living conditions, a crackdown on corruption, and other political reforms. Adding to the tensions was the visit of Mikhail Gorbachev on May 15, 1989. Western television crews arrived in Beijing to set up their cameras for the event and were able to cover the protestors. The international attention only fueled the students' protest and placed more pressure on the Chinese government. Many of the events planned for Gorbachev's visit had to be cancelled, as the ranks of the demonstrators swelled to almost a million. The government declared martial law and sent in the troops. The ensuing massacre was broadcast live to audiences around the world and created a problem that the Bush administration had not anticipated. According to James Baker, he was informed of the Tiananmen Square incident when he called his eldest son, James, to arrange a game of golf at the Chevy Chase Country Club. "I don't think you're going to be playing any golf today," Jamie replied before telling his father that CNN was showing tanks rolling through Tiananmen Square.[23] Thanks to CNN, the U.S. public knew about the crisis before the secretary of state. Public outrage in the United States was intense and President Bush immediately issued a statement from Kennebunkport, Maine, that he "deeply deplore[d] the decision to use force."[24] Bush followed this up with a call for sanctions, but he secretly sent a lengthy private letter to Deng Xiaoping assuring the chairman that, despite what was said in public, the Bush administration had no intention of destroying the relationship between the two countries.[25] This was characteristic of Bush's style of diplomacy, having similarly warned Gorbachev not to read too much into "empty cannons of rhetoric."[26] Just as Bush used these "empty cannons" against Gorbachev with regard to Lithuania, he was now urging Deng to ignore the sanctions being discussed in the U.S. Congress and work through back channels to resolve the difficulty between the two sides.[27] Deng agreed to such a back channel meeting, and Brent Scowcroft and Larry Eagleburger were sent on a secret mission to China, so secret that their plane was almost shot down upon entering Chinese airspace. Scowcroft's trip, which was not made public until six months later, was meant to "personally underscore the United States' shock and concern about the violence in Tiananmen Square, and to impress upon the Chinese Government the seriousness with which this incident was viewed in the United States."[28] This face-to-face dialogue was considered by Bush to be more effective than an emotional response and was followed up with a second trip by Scowcroft following the Malta Summit. Bush renewed China's Most Favored Nation trading status in 1990 to a chorus of protests and two bills by Congress to overturn the President's action, but Congress adjourned before either bill could be taken up by the Senate. Bush, however, was reluctant to upset the process of normalization that had been initiated by Nixon in 1972, instead preferring a deliberate response while reminding the U.S. public that "those demonstrations took place in the first place because of U.S. seeds of democratic reform."[29] President Bush had a personal understanding of one of America's greatest Cold War strategic successes, having turned down ambassadorships in Paris and London to accept the job as chief of the U.S. Liaison Office in Beijing in 1974:

I wanted a measured response, one aimed at those who had pushed for and implemented the use of force: the hard-liners and the Army. I didn't want to punish the Chinese people for the acts of their government. I believed that the commercial contacts between our countries had helped lead to the quest for more freedom. If people had commercial incentives, whether it's in China or in other totalitarian systems, the move to democracy becomes inexorable. For this reason I wanted to avoid cutting off the sales and contacts. It was important that the Chinese leaders know we could not continue business as usual and that the People's Liberation Army realize that we wanted to see restraint. What I certainly did not want to do was completely break the relationship we had worked so hard to build since 1972. . . . While angry rhetoric might be temporarily satisfying to some, I believed it would hurt our efforts in the long term.[30]

Angry rhetoric was exactly what the American public wanted. Although it might have been a solid diplomatic decision to show restraint, and although the United States was the first major government to impose sanctions on China after Tiananmen, what the public really wanted was to see a little righteous indignation from their president. Having failed to accommodate the public mood, Bush was heavily criticized by the press and Congress. Careful, reasoned action may have allowed Bush to be confident that he had not "set aside the passion of [his] conviction," but to the American public Bush had once again missed an important opportunity.[31] It was on this note that President Bush embarked on his trip to Eastern Europe. It should have been a victorious follow-up to his successful NATO summit, but Tiananmen and the criticism of Bush's restraint cast a shadow over his trip to Poland.

Bush's Trip to Eastern Europe

Ironically, the first round of parliamentary elections in Poland occurred the same day as the Tiananmen massacre. Solidarity's Civic Committee won 92 of 100 seats in the first round of Senate elections and 160 of the 161 Diet seats that were open for competition. In stark contrast, the governing coalition was only able to fill 5 of the 299 seats reserved for them. Only five of the Communist's candidates were elected, even more humiliating for the government because it was completely unexpected. The result was the legitimization of Solidarity.[32] Coupled with the surprising election results was Gorbachev's public rejection of the Brezhnev Doctrine: "The political and social order in one country or another has changed in the past and can also change in the future. Still, it is exclusively up to the peoples themselves. It is their choice. All interference, whatever its nature, in the internal affairs of a state to limit its sovereignty of a state, even from a friend or all, is inadmissible."[33] The elections in Poland and Gorbachev's rhetoric accentuated the polarization within the Warsaw Pact that pitted the USSR, Poland, and Hungary against Romania, the GDR, Czechoslovakia, and Bulgaria. The closed-door meetings of the Warsaw Pact heads of state and Party leaders in Bucharest, July 7–8, 1989, were filled with tension. Leaders such as Nicolae Ceausescu and Milos Jakes criticized Gorbachev's perestroika and called for action to put an end to the "counterrevolutionary" process that was occurring in Poland. It was becoming increasingly clear that the destruction of socialism's conquests through the policies of Gorbachev had the potential of turning violent, a possibility that made Bush's trip to Eastern Europe even more imperative. The situation in Poland became more complicated because the gains by Solidarity had placed in jeopardy the election of General Jaruzelski, whose election was one of the central elements of the Roundtable agreements. Also, Poland was informally asking the United States for $10 billion in assistance over the next three years. It was under these conditions that Bush arrived in Warsaw on July 9, 1989. It was important for President Bush to show that he was backing the political and economic reform efforts in Eastern Europe; due to its own huge deficit, however, the United States could not deliver substantial aid. As Scowcroft conceded, the United States could no longer "pick up the check for everything."[34] Although the Bush administration might have liked to make possible a new Marshall Plan, they needed to share the economic burden with Western Europe. The proposal by Bush called for the rescheduling of Poland's $39 billion foreign debt, a request for $325 million in new loans from the World Bank, and $100 million from the United States, a package inadequate for the needs of Poland. At a joint session of the newly elected Polish parliament, President Bush voiced his support of the momentous changes in Poland's political system, saying that "the Western democracies will stand with the Polish people" but warned that "the road ahead is a long one, but it is the only road which leads to prosperity and social peace."[35] Bush wanted a gradual process that encouraged change while maintaining order, a preference which led him to support Jaruzelski over the Solidarity candidates. Jaruzelski, who was considering not even running for president because of Solidarity's victory in the parliament election, asked for Bush's advice during a private conversation. Bush urged the senior Communist leader to run for office because he felt that "Jaruzelski's experience was the best hope for a smooth transition."[36] Later, General Jaruzelski would write in his memoirs that President Bush's support played a crucial role in his election to the presidency.[37] It was certainly ironic, as even Bush admitted, for a U.S. president to talk a Communist leader into running for an election, but Bush realized that a peaceful, controlled process would be the best course for change.

From Poland, Bush traveled to Hungary, the first U.S. president to do so. Bush stepped to the podium, waved off an umbrella, and dramatically ripped up his speech. The crowds cheered him on as he spoke briefly of his support of the reform efforts being undertaken in Hungary. Near the end of his speech he noticed an elderly woman who was standing near the podium, soaked from the rain. He quickly took off his raincoat and wrapped it around her shoulders. The crowd erupted and Bush walked into the crowd, shaking hands and wishing them well. It was a dramatic moment and one that showed the people of Hungary that the United States was committed to establishing a partnership with Hungary to promote lasting change. Bush then flew to Paris for the G-7 summit in hopes of convincing them to share the burden of helping Eastern Europe's economic distress. He did just that, achieving the aims that he had promised to both Poland and Hungary and making the trip to Eastern Europe a very successful one. Energized and growing more confident, Bush decided that it was time to consider a meeting with Gorbachev.

Collision Course

At the same time as Bush's trip to Poland and Hungary, Gorbachev was making a highly publicized trip to West Germany, calling for immediate cuts in short-range nuclear missiles in NATO. The proposals had gained Gorbachev attention in Germany, but the proposals were designed to disrupt the gains that Bush had made at the NATO summit and create rifts within the alliance. Tactics such as this confirmed Bush's decision to move cautiously in regard to Gorbachev. Bush and Gorbachev traveled Europe with competing messages: whether or not the West needed to wait for concrete actions by the Soviet Union. The ferment that was growing in Eastern Europe, however, was not going to wait for the West to decide between the competing views. The Bush administration knew that, as the changes in Eastern Europe accelerated, Gorbachev would face increasing pressure from hard-liners to intervene. After all, Eastern Europe was a buffer zone that separated the Soviet Union from the West and, if its once-reliable allies began to slip away, the Soviet Union would lose much of the security that it had depended upon. It became increasingly unclear whether or not the Cold War would end with violence. The Bush administration knew that "dying empires rarely go out peacefully."[38] Bush became even more determined that the cataclysmic changes in world structure that were about to occur would take place without a shot being fired; as Bush cautioned "there could still be more Tiananmens."[39] Realizing the growing need for a face-to-face meeting between the two men, Bush started the first draft of a letter on the flight home from the G-7 meeting in Paris that asked Gorbachev to a meeting without "thousands of assistants hovering over our shoulders, without the press yelling at us every 5 minutes about 'who's winning'"; a meeting "to reduce the chances there could be misunderstandings" and develop a relationship "on a more personal basis."[40] Bush felt that the negotiations for a proposed meeting between the men should be done secretly as to avoid any outside pressures or competing public agendas. Consequently, he decided to bypass the normal channels of communication by only telling Scowcroft, Baker, and Chief of Staff John Sununu about the letter. The final draft was presented to Marshal Sergei Akhromeyev, Gorbachev's principal military advisor, at the end of July when he was visiting Washington, D.C., to discuss arms control. Akhromeyev could be trusted to deliver the letter in absolute secrecy, and Gorbachev responded within days of receiving it. His messenger delivered Gorbachev's approval of the proposal, suggesting that the two leaders could meet as early as September. The only problem was finding a location. The two sides wrangled over location for weeks before President Bush's brother, William "Bucky" Bush, suggested the island of Malta. Malta would have two benefits. Gorbachev had already planned a state visit to Italy at the end of November and could easily adjust his schedule to include a trip to the island, and Bush, as an old navy man, liked the idea of holding the conference at sea, recalling the Roosevelt-Churchill shipboard meeting in Placentia Bay, Newfoundland, in 1941. A meeting aboard a ship would also limit the number of press and staff that could attend. Bush's national security advisor, Brent Scowcroft, explains the significance of the meeting:

> It was primarily more of a trust-building meeting. [Bush] had wanted from the onset of his administration to talk with Gorbachev, and I think Dick Cheney had held him back because historically the Soviet Union always profited by summits because there was an atmosphere that, you know the Cold War was over; we didn't have to worry. And that always made it harder for us to get appropriations through Congress and so on. So we didn't want—I didn't want, and Cheney didn't want—a summit until we had something specific to get from it, that is an arms control agreement or something else. And early in the ad-

ministration we didn't have anything yet. So the president acquiesced in holding off a summit. Then in the summer of '89, as a result of his trip through Eastern Europe and what he saw there and his meeting with his European allies at the G-7 summit, he decided that he had to talk with Gorbachev, that things were moving too fast, that there was too much danger of misunderstanding, and so he had to talk with Gorbachev. But he, in fact, he didn't even want to call it a summit. He wanted to call it an exchange of views—not to make agreements, which is what summits usually are—but just to exchange views. And he was delighted with the idea of a summit out away from everybody where the press couldn't be hovering around and where there would be little pressure for either side to try to make negotiating points or debating points.[41]

Both Gorbachev and Bush looked forward to the Malta conference as a potential breakthrough in the U.S.-Soviet relationship. Soon, however, events in Europe would add an even greater importance to the meeting in Malta.

Gorbachev faced a crisis not on the agenda for Malta when nationalists in the Baltics began calling for independence, claiming that the 1939 agreement between Hitler and Stalin, which led to the annexation of Latvia, Lithuania, and Estonia, had been illegal. Baltic nationalism threatened the integrity of the Soviet Union itself, potentially spreading throughout the Soviet Union where Gorbachev's strategies for political and economic reforms had made it increasingly difficult to maintain order. The United States had never recognized the Soviet annexation of the Baltic states, and the risk of breaking a fifty-year-old precedent of U.S. policy made it difficult for Bush to call for gradual change in the Baltics. Yet Bush worried that separatism would lead to a civil war that could end disastrously for the United States if nuclear weapons fell under uncertain control. Gorbachev seemed receptive to greater autonomy for the Baltics, but if they pushed for separation, Gorbachev might feel pressure to resort to force. Separatism was already spreading to other parts of the Soviet Union. In Ukraine, nationalists had marched in Kiev in support of independence, and, no matter how much he believed in perestroika, Gorbachev could not lose the Soviet Union's second-largest republic, its primary source of food. A meeting between Gorbachev and Margaret Thatcher demonstrates just how delicate of a situation the outbreak of separatism in the republics had become: "Over luncheon with Thatcher, Gorbachev dismissed the problem of nationalism with the sweep of his hand. Recalling Charles de Gaulle's remark on how difficult it was to preside over a country that manufactured more than 120 different kinds of cheese, he said, 'Imagine how much harder it is to run a country with over a hundred and twenty different nationalities.' 'Yes!' interjected Leonid Abalkin, a deputy prime minister who served as economic advisor to Gorbachev. 'Especially if there's no cheese!' "[42] Even Gorbachev could not continue to gloss over the mounting problems that his political and economic reforms were causing in the Soviet Union.

The Fall of the Berlin Wall

Another problem was the situation in East Germany. In May 1989, Hungary dismantled the barriers along its border with Austria, making it possible for "vacationing" East Germans to slip across into Austria and make their way to West Germany. When Hungary officially opened its borders on September 10, over ten thousand East Germans poured across and made their way to the West. It was a public humiliation to the Warsaw Pact and threatened its cohesiveness. It was even a worse situation for the East German government as the rising discontent forced a series of resignations within the government. Repression was now seen as an unlikely option by the government. Gorbachev claimed that what was occurring in East Germany did not directly affect the Soviet Union and ordered the Soviet troops stationed in East Germany not to get involved. This, in effect, demonstrated the end of the Brezhnev Doctrine, which asserted the Soviet right to provide assistance, including military assistance, to any Communist nation where Socialism was in jeopardy. As Secretary of State Baker recalls, the Bush administration could no longer doubt that Gorbachev's deeds matched his words: "What it proved to us was that the Soviet leadership had, in fact, as they had told us they had, ruled out the use of force to keep the empire together. That was the critical factor. They told us early on they weren't going to use force to keep the empire together. And when they didn't that proved that they were telling us the truth and that they could be trusted and that we could do business with them."[43] East German leader Egon Krenz made a frantic call to Gorbachev asking for instructions. Gorbachev told him that the Soviets would not get involved and suggested that he open his borders. East Germany announced on November 9, 1989, that it was relaxing its border-control policy with West Germany. Citizens of East Germany could now leave the country without having to obtain special permission. Ironically, several mistakes were made by the East German government that allowed for the historic change. The announcement did not mention the city of Berlin, which usually received separate status and had stricter exit visa requirements. Also, the new policy was not meant to take place until after it had been presented to the legislature; however, Günter Schabowski, a Politbüro member and reformist Communist, took it upon himself to announce the policy at the end of his daily press conference. As two Bush officials would later conclude, "the hapless East German government had opened the Berlin Wall by mistake."[44] Confused officials and observers did not understand exactly what was meant, and rumors began to spread that all travel restrictions were dropped. Crowds formed along the Berlin Wall as border guards waited for instructions that would not come. Finally, guards gave in to the crowds, and people crossed over into West Berlin. The atmosphere turned electric as jubilant crowds from both sides of the wall began a celebration of the wall's collapse.

"I'm not going to dance on the Berlin Wall"

In Washington, President Bush watched the celebration on television. Bewildered, he remarked to his aides: "If the Soviets are going to let the Communists fall in East Germany, they've got to be really serious—more serious than I realized."[45] Bush's press secretary, Marlin Fitzwater, knew that the president needed to give the press his view on the historic changes taking place in Germany:

> When the wire stories began coming in that people were breaking down the wall, I saw it the same way the White House press corps did: as a big news story to be handled immediately. I took the wire stories to the president, who was sitting in his study off the Oval watching on CNN as people climbed the wall and toppled over to the other side. He read the wires slowly, as if making an independent determination of their truth. "Do you want to make a statement?" I asked. "Why?" the president said. He knew me well enough to know that my question was really a recommendation. "Why?" I repeated. "This is an incredibly historic day. People will want to know what it means. They need some presidential assurance that the world is OK." The president just looked at me. He understood the historic point, of course, but his vision was taking him into a future of German reunification, diminished communism, and a new world order to be established. "Listen, Marlin," he said, "I'm not going to dance on the Berlin Wall. The last thing I want to do is brag about winning the cold war, or bringing the wall down. It won't help us in Eastern Europe to be bragging about this." "I understand that, sir," I said, "but we have to show that we understand the historical significance of this. You don't have to brag."

Figure 6. At his press conference in the Oval Office following the fall of the Berlin Wall on November 9, 1989, Bush urged caution, labeling the momentous occasion as simply "a good development." *Courtesy of the George Bush Presidential Library*

I paused to let him formulate a message in his mind, then added, "We can just bring the pool into the Oval Office, you will sit at your desk, and the whole thing will be very dignified and presidential." "OK," he said.[46]

Reporters were herded into the Oval Office where President Bush was discussing the situation with Baker, Scowcroft, and Sununu (fig. 6). Bush sat at his desk with briefing books stacked on his desk, one opened to a map of Germany, as reporters huddled around the desk to record a brief statement from the president. Speaking matter-of-factly and with little enthusiasm, Bush labeled the fall of the Berlin Wall as "a good development." He went on to add, "I don't think any single event is the end of what you might call the Iron Curtain. But clearly, this is a long way from the harshest Iron Curtain days. . . . Our objective is a Europe whole and free. Is it a step towards that? I would say yes. Gorbachev talks about a common home. Is it a step towards that? [with a shrug of his shoulders] Probably so."[47] When asked by a reporter if there was a danger that things were accelerating too quickly, Bush responded, "We are handling it in a way where we're not trying to give anybody a hard time. We're saluting those who can move forward with democracy. We're encouraging the concept of a Europe whole and free. And so we just welcome it."[48] Lesley Stahl of CBS challenged his less than enthusiastic response:

> **Stahl:** In what you just said, that is a sort of victory for our side in the big East-West battle. But, you don't seem elated.
> **Bush:** I'm elated. I'm just not an emotional kind of guy. . . . We'll have some suggest more flamboyant courses of action for this country, but I think we are handling this properly . . . and so, the fact that I'm not bubbling over, maybe it's getting along towards evening because I feel very good about it.[49]

While the president was responding to the criticism that he was not elated, he was leaning back in his leather chair, looking down into his lap and fiddling with a pen. Fitzwater stood in the background, leaning against the wall, knowing that the president was not doing well: "From the beginning, he seemed uninspired. As he continued, the president did the one thing that made every Bush staffer start to sweat. He started sliding down in his chair. It was the absolutely ironclad signal that he didn't like what he was doing, didn't want to be there, and probably going to show it. Soon he was talking in a monotone, his head bowed and hands folded across his chest."[50] To the U.S. public, Bush seemed distracted and disinterested. He was out of touch with the dramatic changes that they watched on television. At a time when he could have used a strong public performance to lead the nation in its celebration of the end of the Cold War, President Bush seemed to be asleep on the job. Even Bush admitted that the press conference was "awkward and uncomfortable," but, even as he was answering questions, his mind "kept racing over a possible Soviet crackdown, turning all the happiness to tragedy."[51]

Bush knew that the Cold War was still far from over, and he knew that how he reacted to the dramatic events could have a significant impact: "As positive events rapidly unfolded in Eastern Europe and in the Soviet Union, we recognized that if we handled things properly, there was a real opportunity to see more freedom in Eastern Europe, to see the liberation of the Baltic States, and to see dramatic, positive changes in the Soviet Union."[52] As Fitzwater recalls, Bush was more concerned with ending the Cold War than with his image:

> First of all, he didn't give a damn about his image. And I specifically raised it 'cause I went to him and said, you know, the wall is coming

down and you need to say something here that's going to be strong and show that the president recognizes what's happening and it'd be good for your image and so forth. And he said to me he didn't care about image. That this was not a time to be worrying about that sort of thing. And that he wanted to respond in a way that Gorbachev would understand and that would be supportive of moving ahead in the future relationship. I mean, it's one of Bush's more admirable traits in the sense that he had enormous discipline in order to do what he thought was right for the country even at the personal risk of bad press and bad publicity and image consideration. And he wouldn't do it.[53]

Secretary of State James Baker also defended Bush's decision: "I still think that history will prove that he was absolutely right in not trying to stick it in the eye of the Soviets, not trying to goad them or, as everyone put it at the time, 'dance on the wall.' That would have been a terrible mistake politically and diplomatically."[54] Certainly, Bush had very sound reasons for reacting in the cautious manner that he did. He feared that a Western celebration of the wall's collapse might encourage a backlash by hard-liners in East Berlin and Moscow. But to a skeptical public, Bush's actions built upon the images created by his lengthy foreign policy review and his reaction to the Tiananmen Square massacre to show that Bush, as a symbolic leader, did not live up to his promise to follow in the steps of Reagan.

What the public did not know was that Bush was acting on a request sent to him by Gorbachev that very day. As Bush recalled, "On the day the Wall opened, Gorbachev sent messages to Kohl warning him to stop talking of reunification, and cabled me urging that I not overreact. He worried that the demonstrations might get out of control, with 'unforeseen consequences,' and he asked for understanding. This was the first time Gorbachev had clearly indicated genuine anxiety about events in Eastern Europe. Heretofore he had seemed relaxed, even blasé, about the accelerating movements in the region away from communism and Soviet control. It was if he suddenly realized the serious implications of what was going on."[55] To go against the wishes of Gorbachev would have been counterproductive and seriously jeopardized the gains Bush hoped to accomplish at the upcoming Malta meeting. James Baker explained Bush's fear: "He feared that it would make it tougher for us to continue to move forward positively with Gorbachev. You don't stick it in somebody's eye when something as fundamental and as big and important as that happens. You celebrate it, but you do so in a more statesman-like way . . . and even today when we talk about winning the Cold War, [Gorbachev] takes offense at that. He says, 'You didn't win the Cold War; we came to an understanding, a peaceful resolution of our differences.'"[56] Even with Bush's acquiescence to Gorbachev's request, there was no denying that change was taking place at an unprecedented rate and that the fall of the Berlin Wall demonstrated that change to the world. According to Brent Scowcroft, the fall of the Berlin Wall underscored the necessity of the two leaders talking because "unexpected events could turn into a crisis very easily. Gorbachev was very frightened by the fall of the Berlin Wall."[57]

The Malta Conference

Bush met with his National Security Council on November 30, 1989, in the cabinet room of the White House.[58] It would be the last meeting before his departure for Malta: "I don't want to be begrudging. I don't want to seem halfhearted. The purpose of what I'm going to be doing over there is to show Gorbachev that I support him all the way."[59]

The private statement by the president expressed his desire to use the Malta conference to act boldly and shed his public image. He did not mind being labeled as cautious, but he could not stand being called timid. Up to this point, Gorbachev had been the one to propose bold new initiatives, and Bush had been the one who was seen as timid. He wanted to use Malta to reverse that situation. Bush was determined not to be "out proposed" this time. To that end, the Bush team had been working diligently to prepare a list of twenty possible initiatives that Bush could use in his initial presentation to Gorbachev. In the end, the list was trimmed to seventeen specific proposals. As newspapers began to observe, the goals for the meeting were changing: "The Malta meeting is indeed a summit. No one any more on the U.S. side talks about a 'get acquainted' meeting."[60] Gorbachev, on the other hand, had purposefully not come up with a list of proposals, taking Bush at his word that there would not be an agenda at the meeting. In past meetings, such as Reykjavik and Baker's meeting with the Soviet leader earlier in the year, Gorbachev had been accused of diplomatic sneak attacks. Gorbachev was determined not to receive the same criticism at Malta. Dating back to his UN address the previous year, Gorbachev had spent the past year proposing bold initiatives. Now, he needed to attempt to consolidate whatever progress he had already made. He knew that any further arms control proposals at this point might create a backlash from hard-liners in the Soviet Union. Gorbachev also knew that, even though the Bush administration was beginning to overcome the earlier doubts concerning his sincerity, there was still strong doubt as to whether or not he could remain in power.

Nervous over the unsettling pace of events in Eastern Europe and the increasing uncertainty of the Warsaw Pact, Gorbachev desperately needed the United States to reaffirm the superpower status of the Soviet Union and his own status as Bush's equal.[61] One French newspaper described the Soviet leader's mission at Malta: "Mr. Gorbachev is racing against time to preserve the USSR's great-power interests."[62] It was becoming increasingly evident with the unfolding of events in 1989 that Gorbachev was the leader of a superpower in decline. He hoped to use Malta to portray to the world a U.S.-Soviet partnership that was based on mutual understanding and mutual respect between equals. A letter to Bush from former president Richard Nixon cautioned him that Gorbachev's actions masked a political necessity: "There is no question but that he is a remarkable new kind of leader of the Soviet Union, and we welcome the initiatives at home and abroad that he had already taken. But when you examine the evidence, it is clear that what he is doing is making a virtue of necessity. This does not make him a virtuous leader."[63] Bush knew that Gorbachev was fighting for his political survival: "I worried that we were dealing with a ticking bomb. We could not see what inside pressures were building against Gorbachev and his programs. We were getting hints from Moscow that one of Gorbachev's objectives at Malta was to gain some sort of 'understanding' for his situation and for the measures he might take to crack down. I could not give him that, and if I did, it would have a lasting historical, political, and moral price."[64] Bush also knew, however, that it was in his own best interests to publicly support Gorbachev in order to bring a stabilizing influence to the dramatic changes that were taking place. He made clear his support in his departure statement before leaving for Malta: "America understands the magnitude of Mr. Gorbachev's challenges. And let there be no misunderstanding: We support *perestroika*."[65]

Bush's eight-and-a-half-hour flight from Andrews Air Force Base to Valletta, Malta, did not provide him with the rest he would need for the meeting. His sleep was interrupted with phone calls from Washington, D.C., concerning a military coup attempt in the Philippines that attempted to oust Pres. Cory Aquino. By the time they reached Malta the next morning, the Bush team was a little worn down. During the Malta conference, Bush would stay on a guided missile cruiser anchored in Valletta harbor, the USS *Belknap*—the flagship of the Sixth Fleet (fig. 7). Also anchored in the harbor was a Soviet missile cruiser, the *Slava*, where the first meeting was scheduled to be held. The third ship that was scheduled to be involved in the talks was a large Soviet cruise ship, the *Maxim Gorky*, which was berthed at the dock and the place where Gorbachev would be staying (fig. 8). Bush spent the

Figure 7. During the Malta conference, Bush stayed aboard the USS *Belknap* *(right)*, which was anchored near a Soviet SLAVA-class missile cruiser *(left)*. *Courtesy of the George Bush Presidential Library*

first day taking care of protocol with a visit to Malta's prime minister, a visit to the USS *Forrestal*, and some time settling in aboard the *Belknap*. By the next morning, the weather had made a turn for the worse with twenty-foot waves and gale-force winds pounding the ships in the harbor. The venue for the first meeting was changed to the *Maxim Gorky*, which was in a far more protected position at the dock. Scowcroft recalls the feeling of "anticipatory tension" in the room as both sides greeted each other across a long table (fig. 9).[66] Before leaving for Malta Bush had announced in his departure statement that his discussions would enable the two leaders to become "better acquainted" and that he would "*not* be negotiating" but rather "talking about our hopes and concerns for the future."[67] Despite his public announcement, Bush began his presentation of the seventeen proposals that his team had prepared. An hour and ten minutes later, Bush finished talking.[68] After presenting his avalanche of proposals, Bush joked to Gorbachev, "This is the end of my non-agenda."[69] Gorbachev, of course, did not have any proposals of his own, instead using his time to talk passionately about his desire to achieve a new U.S.-Soviet relationship in which each side would work to help the other overcome its problems. As Fitzwater recalled, Bush then leaned across the table and interjected that he had already begun

Figure 8. Gorbachev preferred to stay on the more luxurious cruise ship, the *Maxim Gorky*, berthed at the dock. Because of the bad weather, the meetings were held on the *Maxim Gorky. Courtesy of the George Bush Presidential Library*

Figure 9. The first meeting of the Malta conference aboard the *Maxim Gorky*, Dec. 2, 1989. *Courtesy of the George Bush Presidential Library*

to move in that direction of mutual support: "'I hope you noticed that I didn't dance on the wall when it came down.' And Gorbachev said, 'I did and I appreciate it very much.' And they talked then about the language they would use to describe the new relationship in a post–Berlin Wall situation."[70] The only real tense moment of the first meeting came when Gorbachev brought up the fact that the Bush administration had been using the phrase "Western values" in speeches and public statements to describe successful reform efforts in Eastern Europe and the Soviet Union. As James Baker recalled, Gorbachev felt that the term portrayed him as a loser and the USSR as having no values or, at least, not good ones. After some discussion, Baker suggested that they change the phrase to "democratic values," thus ending the friction and forging "a new degree of cooperation, at the level of both personalities and principles."[71] After the morning meeting, Bush went back to the *Belknap* to have lunch with his advisors before meeting with Gorbachev over dinner, but, as the weather continued to worsen, it became apparent that the evening meeting would have to be cancelled. At the end of the next day's meeting, Gorbachev asked Bush to share in a joint press conference in which Bush announced that they had gained a "deeper understanding of each other's views" and that the "cooperative U.S.-Soviet relationship" would make "the future safer and brighter."[72] The joint press conference and Bush's statements provided Gorbachev with the symbolism of a new unity that he desperately needed, a unity that was built on the new relationship that the men had been able to achieve in the two-day meeting.

Certainly, the Malta meeting turned out to be very successful for both Gorbachev and Bush. More importantly, it was a key event in the ending of the Cold War. As Bush's press secretary argued, it was the pivotal point in the change of the U.S.-Soviet relationship:

I would say that [Malta] was the pivotal point at which the West first recognized that Communism was changing and may collapse. And we met with the purpose of trying to define how that could happen, what our role would be, and how we could help guide the future of whatever Russia emerged. . . . And I remember a memo from General Scowcroft to President Bush . . . for Malta that laid out three different scenarios of what might happen in the Soviet Union. And one was that Gorbachev was killed or thrown out of office by hard-line Communists. The other was that Gorbachev did actually change things but it created so much chaos and corruption that the whole country fell apart. Another one was that it kind of worked moderately well—they changed the politics and so forth, but the economy slipped away, and he would be eventually replaced by somebody else who might be able to run the country. But the point is not how well those three scenarios reflected what actually happened, but the point is that that memo indicated that that was the point at which we recognized as a country, as a president, that Communism was gone or on its way and were making plans for the post–Cold War world.[73]

Brent Scowcroft agreed that Malta changed the relationship between the two countries, but he saw the affect that the meeting had on the Bush-Gorbachev relationship as being just as important: "I think the relationship between the two leaders changed. That was the most dramatic . . . that they got comfortable with each other. . . . They would occasionally call each other on the phone and so forth. So the personal relationship changed, and that was very beneficial."[74] At Malta, Gorbachev told Bush that he did not consider him an enemy anymore and actually wanted the United States to maintain a presence in Europe. Secretary of State Baker considered that statement to be the most important statement of the meeting because it "showed that the relationship had moved from confrontation to cooperation."[75] And even though no agreements were signed at Malta, the meeting was important because it built trust between the two sides and the two leaders: "There were not a lot of specifics that were accomplished there, but it was a very good trust-building meeting. And remember that I had been having meetings with Shevardnadze before Malta at which I had become convinced that the Soviet leadership was real when they were talking about reform and when they were talking about renouncing the use of force. President Bush needed to hear that and see that and experience that himself with the head of the Soviet Union."[76]

From Malta, Bush flew to Brussels, Belgium, to speak at NATO headquarters. It was important for Bush to brief his allies about the meeting that he had just finished with Gorbachev. He certainly did not want them to feel that they were being left out of discussions that directly affected their countries. It would also be the Bush administration's first opportunity to put their spin on what was achieved at Malta. To that end, the three senior advisors that traveled with Bush to Malta all appeared on U.S. television while Bush continued to brief the Alliance. Brent Scowcroft appeared on ABC's "Good Morning America"; James Baker gave an interview to "CNN Headline News"; and John Sununu made an appearance on "CBS Morning News." All insisted that the Malta meeting had been a great success.[77] The new understanding became even more important as the revolution that was taking place in Eastern Europe took a bloody turn. Nicolae Ceausescu, the leader of Romania who criticized Gorbachev's reform efforts and brutally crushed dissent in his own country, was toppled by a national uprising and executed, along with his wife, on Christmas Day. It was a symbolic act that the communist domination of Eastern Europe was at an end and a reminder of how quickly incremental reforms could give way to violent change. The U.S.-Soviet relationship that was fostered by Malta would be key in insuring that reform meant political and economic progress rather than chaos and disorder. The revolutions of 1989 had begun a transformation in the geopolitical landscape that would continue to shape the future of Europe.

At the beginning of the year, President Bush had decided to make a fundamental change in the foreign policy approach he had inherited from his mentor, Ronald Reagan.[78] By the end of 1989, he was satisfied with his choice: "I think we followed the right course from the outset, even if we had no way of anticipating what was to happen in the Soviet bloc. We had chosen to switch our focus from Moscow to Central and Eastern Europe in part to test the limits of Gorbachev's commitment to reform, openness, and 'new thinking' in foreign policy. It was fortunate that we began the Administration with this change. By concentrating on Eastern Europe and delaying engaging the Soviets on arms control, we were able to pick up immediately on the promising developments in Poland. We were in on the ground floor and could encourage and take full advantage of the wave of liberalism as it moved through the region."[79] Bush, who had begun 1989 with intense criticism from the press over his long strategic review, had ended the year on a high note. The next step, however, would be perhaps more difficult. The fall of the Berlin Wall, which had symbolized the changing face of Europe, also vaulted the question of German reunification to the center of the world's attention. It would not only test the new U.S.-Soviet relationship, it would also be a test for NATO and the leader of that alliance, George Bush.

Chapter 3

Personal Diplomacy

The Reunification of Germany

In September 1983, Vice President Bush made a trip across North Africa and through Central Europe serving, as was often the case, as President Reagan's diplomatic surrogate. From the safety of Vienna, Bush offered a denunciation of the Iron Curtain: "Can a wall, can guard dogs and machine guns and border patrols deny hundreds of years of European history? Can they create and enforce this fictitious division down the very center of Europe? . . . We [the United States] recognize no lawful division of Europe."[1] More unequivocally, President Reagan made a similar point challenging Gorbachev at Berlin's Brandenburg Gate in September 1987: "General Secretary Gorbachev, if you seek peace, if you seek prosperity for the Soviet Union and Eastern Europe, if you seek liberalization: Come here to this gate! Mr. Gorbachev, open this gate! Mr. Gorbachev, tear down this wall!"[2] Reagan's words were of speechwriters, not foreign policy advisors. In practice, Reagan did not want to jeopardize his goals of nuclear arms reduction with a direct clash over the political division of Europe, something the Soviets had fought fiercely to protect. Reagan's strong rhetoric was never matched by actual policies, a contradiction that mirrored that of other western leaders who, while feeling the obligation to publicly support German reunification in the abstract, actually supported the status quo. As former British Prime Minister Edward Heath put it in 1989, "Naturally we expressed our support of German reunification because we knew it would never happen."[3] British

Prime Minister Margaret Thatcher agreed with Heath: "Although NATO had traditionally made statements supporting Germany's aspiration to be reunited, in practice we were rather apprehensive."[4] According to this argument, the Four Powers agreement of June 5, 1945, which divided Germany, was actually a stabilizing influence on Europe, a position held by the Reagan administration.[5] On the evening of November 9 and early morning of November 10, 1989, this argument lost relevance; the status quo collapsed with the wall. This new reality created enormous problems for both the East and the West; however, most observers still viewed reunification in terms of years, not months. There were simply too many unsolved problems, and some feared that dramatic changes taking place in Germany would lead to violence or possibly a new phase of the Cold War. The problems seemed multifaceted. The German Democratic Republic (GDR) and German Federal Republic (FRG) were two separate German states with markedly different systems of government; Soviet and U.S. troops occupied East and West Germany, respectively. Many East Germans liked socialism and feared being "second-class" citizens; West Germans condemned the shaky East German economy.[6] Internationally, there was a fear of new German nationalism: Britain and France still had vivid memories of two devastating world wars. America worried that a unified Germany would abandon NATO; the Soviet Union considered East Germany the heart of the Soviet security system, an important trading partner, its most loyal ally, and its most visible "spoil of war" that continued to be an important symbol to protect against political decline. Both the East and West seemed to have more to lose than to gain by German reunification. Yet in just 10 months, the partition of Germany would end, and a 45-year-old problem would be resolved. As historian Timothy Garton Ash put it, "More happened in 10 months than usually does in 10 years."[7] The rapid and peaceful process toward reunification was a testament to skillful leaders using behind-the-scenes personal diplomacy, plus a bit of good timing.

This process was in its embryonic state when Chancellor Helmut Kohl spoke by telephone to President Bush on November 10, 1989: "I've just arrived from Berlin. It is like witnessing an enormous fair. It has the atmosphere of a festival. The frontiers are absolutely open. At some points they are literally taking down the wall. . . . I hope they will continue to be calm and peaceful."[8] During the conversation, Kohl expressed concerns about East German refugees and West German financial support for the GDR. Kohl did not mention reunification; he did not have to. Both men knew that it would have to be discussed eventually. But for now, Bush was content to let events take their course. He needed to wait for Soviet reaction to the events in Berlin before he made any decisions. Focused on his upcoming meeting at Malta with Gorbachev, now less than a month away, Bush told Kohl that they needed to decide what to tell Gorbachev concerning the German question. The call itself was quite remarkable in that, in the middle of reacting to one of the most momentous events in German history, the German chancellor had called to give a report of the situation to the U.S. president and ask his advice. Kohl told Bush to tell the American people that "without the U.S. this day would not have been possible."[9] President Bush could have used this call as the centerpiece of a dramatic press conference now that it was clear that the wall had been permanently opened. It certainly would have helped answer the criticism of his guarded press conference in the Oval Office, during which he reacted tentatively to the initial reports of the wall's collapse. Instead, the report of this call appeared in a brief statement by Press Secretary Marlin Fitzwater.[10] As two of Bush's NSC staff members later admitted, "This was characteristic of Bush and his national security staff—often well reasoned on substance but inattentive to the ceremonial dimension of the presidency."[11] Though attentive to his diplomatic responsibilities, Bush ignored his duties to the U.S. press.

Bush would not have to wait long for the Soviet response; later that evening the White House received a cable from Gorbachev, who wanted an immediate meeting of the Four Powers to address the German situation.[12] Gorbachev warned that the "chaotic situation" could have "unforeseen consequences." President Bush recalls Gorbachev's reaction: "The Soviet reaction to the opening of the wall was one of outright alarm. . . . Gorbachev sent messages to Kohl warning him to stop talking of reunification, and cabled me urging that I not overreact. He worried that the demonstrations might get out of control, with 'unforeseen consequences,' and he asked for understanding. This was the first time Gorbachev had clearly indicated genuine anxiety about events in Eastern Europe. Heretofore he had seemed relaxed, even blasé, about the accelerating movement in the region away from communism and Soviet control. It was as if he suddenly realized the serious implications of what was going on."[13] Bush and his advisors felt that the Four Powers conference was a bad idea, but before a response was sent to Gorbachev, it was important that the West agreed on a common approach. As the leader of the Western alliance, Bush assumed the responsibility for orchestrating the response. Scowcroft phoned Kohl's advisor, Horst Teltschik, to get his opinion. Secretary of State James Baker then called West German Foreign Minister Genscher and British Foreign Secretary Douglas Hurd. All agreed to reject Gorbachev's demand for a Four Powers conference. Bush proposed a response that (1) ignored Gorbachev's warnings, (2) welcomed his public support of the East Germans' decision to open their borders, (3) reaffirmed the desire to maintain public order, and (4) voiced confidence that the West German government was committed to incremental change that would not destabilize Eastern Europe. For the time being, Bush chose a passive policy, which supported self-determination but with a tone that would not further alarm the Soviets. He would not yield to Gorbachev's insistence on Four Powers intervention, nor would he jump to premature conclusions on reunification. Margaret Thatcher, François Mitterand, and Kohl agreed with the statement that Bush sent to Gorbachev on November 17, 1989; it would give all sides time to properly evaluate the events in Germany and crystallize their views concerning what would take place next.[14]

The issue of German reunification was problematic for Bush because, as leader of NATO, it was his responsibility to create a consensus among the members of the Alliance. Bush's greatest challenge would be convincing Great Britain to go along with German reunification. Britain had traditionally felt that they had a "special relationship" with the United States and was the leading supporter of the U.S.-led NATO framework, which gave Britain greater authority than its economy and military strength warranted.[15] Margaret Thatcher had been the most vocal supporter of this "special relationship" during the Reagan administration, but when Bush took control of the White House, as Thatcher noted in her memoir, "for . . . partly personal chemistry and partly genuine differences of policy—that relationship had become somewhat strained."[16] Thatcher realized something that many Americans did not: George Bush had markedly different policies than Ronald Reagan. For her part, Thatcher preferred Reagan and was uncomfortable with the astonishing pace of change, warning that "times of great change are times of great uncertainty, even danger."[17] Germany certainly was seen as a source of danger by Thatcher, who felt that aggression and self-doubt were an intrinsic part of Germany's national character. Thatcher's foreign policy was animated by an anti-German prejudice common among persons of her generation. This deep-seated feeling was evident in her remarks to one of her foreign policy advisors in which, while watching the collapse of the Berlin Wall, she reminded him that she had "been through the war" and knew "perfectly well what Germans are like and what dictators can do and how national character basically doesn't change."[18] Thatcher's fears, however, were not simply based on painful memories from her youth. She was worried about how a united Germany would affect the power balance in Europe, fearing that a reunited Germany would simply be "too big and powerful to be just another player"; it would be a "destabilizing rather than a stabilizing force in Europe."[19] She also worried that the reunification of Germany would undermine Gorbachev, leading to demands for border changes throughout central Europe. She was even more worried about Germany's economic expansion, which led Thatcher to prefer a truly democratic East Germany to formal reunification. To that end, she sent Bush a message urging that the priority should be to see genuine democracy established in East Germany and that "German reunification was not something to be addressed at present."[20]

France would also be a problem for Bush. France hoped to strengthen the Alliance via Europeanization, which encouraged European cohesion through conventional military cooperation with the West Germans and cooperation with the British on nuclear weapons. This framework emphasized gaining greater independence from the hegemonic power of the United States, a stance which certainly infused Europeanism with an anti-American undercurrent. The Bush administration would not give into this line of thinking; as Brent Scowcroft insisted, the United States would continue to be a European power "with a substantial military and political presence" and with "an abiding and permanent interest in European security."[21] Parts of France's position could be used by Bush to push for a consensus because, even though it undercut Atlanticism (U.S. hegemony), the goal of France was a more independent West European power center. The source of stability for Western Europe was threefold: NATO (defense), the European Community (economic), and the Conference on Security and Cooperation in Europe (political). The source of stability for the East was imposed from the outside—the monopoly of power by the Communist party and the readiness of the Soviet Union to use force to maintain its appointed leaders in power. With that system of coercion quickly crumbling, stability in Eastern Europe, and by means of proximity, Western Europe, was in doubt. Both Thatcher and Mitterand accepted the Germans' right to self-determination, but they did not believe that the Germans had a right to upset the political realities of Europe. Bush focused on stability in Europe, noting that NATO, unlike the Warsaw Pact, provided a solid framework for cooperation in an integrated Europe. This brought protests from Thatcher who, for largely economic reasons, did not want Germany to be part of an increasingly integrated European Community and, instead, wanted to keep both NATO and the Warsaw Pact intact in order to maintain part of the old order.

Consensus within the Alliance was not Bush's only problem in respect to German reunification. East German dissident groups were demonstrating to reform the Communist regime while keeping a separate state, and, in

West Germany, Chancellor Kohl did not yet have a mandate for reunification because of fear that a union would disrupt the economy. An opinion poll taken the month before the fall of the Berlin Wall showed that only 56 percent of West Germans favored reunification.[22] Given the lack of consensus inside Germany, Bush needed a plan that left domestic concerns to be worked out between the two German states. There were also fears from countries surrounding Germany, particularly Poland, that a unified Germany would try to alter the Helsinki Accords, which guaranteed its post–World War II borders. East and West Germany could not be disentangled from any international treaty and occupation status before assurances could be worked out to the satisfaction of neighboring countries. The most difficult job for Bush, however, would be convincing the Soviets to allow a reunified Germany that remained within NATO. The Soviet position on reunification came from concern for their security arrangements. East Germany, with its approximately 370,000 Soviet troops, was the center of the Warsaw Pact. Rather than a mutual defense system, the Warsaw Pact was in essence a series of bilateral agreements between each member and the Soviet Union. If reunification resulted in a united Germany within NATO, it would mean an impossible disparity between NATO and the remainder of the Warsaw Pact.[23]

Before each side had a chance to develop its own policies, Chancellor Kohl surprised everyone with a speech before the Bundestag on November 28, in which he outlined a ten-point plan for German unity:

1. Establish measures to provide unhindered travel between East and West Germany.

2. Expand technological cooperation with the GDR.

3. Expand economic aid to the GDR if "fundamental change of the political and economic system in the GDR be agreed upon and put irrevocably into effect." This would require free elections without SED (Socialist Unity party) monopoly of power and the dismantling of centralized economic planning.

4. Establish a "contractual community" with the GDR to cooperate institutionally on a variety of common problems.

5. Proceed, after free elections in the GDR, to develop "confederate structures between the two German states and, eventually, a federal system for all Germany, which would include joint governmental committees and a common parliament.

6. Embed the development of inter-German relations in the pan-European process and in East-West relations.

7. Strengthen the EC (European Community), encourage European integration, and allow Eastern European countries entrance into the EC once they have met certain prerequisites.

8. Speed up development of the CSCE (Conference on Security and Cooperation in Europe), including new institutions for East-West economic cooperation and environmental relations.

9. Support rapid progress in arms control.

10. Peacefully overcome the division of Europe and support reunification through a policy of self-determination by the German people.[24]

The ten-point plan was actually a modest proposal that was only meant to establish an outline for reunification, not speed up the process. What it did, however, was encourage all sides to take the issue of reunification seriously. The speech had been made without consultation with any NATO countries, something particularly upsetting to Mitterand, who had met with Kohl just three days earlier. The Soviets immediately dismissed the ten-point plan as unrealistic.[25] From that point on, each side suggested corrections and alternatives to Kohl's plan. Soviet officials suggested, at various times throughout this period, the following counterproposals:

1. The dissolution of NATO and the Warsaw Pact and their replacement by permanent all-European security structures.

2. A European-wide referendum on the international and security aspects of German unification.

3. The neutralization and demilitarization of Germany.

4. A military-political status for Germany in NATO similar to that of France.

5. Continued, though modified, exercise of Four Powers occupation rights in Germany.

6. The formation of a center in Berlin to control all military forces in Germany.

7. Membership of Germany in both NATO and the Warsaw Pact.

8. Membership of the Soviet Union in NATO.

9. Membership of the FRG in NATO and associate status for the eastern part of Germany in the Warsaw Pact.[26]

The dramatic differences in these proposals demonstrate the vulnerability of the Soviet Union. Even when reunification took on the aura of inevitability, Gorbachev did not want to give the appearance of acceding to Western demands. The initiatives proposed by the various sides quickly began to fall into three broad categories: a major conference that would be comprised of all CSCE members and convened to negotiate the final peace settlement of World War II; a Four Powers conference to resolve what had been agreed on at Potsdam in 1945 as provisional arrangements; or a German-only solution that left the FRG and the GDR to handle matters without any outside interference.[27]

The Bush administration developed a plan that combined the German-only approach with the Four Powers meeting demanded by the Soviets. This "Two-plus-Four" plan would give the two German states control over internal matters while allowing the Four Powers to oversee the external aspects of reunification. The plan provided a diplomatic process for carrying out rapid reunification in a way that all countries involved might accept. Most importantly, it gave Moscow a chance to participate in part of the process toward reunification as it was happening rather than after the process finished—an important point for Gorbachev, who did not want to appear as caving into Western demands. Not all of Bush's advisors initially embraced the Two-plus-Four approach. There was disagreement between the NSC, who had reservations about the plan, and the State Department. Scowcroft did not like the idea of involving the Four Powers, because he feared that the Soviet Union might end up dominating the process. There was a greater concern, however, that the FRG and Moscow might work out a private deal, as had happened in the past.[28] In the end, Baker was allowed to begin negotiations on Two-plus-Four, and the administration undertook an intensive campaign of personal diplomacy to convince others that the Two-plus-Four approach was best. Baker explained the plan to Hans-Dietrich Genscher who, realizing that it would give great-power legitimacy to reunification, agreed with the plan as long as the "Two" preceded the "Four" so as to avoid any appearance of the Four "negotiating *about* Germany."[29] This talk along with Bush's conversation with British Foreign Secretary Douglas Hurd on January 29 and Scowcroft's conversation with Kohl's assistant Horst Teltschik on February 3 meant that the Two-plus-Four plan had been explained to both the British and Germans, both of whom seemed favorably disposed. Baker traveled to Moscow to present the plan to the Soviets, stopping along the way to discuss matters with French Foreign Minister Roland Dumas. Baker met with Shevardnadze on February 7 and Gorbachev on February 9. Baker recalls that although German reunification was still "a very tough topic" as far as Shevardnadze was concerned, he felt that Gorbachev might be willing to at least consider the U.S. proposal, but only if Germany was unified outside of NATO.[30] Despite the continued reservations on the part of the Soviets, Baker paved the way for Gorbachev's meeting the following day with the West Germans.

On Saturday, February 10, 1990, Chancellor Kohl and Foreign Minister Hans-Dietrich Genscher flew to Moscow to meet with Gorbachev. Kohl's preparation for the meeting included considerable help from the Americans as Baker had given him a summary of his discussions with Gorbachev, including Gorbachev's concerns about a united Germany and the hope that Gorbachev might accept the Two-plus-Four plan. Baker urged Kohl to calm Soviet fears by stressing that Germany's borders were permanent. Bush also sent Kohl a letter, pledging full U.S. support and asking him to make it clear to Gorbachev that the neutralization of Germany was out of the question and that all of a united Germany would remain in NATO: "I was deeply gratified by your rejection of proposals for neutrality and your firm statement that a unified Germany would stay in the North Atlantic Alliance. . . . As our two countries journey together through this time of hope and promise, we can remain confident of our shared ability to defend the fruits of freedom. Nothing Mr. Gorbachev can say to Jim Baker or to you can change the fundamental fact of our deep and enduring partnership."[31] Kohl was ecstatic over the letter, hailing it as "one of the great documents in German-U.S. history."[32] By giving Kohl the strongest possible guarantee of U.S. support, Bush lessened the chance that West Germany might abandon NATO in order to hasten reunification. In a phone call soon after the meeting, Kohl reassured Bush that he had made it clear to Gorbachev that neutralization was out of the question and relayed his belief that Gorbachev could be persuaded to agree:

> **Kohl:** I told Gorbachev again that the neutralization of Germany is out of the question for me.
> **Bush:** Did he acquiesce or just listen? How did he react?
> **Kohl:** My impression is that this is a subject about which they want to negotiate, but that we can win that point in negotiations. The modalities will be important, but I do believe we can find a solution.[33]

The historic meeting between Gorbachev and Kohl was important because Gorbachev finally accepted that German reunification would be decided by the German people. He still, however, was not ready to relinquish his right to shape the external aspects of reunification or accept a unified Germany in NATO. As Kohl told Bush in the telephone conversation, this still needed to be negotiated.

NATO and Warsaw Pact foreign ministers met in Ottawa, Canada, in February 1990 to discuss arms control matters, including Bush's Open Skies proposal. While arms control was the official agenda, unofficial private meetings centered on Germany. Bush had sent Baker to reach agreement on Two-plus-Four. Gorbachev, meanwhile, had sent Shevardnadze with a mandate to wrap up a CFE (conventional forces in Europe) agreement. After Baker, Hurd, Dumas, and Genscher reached agreement, they presented the plan to the Soviets. Baker handed the Two-plus-Four announcement to Shevardnadze, who agreed to forward it to Gorbachev. Gorbachev gave his consent, provided that it did not mention the mid-March East German elections and that the announcement promised to deal with issues of security for neighboring states. These demands were meant to placate his allies in East Germany and Poland. Baker was delighted with the agreement, especially when Shevardnadze informed him that Gorbachev had dropped his demand of symmetrical force levels in Europe, thus clearing the last hurdle for a CFE treaty. In Ottawa, when the joint statement on Two-plus-Four was made to the press, the NATO foreign ministers that had been left out of the ad hoc meetings were furious. They were not the only ones infuriated by the announcement as hard-liners in Moscow were upset that Gorbachev had made this agreement before resolving the West's demand that Germany remain in NATO. Kohl, however, was overjoyed, declaring that Germany was "jumping with a single leap" toward reunification: "We have never been so close to our goal, the unity of all Germans in freedom, as we are today."[34] The Ottawa announcement was important symbolically because it demonstrated that there was a certain degree of consensus that German reunification would happen and a process was now in place to manage it. Reunification had now moved to the planning stage, but there were still significant problems. As one Bush administration official noted, "the road to unification still led through Moscow."[35] Despite Gorbachev's eagerness to accommodate Baker and Kohl, the Soviet hierarchy was still not ready to accept reunification. Many officials in the Soviet Union and East Germany wanted to retain influence by channeling the process through a German confederation, something that would require a victory by the Communists and Social Democrats in the upcoming March elections in East Germany. According to polls, this seemed likely.[36]

Helmut Kohl met with President Bush at Camp David on February 24, 1990. Bush wanted a relaxed atmosphere in which he could talk openly with Kohl (fig. 10). Their many phone conversations had established good rapport, and now Bush wanted to capitalize on the relationship that he had so carefully fostered in order to coordinate the path to reunification, keep Germany committed to NATO, and renew German commitment to the Oder-Neisse line as its permanent eastern boundary. As for the border issue, Kohl proposed that the United States should mediate the dispute. Bush

Figure 10. Bush practicing personal diplomacy during a walk with Chancellor Kohl at Camp David, Feb. 25, 1990. *Courtesy of the George Bush Presidential Library*

accepted Kohl's offer and resolved the Polish-German border issue by the end of March, largely thanks to private mediation between Kohl and Polish Prime Minister Tadeusz Mazowiecki. The NATO issue was a bit more complex. Kohl agreed that a united Germany should be a member of NATO; however, the precise definition for Germany's NATO membership was not yet clear. Should Germany's membership be similar to France's and not participate in NATO's military structures? Should there be a transition period? Should NATO forces and nuclear weapons be prevented from being stationed on East German soil? These questions had clearly not been resolved by Kohl, something that concerned President Bush because he did not want another France in NATO. Bush wanted Germany to remain in NATO, felt that U.S. troops and nuclear weapons should remain in Germany, and believed that the territory of the former East Germany should have a "special military status" that would allow its integration into NATO. Bush also made it clear to Kohl that Soviet opposition to full German membership in NATO would not be tolerated: "The Soviets are not in a position to dictate Germany's relationship with NATO. What worries me is talk that Germany must not stay in NATO. To hell with that! We prevailed, they didn't. We can't let the Soviets clutch victory from the jaws of defeat."[37] Bush's strong words showed that this point was not up for negotiation. Kohl suggested that the Soviets might acquiesce for the right price and that convincing the Soviets about membership might "end up as a matter of cash. They need money."[38] He went on to say that the trick would be to get the Soviets to tell the West the real price for agreeing to German membership in NATO. The Camp David meeting was instrumental in allowing the United States to coordinate the objectives and procedures for the upcoming Two-plus-Four negotiations. Following the Camp David meeting, the NSC staff prepared a blueprint for the talks to limit their scope, circulating the plan to its allies so that the position of the West would be clear:

- Four Power rights, including the fate of Berlin: decide in Two-plus-Four.
- Borders: decide in Two-plus-Four with sovereign German voice.
- NATO's obligations toward the former GDR: sovereign German decision; no discussion in Two-plus-Four.
- German forces in GDR: sovereign German decision; could be discussed in Two-plus-Four.
- Soviet troops in GDR: sovereign German decision and subject for bilateral German-Soviet agreement; could be discussed in Two-plus-Four.
- Nuclear weapons in FRG: to be decided by Germany or in arms control negotiations; no discussion in Two-plus-Four.
- German NATO membership: sovereign German decision; no discussion in Two-plus-Four.
- Prohibition of German nuclear, biological, and chemical weapons: sovereign German decision; could be discussed in Two-plus-Four.
- Size of the Bundeswehr: to be decided by Germany or in arms control negotiations; no discussion in Two-plus-Four.[39]

This plan would be used at the Two-plus-Four meetings and for future consultations with allies. It is clear by the clarity and level of detail in this list that the Bush administration was setting down the law to its allies in order to ensure Western solidarity, something on which the U.S. strategy depended. The belief that Soviet compliance was a matter of money proved important as the United States and West Germany began work on an "incentives package" for the Soviet Union. In the press conference following the Camp David meeting, the United States and West Germany appeared to be in full agreement. Bush called Thatcher, Mitterand, and Gorbachev the following day to brief them, in very general terms, on what had happened.[40] All knew that nothing could be resolved until the March 18 elections in East Germany, and most observers in the West feared that even though the Communists would probably lose, the voters would turn to the

Social Democrats, making it hard for Kohl and the Christian Democrats to regain momentum.

There were two basic possibilities for reunification according to the Basic Law of West Germany. Article 146 allowed for a constitutional assembly following all-German elections to create a new political state with a new constitution and new form of government. The Soviets hoped that the result would be a weak confederation. The other lawful possibility was for East Germany to dissolve and be absorbed through a direct takeover by West Germany under Article 23, thus creating a larger, more powerful FRG with its current system of government intact. Led by Kohl, the official West German position favored using Article 23. East Germans would have their chance to voice their opinion when the first free general elections in the GDR were held on March 18, 1990. With an amazing 93 percent voter turnout, the Alliance for Germany garnered more than 48 percent of the vote; the Social Democrats (SPD) received 22 percent; and the ex-Communists, the Party for Democratic Socialism (PDS), received 16 percent of the vote.[41] It was a decisive vote for the absorption of East Germany into the more prosperous West: over 75 percent of the vote went to parties promoting reunification, a mandate for Kohl's plan for unity. The new East German government was dedicated to a rapid West German takeover under Article 23, giving Kohl complete control of internal unification. President Bush phoned Kohl to congratulate him on a stunning victory, exclaiming, "You're a hell of a campaigner!"[42] Having already begun discussions with the SPD-East leader in anticipation of victory, the election caught the Soviets by surprise, which resulted in the Soviet position becoming weaker after the elections.

While Kohl continued handling the internal aspects of reunification, it was up to the United States, as Baker recalls, to address the major task of leading a fundamental change in NATO and the CSCE: "A unified Germany would alter the fundamental geo-strategic, political, and economic architecture of Europe. That meant that NATO had to become a more political institution, CSCE had to be strengthened, and a clear and complementary division of responsibilities among these institutions and the European Community would have to be defined."[43] Resolving German reunification meant taking a fresh look at European security as a whole, and Secretary Baker had mapped out his plan for a new European architecture in December 1989. Now the position of the United States needed to go even further. A fundamental change in NATO's strategy would have to be made if it were to incorporate a unified Germany without angering the Soviets. It was necessary to convince the Soviet Union that Europe's political and security institutions were evolving. The Soviet Union needed to feel unthreatened by a NATO strengthened by the addition of a unified Germany. After all, the Soviet Union still had 350,000 troops stationed in the GDR and had the legal right to refuse to give up their Four Power rights and remain a military presence in Germany. The best approach for the United States was to convince them that such an action would isolate them diplomatically. As Bush's advisors believed, they needed to make clear to the Soviets that "the cost of continued rigidity would be a deterioration in the smooth, stable relations so essential to the benign international environment in which the Soviet leaders could concentrate on domestic reform."[44] In order to achieve this level of isolation, there had to be complete solidarity on the part of the West. Now that the German election made it clear that unity could not be halted, Mitterand and Thatcher began to play a more constructive role. Bush met with Thatcher in Bermuda and Mitterand in Key Largo, Florida, to discuss the goals of the upcoming Two-plus-Four conference. Bush sent letters after these meetings and his meetings with Kohl to reiterate what had been agreed upon so that the Western position on NATO and Two-plus-Four was clear. He would then make statements to the press to provide public repetition of the agreements, speaking as the official voice of a solidified West, thus locking up debate. Bush dramatically improved the solidarity of the West's position by the end of April, shortly before the first meeting of the Ottawa Group was held in Bonn on May 5, 1990. The day before the Ottawa Group met, Bush spoke on the future of NATO at a commencement address at Oklahoma State University, once again using a low-profile media event to make an important policy speech. Bush had previewed his ideas to NATO leaders in the days leading up to his speech, meeting with Thatcher, Mitterand, and Kohl, and talking via telephone to NATO Secretary General Wörner. As with previous dealings with NATO leaders, Bush wanted to make sure everyone was on the same page—his. Bush proposed an early NATO summit to review NATO's political role in Europe, review its strategy in conventional defenses and nuclear weapons, and establish a consensus on the future of CSCE. This "wide-ranging NATO strategy review for the transformed Europe of the 1990s" was meant most of all to signal to Gorbachev that NATO was changing and would not be a threat: "As military threats fade, the political dimension of NATO's work—always there but seldom noticed—becomes prominent. . . . Our enemy today is uncertainty and instability."[45] In the same speech, however, Bush also sent a message that Germany would remain a "full member of NATO."[46] He made it clear that the West was committed to changing NATO's traditional role, which had been one of defense against a massive Soviet attack on Western Europe, and re-inventing it as a political alliance. This idea built on a speech Secretary Baker made before the Berlin Press Club the previous December in which he called for a "new architecture" for a new era: "As we construct a new security architecture that maintains the common defense, the non-military component of European security will grow. Arms control agreements, confidence-building measures and other political consultative arrangements are going to become more important. It is in such a world that the role of NATO is going to evolve. NATO will become the forum where the Western nations cooperate to negotiate, to verify and to extend agreements between East and West."[47] NATO had to adapt to a new role if the United States was to stay in Europe. Gorbachev had suggested doing away with NATO and the Warsaw Pact in favor of other European alliances, a suggestion that forced Bush to demonstrate that NATO, the EC, and CSCE were complementary, not competitive. To further that goal, the Bush team put together a proposal that would, as Brent Scowcroft put it, "help Moscow save face," and transform the alliance in four areas:

1. It would emphasize its political mission and develop cooperation and partnership with former adversaries. The alliance pledged never to be the first to use force, proposed a non-aggression pact with members of the Warsaw Pact (not with the Pact itself), and invited those governments to establish diplomatic missions at NATO headquarters in Brussels.

2. It called for changing the character of conventional defense by moving away from "forward defense" and relying increasingly on more mobile, truly multinational forces. The document also proposed conventional arms control negotiations (after the conclusion of a CFE treaty) to further limit offensive military manpower in Europe.

3. It announced a new NATO nuclear strategy, modifying "flexible response" to reduce reliance on nuclear weapons and make them "truly weapons of last resort."

4. It proposed strengthening the CSCE process by giving it a new mandate to promote democratic institutions, operational capacity in the area of conflict prevention, and, for the first time, an institutional structure through a new secretariat and other bodies.[48]

These proposals would be made at the NATO summit to help resolve the obstacles to Soviet acceptance of German reunification within NATO.

Persuading Gorbachev to give his approval for German membership in NATO, however, would require more than just a change in NATO. Kohl urged Bush to agree to Gorbachev's request for financial assistance, but Bush could not give Gorbachev the twenty billion dollars for which he had asked, not while the Soviets were still blockading Lithuania and not until Gorbachev made economic reforms to demonstrate that the money would not be wasted. What the United States actually offered was the image of a deal being struck between the two superpowers. Gorbachev desperately needed this image, even if the economic assistance came from a different source. The Bush administration planned a Washington summit at which they would shower Gorbachev with attention. Gorbachev arrived on May 31, 1990, and was greeted with a parade of soldiers wearing ceremonial Revolutionary War uniforms of the Old Guard from Fort Meyer. Gorbachev and Bush reviewed the fife and drum corps on the South Lawn of the White House against the backdrop of the Washington Monument before moving into the Oval Office for a private meeting at which Gorbachev hinted at financial help. Bush planned the type of summit that Gorbachev needed to boost his image. Unlike Malta, the Washington summit was full of ceremonial events, where Gorbachev mingled with prominent business leaders, intellectuals, and celebrities. By the end of the summit, Gorbachev would receive various honors, including the *FDR for Freedoms Medal* from the Franklin Delano Roosevelt Institute, the Peace Prize from the Albert Einstein Peace Prize Foundation, and the Martin Luther King Jr., Non-violent Peace Prize. The first day concluded with a formal State Dinner honoring President and Mrs. Gorbachev. The dinner had a long and varied guest list ranging from political leaders, such as Henry Kissinger and Richard Gephardt, to movie stars, such as Morgan Freeman and Jessica Tandy.[49] In his toast Bush laid it on thick: "Mr. President, you deserve great credit for the course you've chosen—for the political and economic reforms you've introduced—and for creating within the Soviet Union a commitment to change. As I said this morning as I welcomed you to the White House, we want to see perestroika succeed—we want to see this transition now underway in the Soviet Union maintain its momentum."[50] Of course, this type of praise and effort by the Bush administration to boost Gorbachev's image was not meant as a one-way gesture, and Bush hoped Gorbachev would move to embrace NATO membership for Germany. At 4:30 the next afternoon, both sides crowded into the Cabinet Room to discuss Germany. At first, Gorbachev seemed unwilling to soften his position on NATO membership for a united Germany. Bush had tried all the standard arguments but to no avail. Then, as Bush recalls, he tried something else: "I tried a new track. I reminded Gorbachev that the Helsinki Final Act stated that all countries had the right to choose their alliances. To me, that meant Germany should be able to decide for itself what it wanted. Did he agree? To my astonishment, Gorbachev shrugged his shoulders and said yes, that was correct. The room suddenly became quiet. Akhromeyev and Valentin Falin looked at each other and squirmed in their seats."[51] Amazingly, the leader of the Soviet Union had, on his own and without consulting his advisors, now conceded that German membership in NATO was a matter for the Germans to decide. Knowing that Kohl had already publicly stated that Germany wanted to join NATO, Gorbachev had just given Germany the right to make that decision without having to gain approval from the Four Powers. The U.S. side almost could not believe what they had heard: "Bob Blackwill slipped me a note asking whether I thought I could get Gorbachev to say that again. I nodded to him. 'I'm gratified that you and I seem to agree that nations can choose their own alliances,' I said. 'Do you and I agree that a united Germany had the right to be non-aligned, or a member of NATO, in a final document?' asked Gorbachev. 'I agree with that, but the German public wants to be in NATO,' I replied. 'But if they want out of NATO, we will respect that. They are a democracy.' 'I agree to say so publicly, that the United States and the USSR are in favor of seeing a united Germany, with a final settlement leaving it up to where a united Germany can choose,' said Gorbachev."[52] Gorbachev's concession angered his own side: "By this time, the dismay in the Soviet team was palpable. Akhromeyev's eyes flashed angrily as he gestured to Falin. They snapped back and forth in loud stage whispers in an agitated debate as Gorbachev spoke. It was an unbelievable scene, the likes of which none of us had ever seen before—virtually open rebellion against a Soviet leader."[53] Despite this opposition, Gorbachev refused to recant his concession to Bush's major point. He suggested that the foreign ministers work out the details. Shevardnadze refused, saying that it was a matter for the presidents to decide. The United States had managed to get a major concession from the Soviet leader and were not about to let him forget his pledge (fig. 11).

The rest of the summit went as planned, with discussions of other pressing matters. There were no further discussions of Germany between Bush and Gorbachev during the summit. Instead, Gorbachev pressed for a trade agreement that included Most Favored Nation (MFN) status. He seemed almost agitated at times, desperate to go home with some tangible accomplishment from the summit, and, considering Gorbachev's newfound flexibility on Germany, the Bush administration was inclined to accommodate him. The only problem was the situation in Lithuania, which necessitated that the trade agreement would have both a public side and a private one. The United States would sign the grain and trade agreements but would not send the package to Congress until the Soviets passed legislation on

Figure 11. Bush and Gorbachev in the Cabinet Room during the Washington Summit on May 31, 1990. By the end of this meeting, Gorbachev had conceded that NATO membership was a matter for the Germans to decide. *Courtesy of the George Bush Presidential Library*

emigration, something that had been a precondition for MFN status. The package would also not be sent for congressional approval until the Soviets lifted the economic embargo on Lithuania and began negotiations. With those stipulations, the trade agreement was signed and Gorbachev had a tangible accomplishment to take back with him to bolster his support at home. Gorbachev's accomplishment came at considerable public expense for President Bush. Unaware of the secret conditions behind the agreement, the press attacked Bush for abandoning Lithuania. The next day the two men traveled to Camp David for more relaxed discussions (fig. 12). Bush had gotten Gorbachev to be flexible on German membership in NATO, and Gorbachev had gotten his trade agreement to help his struggling domestic economy. At the press conference at the end of the summit, Bush sought to get Gorbachev's pledge on record (fig. 13): "On the matter of Germany's external alliances, I believe, as do Chancellor Kohl and members of the Alliance, that the united Germany should be a full member of NATO. President Gorbachev, frankly, does not hold that view. But we are in full agreement that the matter of Alliance membership is, in accordance with the Helsinki Final Act, a matter for the Germans to decide."[54] The

Figure 12. Informal discussions at Camp David, June 2, 1990. *Around the table clockwise:* Bush, Quayle, Scowcroft, Shevardnadze, Gorbachev, Marshal Sergei Akhromeyev, Peter Afanasenko (interpreter), and Baker. *Courtesy of the George Bush Presidential Library*

Figure 13. Gorbachev and Bush sign agreements reached at the Washington summit, June 1, 1990. *Courtesy of the George Bush Presidential Library*

statement had been cleared with the Soviets and, from that point on, Gorbachev never publicly opposed the idea that alliance membership was a matter for the Germans to decide. The Washington summit had been a success. In Copenhagen on June 5, Shevardnadze met with Baker during a session of the CSCE and told him that the Soviet Union would accept a unified Germany in NATO and that the unification process could be completed by the end of 1990. This offer, of course, would be dependant on the United States following through with the assurance that had been promised in the nine-point plan.[55] Baker marched over to Genscher's hotel to get him out of bed to tell him the good news.[56] Gorbachev made it official the following week on June 12 when he publicly announced from Moscow that he would accept a unified Germany as a member of NATO if certain conditions were met. In an amazingly short time span, the Soviet position had moved from an adamant "no" to a "yes, but."

Bush sought to eliminate Gorbachev's remaining reservations at the NATO Summit in London on July 5–6. Despite some objections by Thatcher and Mitterand concerning some of the language used in his proposals, Bush was largely able to push through his plan for a new NATO structure. On his flight from London to the G-7 summit in Houston, Bush sent Gorbachev a personal message transmitted from *Air Force One* that described how the NATO declaration addressed Soviet concerns and how it was written with Gorbachev "importantly in mind."[57] At the G-7 meeting, Bush sought to address Gorbachev's remaining condition: economic assistance. Unfortunately, the international consensus that had helped push through the London declaration did not exist when it came to large-scale aid. Instead, over the objections of Kohl, the leaders asked the International Monetary Fund to start a year-long review of the economic needs of the Soviet Union. Direct assistance would have to wait . . . or come solely from the Germans. That is exactly what happened when Kohl and Gorbachev met on July 14 in the Caucasus at Gorbachev's home. Kohl agreed to assume all GDR economic obligations to Moscow, arrange a credit of DM 5 billion ($3 billion), and pay the costs of Soviet troops in East Germany during the transition period. Finally, Gorbachev was ready to agree to German unification within NATO without conditions or reservations.[58] As Margaret Thatcher cynically assessed, "The Soviets were prepared to sell reunification for a modest boost from Germany to their crumbling economy."[59] Although the final concession was monetary, the Washington summit and NATO declaration had allowed Gorbachev to accept the final terms without, at least in his mind, appearing to concede to Western ultimatums. No matter when or why he decided to concede to the U.S. position, Gorbachev knew that he had to sell German NATO membership to the Soviet people. He would soon find out how good a salesman he had been.

The reunification process went smoothly after the Gorbachev-Kohl Caucasus meeting with the Two-plus-Four talks producing a final document that detailed the international conditions of German reunification, and the *Treaty on the Final Settlement with Respect to Germany* was signed with little fanfare on September 12, 1990.[60] There was little reason for celebration. The true accomplishment had not come during the Two-plus-Four talks, where negotiators quibbled over minutiae. It had come months earlier during the private meetings, letters, and phone conversations between leaders from both the East and the West. It was during those moments that personal diplomacy proved to be decisive. As Dick Cheney recalls, the task was not an uncomplicated one: "Getting Germany reunified as part of NATO, those things look fairly simple now because we got them done but they weren't that easy at the time."[61] The United States in particular used personal diplomacy to achieve what had once been unthinkable. Convincing the Soviet Union to allow a unified Germany to remain in NATO was an important foreign policy achievement for the Bush administration. As Secretary Baker recalls, the Bush administration "took advantage of a very narrow window of opportunity."[62] The first step was to unite Western leaders. Bush accomplished this through extensive meetings, letters, and telephone conversations with those leaders. As Baker recalls, "personal diplomacy was very important" to he and President Bush, because "if you can trust a person on the other side of the table, you have a better chance at getting things done."[63] This was particularly important in relations with Helmut Kohl; Bush had to make sure that the Germans would remain in NATO. Bush ensured Kohl's partnership by offering him full support for his plan for German reunification as long as it was understood that the end result would be a unified Germany inside NATO. As Scowcroft recalls, the Bush-Kohl meeting after Malta was the turning point in their partnership: "It was pivotal because Kohl was sort of out on his own. . . . The other allies didn't want German unification, so Kohl was kind of feeling his way. And they had this meeting and the president said . . . 'I'm not worried. I like your ideas. You go ahead; I'll back you. I'll keep everybody else off your back.' So he gave, in essence, a blank check to Kohl to move ahead."[64] After that meeting it was a steady course as far as Western solidarity was concerned. But getting the Soviets to accept what had been difficult even for some Western leaders to accept would prove much more difficult. The U.S. strategy depended on Western solidarity and Soviet unwillingness, or inability, to take decisive action. Just as having a clear plan of attack was key for the West, disagreements within the Soviet hierarchy weakened their resolve. The Bush administration needed to hold firm in their demands, try to diplomatically isolate the Soviet Union, and hope for a crack in the Soviet position. Getting a defeated Soviet Union to accept an abrupt realignment of the European power balance would require the Bush administration to wait for an opening. According to Scowcroft, that narrow window of opportunity was created when Gorbachev simply could not provide an acceptable alternative to the position taken by the United States:

> There were two problems. First of all, there was the problem of unification itself. And that is that East Germany was the crown jewel of the Soviet bloc. That was the major achievement, if you will, out of World War II. And so it was difficult to say, "Yes, we [the Soviet Union] failed there." And secondly, it was the heart of the Warsaw Pact. It's pretty hard to have a viable Warsaw Pact if East Germany is not in it. So that was the problem with unification. Then there was an added problem: suppose you let Germany unify—What do you do about membership in NATO? Because East Germany was in Warsaw Pact. West Germany was in NATO. And that was a very hard pill for Gorbachev to swallow. And in the end I think that he swallowed it only because he didn't have a better alternative. He toyed around with the idea of a neutral Germany, but I think he decided that that would be more dangerous—to have a neutral Germany loose in Europe—than one tied down by the United States.[65]

Not having an acceptable solution of his own, facing increasing domestic problems, and desperately needing foreign financial assistance, Gorbachev broke with the hard-liners and acquiesced at the Washington summit to allow a unified Germany to remain in NATO. These same hard-liners blamed him for losing Eastern Europe and weakening the Soviet Union.

Chapter 4

A Glimpse of the Post–Cold War World

The Persian Gulf War

The Persian Gulf War has been described by some as the acid test of the end of the Cold War. In the fall of 1990 and spring of 1991, the re-unification of Germany was being finalized, relations between the United States and Soviet Union were continuing to improve, and by the end of 1991, the Soviet Union would cease to exist. It was under this backdrop that President Bush confronted Iraq's aggression in what many in his adminis-tration viewed as the first real crisis of the post–Cold War era and a diffi-cult test of the new U.S.-Soviet relationship. Bush's initial approach to Iraq was one decision that actually mirrored that of the Reagan administration The war between Iran and Iraq began in 1980 and presented a dilemma for the United States in that neither country was considered a Cold War ally; the Reagan administration, however, decided to "aid the weaker, which was Iraq."[1] This was seen as necessary in order to contribute to the adminis-tration's regional security interests and objectives in the Middle East "to prevent the Soviet Union from attaining a position of hegemony in the re-gion by deterring Soviet expansion and by supporting the sovereignty of all countries in the region" and "to maintain continued access for the U.S. and its principal allies to Gulf oil."[2] To that end, the Reagan administration had given Iraq more than one billion dollars worth of Commodity Credit Cor-poration (CCC) credit guarantees to encourage Iraq to import U.S. grain, and the administration approved export licenses that allowed Saddam Hussein to purchase military technology.[3] National Security Directive 26, issued during Bush's first year in office, confirmed the Bush administration's commitment to continuing the policy started by Reagan: "Normal relations between the United States and Iraq would serve our longer-term interests and promote stability in both the Gulf and the Middle East. The United States Government should propose economic and political incentives for Iraq to moderate its behavior and increase our influence in Iraq. . . . Also, as a means of developing access to and influence with the Iraqi defense establishment, the United States should consider sales of non-lethal forms of military assistance, e.g., training courses and medical exchanges, on a case by case basis."[4]

Despite the U.S. government's continued economic engagement with Iraq, the Bush administration was not able to control Saddam's foreign policy moves.[5] U.S. intelligence had repeatedly discovered evidence of Iraq's efforts to develop weapons of mass destruction, including the development of a nuclear weapons program. The immediate international concern, however, came in the form of Iraq's relationship with Kuwait, which had been a financial supporter of Iraq in its war against Iran. Now Iraq owed Kuwait thirty billion dollars for their assistance. Moreover, the two countries were locked in a boundary dispute over the rich Rumaila oil field as well as Iraq's claim of islands off Kuwait. This was more than a boundary dispute. Heavily in debt, Saddam was using the fourth-largest military in the world to make a move for hegemony in the region and to take a leading role in OPEC and the Arab world. On July 25, 1990, U.S. Ambassador April Glaspie met with Saddam in Baghdad and demanded that Iraq clarify its intentions. In the meeting Saddam assured her that he was seeking a diplomatic resolution to the problem with Kuwait, but he lied to her. On August 2, 1990, Iraq invaded Kuwait, a move that caught the Bush administration off guard. They had been assured by Arab leaders in Egypt, Saudi Arabia, and Jordan that Saddam would not attack Kuwait.[6] Now the Bush administration scrambled to form a strategy for response. It was an abrupt transition. As Secretary of State Baker summed up, "Practically overnight, we went from trying to work with Saddam to likening him to Hitler."[7] The process began the morning of August 3, 1990, as a meeting of the National Security Council convened in the Cabinet Room of the White House. A White House press statement the day before had said that the Bush administration was "reviewing all options in its response to Iraqi aggression."[8] In reality, the administration policy was already moving in a singular direction, a fact evident in the opening statements of the NSC meeting. Setting the tone, General Scowcroft argued that "to accommodate Iraq should not be a policy option."[9] The group was in agreement that action needed to be taken. As Secretary Cheney explained at the meeting, there were many levels to consider: "Initially, we should sort this out from our strategic interests in Saudi Arabia and oil. He [Saddam] has clearly done what he has to do to dominate OPEC, the Gulf and the Arab world. He is 40 kilometers from Saudi Arabia, and its oil production is only a couple of hundred kilometers away. If he doesn't take it physically, with his new wealth he will still have an impact and will be able to acquire new weapons, including nuclear weapons. The problem will get worse, not better."[10] Clearly there were economic, diplomatic, and military aspects of this crisis that had to be considered, and, as Deputy Secretary of State Larry Eagleburger injected, the ending of the Cold War made this crisis pivotal: "This is the first test of the post war system. As the bipolar contest is relaxed, it permits this, giving people more flexibility because they are not worried about the involvement of the superpowers. The Soviets have come down hard. Saddam Hussein now has greater flexibility because the Soviets are tangled up in domestic issues. If he succeeds, others may try the same thing. It would be a bad lesson."[11] The two main themes present throughout the free-wheeling debate were the problems with the oil supply and the possibilities for the use of force to roll back the Iraqi aggression. It was clear that the members of the administration quickly recognized this as a problem that would in all likelihood require a show of force, and indeed, President Bush had already begun talks with foreign leaders for just such a response.[12] Subsequent meetings continued to crystallize the U.S. position.[13] There were many nuances and contingencies to the U.S. policy as it was being developed, but President Bush summed up the overriding goal in one exchange by concluding that "all will not be tranquil until Saddam Hussein is history."[14] By the end of the month, they issued National Security Directive 45, which dramatically shifted U.S. policy toward Iraq by clearly stating that the Iraqi occupation of Kuwait placed "vital U.S. interests at risk" and that the United States would defend these interests "through the use of U.S. military force if necessary and appropriate."[15] In the same month, the United States worked on the United Nations Security Council to push through a series of resolutions that condemned the Iraqi invasion of Kuwait and demanded that Iraq withdraw immediately and unconditionally.[16]

Coalition Building

The debate over resolutions in the United Nations clearly demonstrated that the old Cold War rivalries were starting to break down. The United

States was able to convince the Soviet Union to vote for each of the Iraq/ Kuwait UN Security Council resolutions even though it meant voting against a former Soviet client state. As James Baker recalls, this cooperation was evident even before the UN resolution. Baker had been in Mongolia when Iraq invaded Kuwait and decided to fly back through Moscow to discuss the situation with the Soviets, who had a vested interest in Iraq as a client state. To Baker's delight, Soviet Foreign Minister Eduard Shevardnadze, without even clearing it with Gorbachev, joined Baker in a statement condemning the invasion and calling for an arms embargo of Iraq. That level of cooperation between the United States and the Soviet Union against a Soviet client state convinced Baker that "it was certainly clear that day that the Cold War was over."[17] Baker and Shevardnadze issued the joint declaration on August 3, 1990, in the lobby of Vnukovo II Airport outside Moscow. Bush and Gorbachev would echo this statement with a joint declaration of their own on September 9, 1990, in Helsinki, Finland.[18] A small, but in no way insignificant, example of the increasing mood of cooperation also occurred at Helsinki when Bush and Gorbachev agreed to start using first names to address one another in small private meetings. Throughout the rest of Gorbachev and Bush's working relationship, in private meetings, phone conversations, and personal letters, both men would regularly use "Mikhail" and "George" rather than the stiff, formal titles used during the Cold War period by each man's predecessors.[19] The cooperation between the United States and the Soviet Union was so unusually great that it led one British diplomat to make a tongue-in-cheek statement in a cable in August of 1990 that "the person determining Soviet policy in the Middle East these days is James Baker."[20] Clearly Baker viewed the U.S.-Soviet cooperation in the reaction to Iraqi aggression as a historic moment in the Cold War, even claiming that "the entire planet is in this madman's [Saddam Hussein's] debt. His brutal invasion of Kuwait provided the unexpected opportunity to write an end to fifty years of Cold War conflict with resounding finality."[21] Baker's assessment of the situation may have been somewhat overstated, but this was a relationship that had fundamentally changed over the previous few years, and East-West confrontation had given way to at least a limited form of cooperation.

UN Resolution 678

The use-of-force resolution was more difficult to procure than earlier resolutions condemning Iraqi aggression. Time became a factor because the United States chaired the Security Council in November but would have to turn over the chairmanship the following month to Yemen, an ally of Iraq who would undoubtedly try to block any coalition-led resolutions. With such a short timetable, Baker went on a diplomatic offensive, meeting personally with all his Security Council counterparts in "an intricate process of cajoling, extracting, threatening, and occasionally buying votes."[22] Starting on November 3, 1990, Baker traveled to twelve countries on three continents within a span of just three weeks. Along with support for the use-of-force resolution, Baker needed to gain support for three other matters that would become important if force were used: Combat operations would remain under the control of U.S. commanders; coalition members would give their acquiescence to the bombing of Iraq; and member nations would continue to support the coalition even in the case of Israeli retaliation to an Iraqi attack.[23] The third question was particularly delicate in discussions with leaders from Saudi Arabia, Bahrain, Egypt, and, especially, Kuwait. The hawkish leaders quickly agreed to the first two conditions, but most found the third condition troubling. Baker knew that Arab leaders siding with Israel was an unnatural alliance, but with a little diplomatic prodding, he was able to obtain at least a passive agreement to show restraint and give the United States time to deal with such an occurrence.[24] While in Egypt, Baker met with Chinese Foreign Minister Qian Qichen, who was beginning a tour of the Middle East. Since China had veto authority on the UN Security Council, Baker needed to make sure that China would not stand in the way of a use-of-force resolution: "I told Qian that [the United States] could accept a decision on their part not to contribute forces to the multinational effort, but we would *not* [emphasis added] understand if they stood in the way of our pursuing an appropriate resolution at the UN. Although I did not press him either for a response or commitment on the resolution, Qian clearly got the point."[25] Baker left the meeting confident that, at worst, China would abstain from the vote on a use-of-force resolution.[26]

The next day, Baker flew to Ankara, Turkey, and gained similar promises of support before heading to Moscow for a thirteen-hour meeting with Shevardnadze and Gorbachev. The Soviets clearly preferred to continue sanctions rather than a use-of-force resolution; Shevardnadze in particular was fearful that military action might backfire, as it did for the Soviets in Afghanistan. To quiet those concerns, Baker had his military attaché, Gen. Howard Graves, give a detailed classified briefing of the U.S. war plan; briefing the Soviets of U.S. military war plans against a Soviet client state would have been unthinkable even a few years earlier.[27] By the end of the long day, Baker felt that the Soviets, although not enthusiastic about the idea, would not stand in the way of a use-of-force resolution. He relayed his feelings to

President Bush: "My own sense is that in the end they will go along with us. Gorbachev made a real point of saying they'd stick with us. . . . As I said several times, we saw the extraordinary value of them participating with us if force was needed, but understood their problems (internal preoccupation, Afghan syndrome) with not doing so. It would be far harder for us to understand their blocking us from the clearly preferred option of a UNSC resolution. They got the point, and I believe their stake in good relations and desire for partnership with us will lead them in the right direction."[28] Just as he had done with the Chinese foreign minister, Baker used a veiled (or perhaps not so veiled) threat that the Soviets could not veto a use-of-force resolution without expecting it to do serious harm to U.S.-Soviet relations. As Baker himself said in his letter to Bush, "they got the point."[29]

The odyssey continued as Baker flew to London and then Paris. Prime Minister Thatcher was still "skeptical" about a UNSC resolution authorizing the use of force but made it clear that Great Britain would support whatever decision was made by the United States.[30] President Mitterrand, in the words of Baker, was "remarkably" enthusiastic about a use-of-force resolution.[31] Baker then continued his trip by meeting with leaders from other countries that had votes on the UN Security Council. In each case, Baker was able to gain their vote either by bribe or threat. Yemen was one of only two holdouts despite Baker's warning to Pres. Ali Abdullah Saleh that "Yemen was risking $70 million a year in U.S. foreign aid by its behavior" and the possibility of the United States adding Yemen to the terrorism list.[32] Cuba was the other holdout. Despite Soviet pressure and a "not-so-subtle" threat by Baker, Cuban Foreign Minister Isidoro Malmierca made it clear that they would vote against the resolution.[33] Despite Yemen and Cuba, Baker had achieved his goal, and, on November 29, 1990, UNSC Resolution 678 passed twelve to two with China abstaining.[34] The international coalition was still intact, and President Bush now had a UN resolution authorizing the use of force.

Domestic Consensus?

It could be said that this same level of cooperation did not exist within the United States. While President Bush worked during the fall of 1990 to put together an international coalition to address the Iraqi aggression, he had to battle a reluctant Congress to obtain their approval for the use of force to reverse Iraq's aggression. Bush's apparent support for an offensive option angered many Democratic members of Congress, who became emboldened as Bush's approval ratings steadily dropped from 75 percent (August) to 59 percent (October) to 50 percent (November).[35] During a bipartisan leadership meeting at the White House in November 1990, Senate Majority Leader George Mitchell urged the president to "give sanctions time to work," and House Majority Leader Dick Gephardt urged him to continue to use the UN and have "patience—a year or year and a half is a better alternative."[36] Baker described the meeting as "one of the most contentious meetings I can remember with the bipartisan congressional leaders."[37] When the resolutions finally were introduced in both houses on January 10, 1991, the debate mirrored the contention of the earlier meeting in the White House as Democrat after Democrat stood to denounce the president. Edward Kennedy of Massachusetts angrily said, "There is still time to save the President from himself."[38] John Kerry, the junior senator from Massachusetts, agreed, asking if Congress should be expected "to go to war simply because one man—the President—makes a series of unilateral decisions that put us in a box—a box that makes that war, to a greater degree, inevitable?"[39] On January 12, 1991, Congress voted largely along party lines to give President Bush the authority to wage war under the terms laid out in UN Security Council Resolution 678, which called for the use of "all necessary means . . . to restore international peace and security in the area."[40] The vote in the House was 250–183 and in the Senate it was 52–47, the closest vote ever for what was in essence a declaration of war. Despite Gephardt's call for patience, Bush was determined to act, with or without approval from Congress: "In truth, even had Congress not passed the resolution I would have acted and ordered our troops into combat. I know it would have caused an outcry, but it was the right thing to do. I was comfortable in my own mind that I had the constitutional authority. It had to be done."[41] Patience had served him well in his dealings with the Soviet Union, but he saw a greater sense of urgency in the Gulf crisis and stated in a 1991 interview that there had been "nothing of this importance since World War II."[42] Bush would later refer to it as "the Lord's work."[43] This type of symbolic language was uncharacteristic of Bush, who, in stark contrast to Ronald Reagan, had shied away from such language in relation to the Cold War. In marked contrast to the "plodding, almost timid foreign policy style" that his critics had lamented during the first year of his administration, Bush now embarked on a Reagan-style ideological crusade.[44]

Tin-Cup Diplomacy

As Bush continued to build an international coalition against Iraq, he became convinced of the need to share the financial burden of a military option, a need made necessary by the tight budget constraints in the United

States. Bush preferred that the coalition members provide financial assist-ance rather than token military contributions. This so-called "tin-cup" di-plomacy was so successful that out of the estimated $54 billion cost of the war, the United States received $48.2 billion from Saudi Arabia, Kuwait, Japan, Germany, and other allies.[45] Baker bore the primary burden of rais-ing funds with an eleven-day journey to nine countries in September 1990 to garner financial commitments. The easiest, and most substantial, com-mitments came from King Fahd of Saudi Arabia and the Emir of Kuwait, each of whom agreed to pledge $15 billion without protest. Saudi Arabia was desperate for U.S. help and, according to Baker, was prepared to pay virtually any amount for a U.S.-led war that could destroy Saddam's military machine.[46] In the end, the Bush administration's success in raising funds for the Persian Gulf War mirrored their success in convincing the Soviets to allow a reunified Germany in exchange for a cash payment from Western Germany, as well as other financial considerations.[47] Ironically, keeping the Soviets in the coalition was also linked to monetary considerations. After attending the Two-plus-Four ministerial meeting in Moscow on September 12, 1990, to finalize the conditions for the reunification of Germany, Baker received a request from Gorbachev for the United States to ask Saudi Arabia to give the Soviets $4 to $5 billion to help their struggling economy. Baker agreed and convinced the Saudis to give the Soviet Union a $4 billion line of credit, a move that Baker would later recall as being "instrumental in solidifying Soviet support for the use-of-force resolution and keeping them firmly in the coalition throughout the crisis."[48] Gorbachev would later tel-ephone President Bush to thank him.

Complications

With a coalition intact, the greatest fear on the part of the Bush admin-istration was that Saddam would attempt a "partial" withdraw before the initiation of military action by the coalition forces, possibly weakening the resolve of the international coalition and the policy of no compromise put forward by the United States. Scowcroft argues that this would also have been problematic from a strategic military point because "the U.S. could not [indefinitely] maintain force buildup in Saudi Arabia and Iraq forces would still be on the border."[49] The Deputies Committee, which had been meeting on a regular basis since the beginning of the crisis, now met to discuss several "withdrawal" scenarios that they thought were more likely than the twin extremes of continued outright defiance of the UN Security Council and unconditional, rapid withdrawal from Kuwait.[50] Any type of partial withdrawal would be problematic for the Bush administration: "The danger is that a pledge to withdraw or initial withdrawals could prove to be a ploy, to buy time in the hope that the coalition would unravel. It might also simply be a probe, to test how resolute we are. Either way, many individuals in this country would object to our using force just when peace seemed to be at hand. Some coalition partners might second this reaction."[51] The Deputies Committee recommended that the United States should "not negotiate with Saddam over the terms of the withdrawal" and needed "to act quickly and firmly, to place Saddam on the defensive, to shape domestic and international reaction, and to signal to Saddam that anything less than full withdrawal in earnest will be unacceptable and pave the way for conflict."[52] In short, the United States needed to make it clear that a partial withdrawal would not preclude the use of force to implement UN Security Council Resolution 678. The only question, the committee concluded, was "whether we would have sufficient domestic and international political support to actually use force under these circumstances."[53] To help alleviate the political pressure and to prove to critics in the United States and around the world that the Bush administration was going the "extra mile for peace," Bush made an offer to Iraq that Secretary Baker would meet with Iraqi Foreign Minister Tariq Aziz in Geneva, Switzerland, between January 7 and 9.[54] This was a follow-up to an earlier suggestion that Baker travel to Baghdad and Aziz travel to Washington, an idea that fell apart when Saddam stated that he did not have time to meet with Baker until January 12.[55] In calls to coalition leaders, Bush emphasized that Baker would not be negotiating with Aziz and would make it clear that Iraq's only option was to withdraw from Kuwait without concessions. He had made this same statement many times in public by saying, "There can and will be no negotiations, no concessions, and no rewards for aggression."[56] Bush described this as "the last offer of a meeting."[57] It was clear by Bush's conversations with coalition leaders that this was part of the public relations battle and that the Bush administration did not place any faith in the meeting.[58] Indeed the meeting between Baker and Aziz on January 9, 1991, at the Hotel Inter-Continental in Geneva ended, according to Baker, "with President Bush's [ultimatum] letter to Saddam Hussein lying on the table between us."[59]

Lessons from Vietnam

Looking ahead to what appeared to be the inevitability of military operations, the Bush administration was determined to set objectives and clearly define the point at which it would be recognized that the objectives would be achieved. By doing this, Scowcroft hoped to exorcise the "legacy of paralysis" from the Vietnam era.[60] Cheney agreed that the Vietnam legacy had "a significant impact" in the Bush administration's plan for the Gulf War and their desire to not get in a "quagmire."[61] The military establishment had thought the Vietnam War had been mismanaged by the political leadership, and, unlike Pres. Lyndon Johnson who was criticized for being "down in the weeds," Bush went to great lengths to protect the integrity of the chain of command by signing off on the overall plan but not micromanaging the operational use of forces.[62] Other lessons included the use of reserves, not imposing severe restrictions on the military in terms of what targets they could go after, establishing an air plan that "puts together the whole load the first night," and establishing unit cohesion through troop rotation that kept units together with stop loss orders (train in units, fight in units, come home in units) rather than the Vietnam-era individual rotation with tours of duty.[63] It is telling that when writing in his memoir about his decision-making process in the Persian Gulf War, Bush refers to the Vietnam War more than a dozen times, stressing that he did not want "to repeat the problems of the Vietnam War."[64] At first, the Pentagon was reluctant to believe Bush, a fact that was easily apparent on October 11, 1990, during preliminary planning for a ground war. In that meeting the Pentagon presented a plan that, according to Scowcroft, was "designed to show why we shouldn't fight."[65] The plan called for an assault straight up the middle of Iraqi defenses in Kuwait, prompting the Bush administration to refer to it as the Washington Monument plan. Scowcroft felt it "sounded unenthusiastic, delivered by people who didn't want to do the job."[66] Cheney agreed, calling the plan "unimaginative."[67] When pressed for alternatives, the Pentagon responded with requests for more troops, supplies, and weapons. To reassure the military establishment that things would be drastically different from Vietnam, the Bush administration, upon the suggestion of Cheney and with the support of Baker and Scowcroft, made it unofficial policy that the White House would accede to every request for more troops and weapons. The policy was designed "to reinforce the credibility of our commitment and produce a quick and overwhelming victory."[68] As a result, military planners became increasingly more confident that the politicians would do it right without falling back on half measures.

After the January 15, 1991, deadline set by UN Resolution 678 expired, Operation Desert Shield was transformed to Operation Desert Storm, an offensive strike against Iraq meant to reverse Iraqi aggression and force them to withdraw from Kuwait and "restore international peace and security in the area."[69] During the two hours leading up to the attack, the White

House notified the coalition leaders. Once again, President Bush took the lead with personal calls to Gorbachev, Mitterand, Mulroney, and others in an effort to maintain unity. The only leaders to be notified prior to the two-hour window were Prime Minister John Major of the United Kingdom and Prince Bandar of Saudi Arabia, both of whom were contacted a full twelve hours before the attack.[70] Once the attack began, President Bush continued regular communication with coalition leaders throughout the campaign.[71] In those calls, Bush thanked the leaders of the coalition nations for their support and the sacrifices they were making, but the calls were much more personal than just a diplomatic formality. Bush routinely addressed these leaders by their first names, asked about public opinion in their nation and bragged about public opinion in the United States, discussed the progress of coalition forces, discussed concerns such as the attacks on Israel and the difficulty in convincing Prime Minister Yitzhak Shamir to restrain from commencing Israeli retaliation, and talked about the coverage in the media. At one point Bush and President Mitterand lamented the difficulty in waging a war while "being harassed by the media," and Bush stated, "I think CNN has been a great asset to Saddam Hussein."[72] It is interesting to note that while these telephone conversations were certainly important diplomatically to Bush in helping him maintain his hegemony over coalition leadership, they also seemed to provide Bush with a forum to vent/brag about concerns/triumphs of the war effort and offer historians a rare glimpse into the thinking of a president as events of the war unfolded.

The Israel Question

The situation in the Middle East was complicated, to put it mildly, by Israel. At first, Israel itself complicated matters with violence in Jerusalem that left more than twenty Palestinians dead and led to UN sanctions. The United States voted for UN Security Council Resolution 672, and Bush wrote to Prime Minister Shamir urging Israel to comply with the UN's decision: "Mr. Prime Minister, I believe it is essential that we not lose sight of what ought and indeed must be the focus of the international community at present— Iraq's invasion, occupation, and now destruction of Kuwait. . . . I would, therefore, ask that you cooperate with the mission called for by Security Council Resolution 672."[73] Now it was Iraq that could complicate matters by bringing Israel into the fighting and possibly disrupting the fragile coalition. If Saddam began an attack on Israel, Israelis would feel compelled to defend themselves by launching an attack themselves. Bush had been able to build an international coalition that included, and indeed heavily relied on, Arab nations. Asking them to defend Israeli aggression would put the Arab leaders in an awkward position, something Saddam knew very well and hoped to exploit to create divisions within the coalition. According to a White House Situation Room report: "The U.S. is now locked in a psychological battle with Saddam Hussein in which we hope to keep Arab focus on the perfidy of his aggression, while he seeks to define the conflict as poor versus rich, Arab versus foreign, Muslim versus non-Muslim. The majority of Arabs were horrified at Saddam's invasion of Kuwait, but the vast majority also find the military intervention by Israel's protector—especially with troops into the kingdom that keeps the Holy Places—hard to stomach. For most Arabs it is now a choice between negatives, and our battle to keep the second negative the lesser of the two is distinctly uphill."[74] Bush had been working on this problem from the very beginning. It had been one of the issues Baker addressed in his travels to secure the support of UNSC Resolution 678. In a December meeting in the Oval Office with Prime Minister Shamir, Bush had tried to maintain control of the problem: "A preemptive strike by Israel would be very bad. I know your position about responding to an attack and I respect it. But if we could consult first, our preference would be for Israel not to respond until you have seen our reply. We have common objectives and I would like to fulfill them. If there is an attack on Israel, I am concerned that the coalition would stay together for a massive response."[75] Shamir responded positively and stated that Israel fully supported the path taken by the United States, but he made it clear to Bush that the political pressure created by Iraqi attacks on civilians in Israel would make it difficult for him to follow the restrained course of action laid out by the U.S. president and Israel. Shamir did rule out a preemptive strike and agreed to "consult beforehand, before something is launched."[76] It was clear that this was going to be an ongoing concern for Bush in his efforts to hold together his coalition.

That concern became an all-out panic the second day of the air war when Iraq launched Scud missiles into Israel. Although very little damage was done by the first Scud strike, Israeli Defense Minister Arens telephoned Cheney demanding a unit of Patriot air defense missiles and informing him that arrangements were underway for an Israeli counterstrike. Any Israeli counterstrike would require them to fly their planes over Arab territory, either Syria, Jordan, or Saudi Arabia. It was highly unlikely that any of these nations would grant permission and much more likely that they would attempt to intercept the Israeli aircraft. An alternate response would be for the Israelis to use their Jericho surface-to-surface missiles to respond to the Iraq attack in kind. That would also threaten the coalition by bringing Israel into direct military participation in the war. For the moment Bush asked Israel to hold off on any response to give the United States time to take care of the situation. The next day Bush reiterated the point to Shamir, pressing him to "leave it to the coalition to act against Iraq" and warning him that Israeli action could jeopardize Bush's ability to hold the coalition together.[77] Despite this plea, Shamir told Bush that Israel would probably have to respond, and, after continued wrangling over the course of the day, Bush finally told Shamir that the best of the "bad options" would be for Israel to retaliate with missiles by attacking some of the northern airfields in Iraq.[78] This would at least minimize the damage to the coalition. Hoping that even this option could still be averted, Bush sent a Patriot missile team in an attempt to better defend Israel and Larry Eagleburger and Paul Wolfowitz to "hold the Israeli hand."[79] As Scowcroft recalls, sending Eagleburger proved to be the right move and was probably "the deciding factor in dissuading Shamir from retaliating."[80] The Scud attacks continued, but Israel's restraint allowed the coalition to hold—a major diplomatic success for the Bush administration.

The Soviet Initiative

In addition to the situation with Israel, the beginning of an air war in January 1991 produced a major problem for the Bush administration in managing Soviet fears of a ground offensive. Secretary Baker recalls that "Soviet efforts to avoid a ground war became without question our greatest political impediment."[81] Perhaps to reassert Soviet prestige or to somehow restore the patron-client relationship with Iraq, "the United States now found itself occasionally working at cross purposes with its most important strategic partner in the crisis."[82] This was clearly a fight over superpower status. Up to this point, the United States had taken the lead in building the international coalition and certainly was responsible for the bulk of the fighting during the air war. Now, the Soviet Union hoped to even the field by playing the pivotal role in brokering the peace. Gorbachev sent Yevgeny Primakov to Baghdad and invited Tariq Aziz to come to Moscow to develop a new peace proposal. Most of the drafts tied Iraqi troop withdrawal to the lifting of economic sanctions and the voiding of all relevant UN resolutions. Adding to the problem of this type of linkage was the fact that the timetable given for an "immediate withdrawal" was up to six weeks. Despite Gorbachev's insistence to Bush that he had negotiated an "unconditional withdrawal" of Iraqi troops, it clearly was not the immediate and unconditional surrender demanded by Bush.[83] When Gorbachev cabled the proposal to Washington, Bush responded with the first of two "Dear Mikhail" letters that kindly but firmly rejected the proposal. Bush held firm to the idea that any proposal would begin with an immediate withdrawal that would take no more than ninety-six hours to complete, insist upon Iraqi compliance with all the relevant UNSC resolutions, and establish a method for the release of POWs and third-party nationals. In his second letter, Bush once again made it clear to Gorbachev that the proposal was not acceptable: "Mikhail, I do appreciate your efforts, but I worry that incompleteness and ambiguities in the proposal may give heart to Saddam Hussein that he can somehow escape the consequences of his actions and obtain an unclear outcome, which he can exploit politically. . . . The joint efforts of many nations, including the Soviet Union, have brought us to the threshold of a historic rebuff to an aggressor. We must not allow that aggressor now to salvage political gain or the basis of future aggression through negotiation or divisive tactics."[84] Bush followed up on the second letter by sending letters to coalition members telling them that "the Soviet initiative as it currently stands does not meet *our* [emphasis added] requirements."[85] Bush followed up on the letters with personal calls to the coalition leaders reiterating that the Soviet initiative was "not acceptable."[86] Bush emphasized the point rather strongly with his first call, which was to President Mitterand: "The Soviets would clearly like a piece of the action. I see no problem in that, but they should not make the decisions. I don't think that they should carry the ball. They want to play a role but they must not have too big a role and they cannot be the sole broker. The UN has a position, and the coalition has a position. I don't think we need the Soviets to negotiate for us."[87] Gorbachev, however, did not give up and called Bush again on February 21, 1991, to present a modified proposal. Once again Bush rebuffed him, "To be very honest with you, we have no trust anymore in anything the man [Saddam] says."[88] Still determined to avoid a ground war, Gorbachev called again the next morning. Bush and Baker were in the Oval Office when the call came in, but Bush was late to a Rose Garden ceremony and told Baker to talk to Gorbachev until he could return. When Bush returned to continue the call, Gorbachev complained to the U.S. president, "Where does our priority lie in putting a final touch on this settlement? Is it a political approach or the continuation of military operations and the escalation to ground operations. Now, I saw my role in cooperation with you in trying to find a political solution, as trying to protect the U.S. servicemen and peaceful Iraqi civilians from the suffering that may befall them. If you share this understanding then our task is to find a solution that is tough but also implementable."[89] Gorbachev was essentially questioning whether or not Bush, at this point, would consider any settlement or was he firmly committed to a ground war no matter what. Later in the conversation Gorbachev would apologize for becoming "emotional" and using "charged language," but he was essentially right in his assessment that Bush refused to consider any compromise with Saddam.[90] After once again dismissing the proposal, Bush made it clear that the U.S.-Soviet partnership was important: "In spite of that we continue to make clear that we support your role and value your role and believe you are making a contribution. I mean it right from my heart and so does Jim [Baker]. . . . I don't want to see us pull apart even though we have profound differences at this moment on this particular question."[91] At the end of the hour-and-forty-minute call, Bush hung up the phone and told Baker, "It's totally unacceptable."[92] Despite the call, Gorbachev remained in contact with Baghdad, trying to reach an agreement that would be acceptable to Bush. On the day of the U.S. deadline, February 23, Baker was awakened at 12:30 A.M. by a call from Alexander Bessmertnykh claiming that a settlement had been reached and that there was "no longer any reason for a ground war"; Baker now felt that the United States and the Soviets were just "talking past each other."[93] Ground operations began at 9 P.M. (EST). In a call that lasted less than a minute, Baker called Bessmertnykh to inform him. The Soviet initiative had failed.

An Anti-Climactic End

The five-and-one-half-week air bombardment was followed by a land war that lasted exactly one hundred hours. The war was concluded on February 27, 1991, after President Bush announced in a televised address from the Oval Office an end to all Allied offensive combat operations: "Kuwait is liberated. Iraq's army is defeated."[94] As many historians covering the period have stated, even before the cessation of hostilities was declared, "the outcome was never in doubt."[95] But several issues would prove controversial and begin to tarnish the luster of the victory. Convinced that the land campaign had run its course and concerned over excessive carnage and the needless killing of retreating Iraqis, Bush ended the war without pushing toward Baghdad. According to Colin Powell, he, General Schwarzkopf, and all of President Bush's advisors supported the decision to terminate combat operations: "There was no contrary recommendation. There was no disagreement. There was no debate. Although we could have continued combat operations, it was clear that our objectives had been accomplished, and further loss of life was unnecessary."[96] But from the very beginning there were grumblings that the war ended two or three days too early.[97] A year after the war two-thirds of Americans polled agreed that the war ended too soon, a damaging statistic to Bush's hopes for reelection in 1992.[98] The feeling, later seized upon by challengers Ross Perot and Bill Clinton, was that the situation in Iraq was unresolved. Indeed, Saddam Hussein had been severely weakened but not vanquished. But, as one reporter has noted, "limited wars achieve limited results."[99] Bush's limited agenda for the war was to fulfill the United Nations Security Council Resolution 678 and to continue the war in an effort to capture Saddam Hussein would be, according to Bush, illegal under international law, and the coalition that he had so carefully assembled "would have unraveled" and led to a "morass."[100] Secretary of Defense Cheney agrees that capturing Saddam Hussein had never been the objective: "[Capturing Saddam] would have turned what had up to that time been a very successful U.S.-led coalition effort to roll back aggression into a situation where the heavy hand of the U.S. occupies an Arab nation and starts taking down governments. . . . If we crossed over that line and begun to try to dictate who's going to govern Iraq, if we can take down the president of Iraq—hell!—we can take down anybody. . . . It's always going to be a messy situation over there."[101] Although Scowcroft agrees that it was never a goal, he did concede in an interview with Bush biographer Robert Greene that, at the time, the administration did hope that removing Saddam from power would be a "byproduct."[102]

Regardless of the fate of Saddam Hussein, the Persian Gulf War was an important test of the relationship that had been built between the United States and the Soviet Union since the Malta conference. Bush had succeeded in building a coalition that did not mirror the old Cold War rivalries and offered the first glimpse of the leadership burden that the United States would be forced to take in a world where they were quickly becoming the world's lone superpower. Gorbachev both followed the U.S. lead and tenaciously fought to forge a role for the Soviet Union in the conflict in an effort to produce some tangible success that would bolster the world power status for his beleaguered nation. Little did he know that by the end of 1991, the Soviet Union would cease to exist.

Postscript: Bush and the Middle East

Although Bush's role in the Gulf War has received perhaps more attention than any other facet of his presidency, his impact on the Middle East did not end with the conclusion of that war. The Middle East Peace Conference, which was the first ever multilateral Arab-Israeli peace conference, was held in Madrid's Royal Palace on October 30, 1991. For the first time, Israeli and Arab leaders discussed the possibility of a lasting settlement. Representatives from the United States, the Soviet Union, Israel, Syria, Egypt, Jordan, Lebanon, and the Palestinians were all in attendance.[103] The coalition-building undertaken by the Bush administration during the Gulf War made this type of conference possible, and Bush hoped to take advantage of the recent goodwill to advance regional peace and security.[104] As a sign that the Cold War was indeed coming to an end, the United States asked the Soviet Union to co-sponsor the event. In fact, Bush and Gorbachev continued their friendly relationship by meeting for lunch at the Soviet ambassador's residence in Madrid the day before the conference.[105] Gorbachev spent much of the meeting discussing the internal problems that he was having with Yeltsin and other leaders concerning the creation of a new Union Treaty. A Soviet leader openly discussing internal problems, including an admission that he needed more money, with a U.S. president is something that would have been unthinkable during the Cold War. Gorbachev's conversation with Bush was also an indication that the Soviet Union had far too many problems to be heavily involved in the Middle East. The Soviet Cold War presence in the Middle East was coming to an end, leaving the United States with overt supremacy in the tumultuous region.

The conference was a success due in large part to the preparation work done by Secretary of State James Baker. Baker had traveled throughout the Middle East and Europe meeting with leaders concerning the possibility of such a meeting. President Bush joked at the time, "Baker has a sign on his door. It reads '10 to 3.' They're not his hours, but his odds of being there."[106] The conference was merely the first step in a long and difficult process. In fact, Baker told reporters following the conference that it was not really a first step at all: "We have to crawl before we walk, and we have to walk before we run, and today I think we began to crawl."[107] Baker's choice of words was not meant to downplay the importance of the events but to caution that a great deal of work still needed to be accomplished. Baker would look back on this conference as both a personal triumph and one of the great achievements of the Bush administration.[108]

Over the next decade, U.S. influence in the region grew as the withdrawal of Soviet influence created a vacuum that the United States quickly filled. This vast expansion of U.S. influence was a direct result of both the Persian Gulf War and the end of the Cold War. However, the uncontested supremacy of the United States led to a wave of anti-Americanism, centered on the U.S. government's continued support of Israel as well as the lingering presence of U.S. troops in Saudi Arabia, a place considered holy by Muslims. As one political observer noted, this left the United States in "a stronger position strategically and a weaker position politically."[109]

Chapter 5

"When You Lose Your Best Enemy"

The Collapse of the Soviet Union

Although the Bush administration was preoccupied with the Persian Gulf War during the latter part of 1990 and the first part of 1991, the new relationship between the United States and the Soviet Union was becoming increasingly evident. The joint statement by James Baker and Eduard Shevardnadze on August 3, 1990, condemning the Iraqi invasion made it clear, at least to Baker, that the Cold War was over.[1] Later, on November 29, 1990, the United Nations, with Soviet support, would authorize "all necessary means" to compel Iraq to comply with UN resolutions on Kuwait. This, basically, allowed military intervention by the UN forces to end Iraqi aggression against Kuwait. Wanting to illustrate the new U.S.-Soviet relationship, Baker called for actual Soviet participation in the multinational force, a suggestion that was not widely embraced on the U.S. side. Bureaucrats within Baker's own command at the State Department argued that sanctioning a Soviet military presence in the Persian Gulf directly contradicted more than forty years of U.S. diplomacy designed to keep the Soviets out of the region. Colin Powell, Dick Cheney, and Brent Scowcroft also expressed initial misgivings. Robert Gates would describe Cheney as one who wanted to "kiss off the Soviets and considered them a complication in the whole process."[2] Baker recalls that "Powell was especially worried about giving the Soviets a role in a possible attack on Iraq in the future."[3] Powell disputes Baker's claim, adding, "I certainly don't remember any particular conversations."[4] What was more important to Powell was the fact that the United States had the support of the Soviet Union where it really was needed—during votes at the United Nations where a solid bloc of support was needed to pass resolutions against Iraq. Regardless of which view is accurate, there is no denying that Soviet participation in the Persian Gulf War, whether direct or indirect, was an event unthinkable during the Cold War. The coordination of superpower positions on the Gulf crisis showed a level of cooperation that demonstrated just how far the relationship between the two countries had progressed. That does not mean that there was complete unanimity throughout the crisis. But disagreements were worked out in meetings that simply would not have taken place during the Cold War. The Soviets did end up playing a role in the coalition effort, albeit a small one. They sent a few ships to join the international flotilla and monitor the blockade but did not participate in the coalition ground forces. Although their help was not needed, their support was essential. According to U.S. ambassador to the Soviet Union, Jack F. Matlock Jr., Soviet support of the United States during the Gulf War was "the final nail in the coffin" in terms of the Cold War rivalry.[5]

During the course of negotiations with the Soviets over their support for the UN resolutions that would allow the use of force, Secretary Baker had successfully lobbied Saudi Arabia to extend a four-billion-dollar line of credit to the Soviets to help them during their transition into a market economy. It was, Baker insists, instrumental in maintaining the Soviet's support for coalition efforts.[6] It also demonstrated the growing crisis in the Soviet Union. Originally brought to power in 1985, in part because of dissatisfaction with the faltering Soviet economy, Gorbachev had orchestrated a revolution in Soviet economic thinking. However, surprisingly little progress was made in reshaping the Soviet economy. A 1990 State Department evaluation concluded that "Despite all the rhetoric about economic reform, the Soviet economy still operates in much the same way it did when Gorbachev came to power. Enterprise decisions on production, prices, investment, wages, supplies and product mix are still constrained by central planners; innovators have no incentive to innovate, nor workers to work."[7] According to this report, the old central planning system had been disrupted by ballooning deficits, inconsistent reform measures, labor unrest, and national conflicts. No new framework had been utilized to replace the crumbling system, and, consequently, the economy slowly deteriorated between 1985 and 1988 and more noticeably in 1989. In 1990, the GNP declined by 7 to 9 percent, and 1991 looked to be even worse. Under Gorbachev's perestroika, wages and government budget deficits rose significantly faster than production.

This, in turn, caused a "ruble overhang" that led to an explosion of short-ages, rationing, and inflation. The resulting deterioration in living conditions sharpened social and ethnic conflicts throughout the Soviet Union. Gorbachev responded to the growing economic crisis with a "radicalization of rhetoric," assuming the "executive" presidency and announcing a move to a "full-blooded" market. Unfortunately, this rhetoric was not followed by real economic reform programs such as monetary stabilization, the creation of property rights and incentives, microeconomic reform to create enterprise competition, and the creation of a safety net based on income subsidies rather than price subsidies. The report concluded that Gorbachev had been able to survive primarily because no other credible leader had emerged.[8] As Ambassador Matlock concluded, "Public confidence had plummeted just as the public was being allowed to express its views. Nationalism found sustenance in nutrients thrown off by the centrally controlled economy. Economic reform had been bungled—or rather had not been seriously attempted—and the stumbling economy was causing growing distress."[9] Even Gorbachev admitted in his memoirs that "*Perestroika* did not give the people prosperity, something they expected of me, as head of state, based on an ingrained, traditional feeling of dependence."[10] If the economic crisis was not addressed, the people would eventually find a new leader upon which to depend.

Gorbachev's domestic difficulties were complicated by his policies in regard to foreign affairs, which opened the door for the democratization of Eastern Europe, the collapse of the Warsaw Pact, the stand-down of Soviet forces, and German reunification.[11] First, Gorbachev's concessions to the West angered hard-liners in Moscow who increasingly began to view Gorbachev as a traitor, blaming him personally for the country's problems. At a meeting with Gorbachev in November 1990, more than a thousand military officers openly expressed their dissatisfaction with Gorbachev's leadership.[12] Gorbachev was shaken by this meeting and began to fear a military coup. Second, the events in Eastern Europe both directly and indirectly promoted separatist tendencies within the Soviet Union. The doctrine of self-determination, which Gorbachev promoted in Eastern Europe, was used by Latvians, Lithuanians, and others calling for secession. Gorbachev's goals of decentralization and democratization directly worked against his desire to preserve the Soviet Union's political and territorial integrity.[13] Finally, Gorbachev had to worry about maintaining his political authority. Boris Yeltsin was growing increasingly popular. A poll in the Soviet Union at the end of 1990 to select the "Man of the Year" showed that 32 percent supported Yeltsin; only 19 percent backed Gorbachev. This was a dramatic change from the end of 1989 when 46 percent had supported Gorbachev and only 6 percent Yeltsin.[14] It was becoming increasingly apparent that Yeltsin could appeal to the reformers who felt let down by Gorbachev. Gorbachev's approval rating also plummeted, dropping from 52 percent in December 1989, to 44 percent by January 1990, to 39 percent by May, to 28 percent by July, and to 21 percent by October.[15] Gorbachev made a sharp turn to the right politically in an effort to protect against public and political opposition from Yeltsin and his allies on the left. This angered Shevardnadze who, already under intense criticism for his decision to join the United States in support of the Gulf War, resigned on December 20, 1990, and delivered a scathing speech in which he warned "against the onset of dictatorship."[16] The move stunned Gorbachev, whom Shevardnadze had not consulted before making his surprise announcement in the Congress of People's Deputies. Gorbachev stood and blasted the idea that a coup was possible or that there was an approaching dictatorship, charging that Shevardnadze was deserting him at his most difficult time. Certainly, it was a sign that Gorbachev's problems would only get worse.

The U.S. Viewpoint

Gen. Colin Powell made a trip to the Soviet Union in the summer of 1991. Arriving on July 22, Powell met with his Soviet counterpart, Mikhail Moiseyev, and was "dragged" through Red Army exercises and a tour of equipment and facilities until he was "ready to scream."[17] But, as Powell recalls, behind the facade the rot was evident. The Soviet leaders would only let him see the elite troops that they were putting on display to impress him. They denied his requests to see how the Soviet troops who had been pulled out of Eastern Europe were living and denied his requests to talk with ordinary Russians. President Bush, who was scheduled to arrive in the Soviet Union shortly after the general, asked for a report. The resulting observations depicted a military in serious decline and, with it, a deep dissatisfaction in the upper reaches of the Soviet military:

> After traveling across the Soviet Union and talking to a lot of their generals, many of whom just didn't understand the reality of the situation they were in. . . . I said, "You guys, you're going to have to cut back sharply; you're probably going to have to go to a volunteer force," and they just kept dismissing it. . . . I also could sense a deep, deep uncertainty and discomfort among the senior ranks of the Soviet military leaders. They were also very troubled over what they saw in

Figure 14. Gorbachev takes Bush on a tour of Moscow on July 30, 1991. *Courtesy of the George Bush Presidential Library*

Desert Storm and in what they saw in terms of the sophistication of the West and what we could do, and we were no longer that weak-sistered, soft, not terribly competent military that they might have been counting on. And finally, I just saw generation after generation of Soviet weaponry abandoned in airfields. Every time they brought in a new generation of equipment, they just left the other generations laying around. And I could see the Red Army was essentially bankrupting the country, and it could not continue; it was not sustainable.[18]

The problems were not merely with the Soviet military. As Powell recalls, the problems in the Soviet Union had taken their toll on its political leader as well. Gorbachev no longer appeared to be the "supremely confident figure of earlier summits" but rather seemed "beaten down by the incessant battering he was taking" in the Soviet Union.[19] When President Bush arrived in Moscow the following week, he found Gorbachev in better spirits (fig. 14): "Gorbachev was marvelous, and how he could stand up to all the pressures against him I simply did not know. At first I thought he still believed that there would be some windfall of Western money that would help bail out the Soviet economy—he seemed confident as he spoke—but it was soon clear that he was pragmatic and resigned to the fact that he would not get

Figure 15. Bush talking via telephone to Gorbachev, Jan. 11, 1991. *Courtesy of the George Bush Presidential Library*

funds."[20] The fact is that by 1991 Gorbachev was more comfortable talking to President Bush than he was most officials in the Soviet Union. Despite the very tenuous beginning to their relationship during "the pause," Bush and Gorbachev became genuinely friendly after Malta. During the spring and summer of 1991, Bush and Gorbachev spoke on the telephone almost every week (fig. 15).[21] Yet Bush could not give Gorbachev what he really needed— economic aid. The Bush administration's reluctance to provide economic aid to the Soviet Union would fall under heavy criticism, some of the most pointed of which came from the U.S. ambassador to the Soviet Union:

> I think at first, in '89, there was a fear, particularly on Baker's part, that the Soviets would simply get into the international financial and other organizations as trouble makers, as spoilers, and he didn't want to let them in. And it was true that many of these organizations were setup for market economies, and [the Soviet Union] did not have a market economy. But I think that's also a reflection of the fact that Baker hadn't quite grasped that the Cold War really was over and they were looking for advice and help on how to become a capitalist society, though they didn't want to use that word. And I think [the Bush administration was] very slow in grasping that. . . . I knew that [Bush]

would want something new, and I thought that given his background in business and whatnot, to make economic cooperation to bring the Soviet Union into the world economy and to create a market economy there could be, you might say, the watchword for the Bush administration. So I was trying to give him something new. But I think [the Bush administration] didn't really grasp the potential until too late.[22]

The Bush administration did start to address the problem of economic aid to the Soviet Union in the fall of 1990 when Gorbachev's support of U.S. actions against Iraq prompted the Bush administration to be more inclined to help. Bush sent Secretary of Commerce Robert Mosbacher with a group of top executives to the Soviet Union to suggest investment and trade possibilities. The trip demonstrated to Gorbachev the benefits that could come from continued Soviet cooperation with the United States during Security Council votes on Iraq. But as far as producing any real help to the Soviet economy, the trip did little good because, as Jack Matlock explains, "[the trip] was without any strategy and without any real briefing about what we wanted to encourage. They hadn't really given any thought to that, and whereas Gorbachev never came up with something worthy of support, at the same time we never gave him any coherent advice either. And the time to give him that advice was '89, and '90 at the very latest. By 1991 it was too late—things had fallen apart too much. But there could have been a lot more direct support for the reformers there if we'd have gotten involved earlier."[23] Bush did not get involved in helping the Soviet economy early on in his administration and refused to offer large-scale aid, citing ballooning budget deficits in the United States. Matlock takes issue with that excuse: "I think [the Bush administration] could have found the money if they wanted to. Obviously this made it more difficult that there were budget deficits. But I think they could have, and that is what Thatcher . . . when she was no longer prime minister . . . was pressing [the Bush administration] to do: 'George, we need to do it and you don't have to do it all. But, you know, press the Germans.' And, by the way, Major was willing to give very substantial support in January and February '92 after the Soviet Union collapsed. It was no longer Gorbachev, and it was Bush who turned it down."[24] Certainly, Bush quickly found money in his budget to finance the Persian Gulf War. In that case, Bush told the American people that even though they were experiencing financial difficulties at home, the stakes in Kuwait were too great to sit idly by and let aggression stand. When it came to the Soviet Union, however, he treated it more like a corporation evaluating a large-scale investment and deciding not to take a risk.

The Coup Attempt

The Bush administration had always been worried about a coup attempt by the hard-liners in Moscow. In fact, one of the reasons that the Bush administration had been slow in embracing Gorbachev had been their uncertainty over whether or not he would be able to maintain power or, in the event of a coup, whether or not his reforms would prove to be merely temporary and reversible, with a new government relapsing into earlier policies.[25] There had been rumors of a coup attempt in July of 1991. Bush had even warned Gorbachev through a message sent through Ambassador Matlock; Gorbachev dismissed the rumors as false. It was during July that negotiations were taking place concerning a new Union Treaty. The republics had built upon the example of Russia and declared their sovereignty. They then began the task of securing as many rights for themselves as possible. Although most of the republics' leaders recognized that they needed some central authority capable of resolving common problems, they also wanted to tackle their own affairs without interference. The details of the Union Treaty were agreed upon on July 23, 1991—the same month that Boris Yeltsin was officially inaugurated as the president of Russia. The Union Treaty was scheduled to be signed the following month. On Sunday, August 18, just two days before the Union Treaty was scheduled to be signed, information began to filter to President Bush, who was vacationing at his home in Kennebunkport, Maine, that Gorbachev had been removed from office due to "health reasons" and that a "State Committee for the State of Emergency" had been set up.[26] The committee included Vice Pres. Gennady Yanayev, Prime Minister Valentin Pavlov, Defense Minister Dmitri Yazov, KGB chief Vladimir Kryuchkov, Oleg Baklanov, who was in charge of the military-industrial complex, Interior Minister Boris Pugo, and two civilians, Valery Starodubstev and A. I. Tizyakov. These eight men were all hard-liners and now *seemed* to be in control of the Soviet government. That was the problem facing the Bush administration. They really did not know if the coup was successful or what had become of Gorbachev. News reached Washington of a column of ten light tanks rolling toward the city center in Moscow shortly after the announcement of the six-month state of emergency, but little other information was available.[27] Bush immediately engaged in frantic telephone diplomacy, calling John Major, François Mitterrand, and Helmut Kohl to see if they had any more information than he had. Coordinating their responses, all agreed to avoid statements that might give legitimacy to the new coup. Bush conducted an impromptu press conference at Walker's Point at which he described the coup attempt as "extra-constitutional" and a "disturbing development." Admitting that he had few details of the situation currently taking place in the Soviet Union, Bush promised to "watch the situation unfold" before taking any action, warning that it was too early to write off Gorbachev because coups are not always successful—"Coups can fail," he added hopefully.[28] By the end of the day, Bush had received a letter from the plotters explaining the "official" reasons for the coup, which included "a real threat of the country's disintegration, of a breakdown of the single economic space, and the single civil rights space, the single defense, and the single foreign policy."[29] Under these circumstances, the coup leaders felt that they had "no other choice but to take resolute measures in order to stop the slide towards catastrophe."[30] The deep uncertainty and discomfort among the senior ranks of the Soviet military that General Powell had witnessed earlier that year were apparent in the letter, and, although Yanayev claimed that the new regime would honor the international agreements and continue Gorbachev's reforms, there were plenty of reasons to doubt him.[31] Bush flew back to Washington that night still wondering what, if any, action he should take. His daily diary indicates that he was especially concerned with how his administration would be criticized. Reporters were already asking why the Bush administration had not anticipated the coup; Bush, along with many members of his cabinet, was on vacation. The Bush team quickly assembled an eight-point plan for action:

1. Make an assessment. Meet with advisors to determine how we can influence the situation. Perhaps through arms control or economic aid
2. Get Marlin [Fitzwater] back to Kennebunkport
3. Contact the South American leaders and stress to them the necessity for the entire hemisphere to speak out against the coup
4. Make sure the U.S. message is constant and steady
5. Stay in touch with Yeltsin
6. No politics
7. Get our information out to our people so that we speak with one voice
8. Change the work schedule from the relaxed vacation schedule to one that was more formal[32]

The plan of action was more reactive than proactive, but there was little that Bush could do until he learned more about the situation in the Soviet Union. The most important item on the list was the need to stay in constant contact with Yeltsin.

Bush placed a call to Yeltsin the next morning, August 20, 1991. Unlike his repeated calls to Gorbachev, Bush was actually able to reach Yeltsin, who informed him of the situation: "The situation is very complex. . . . President Gorbachev is located in Foros in the Crimea. He is absolutely blocked, no way of reaching him. President [*sic*] Yanayev is using the pretext that Gorbachev is ill, but this is not yet confirmed. Essentially a committee of eight people has taken over the presidency and established a state of emergency in Russian territory and the Baltics. Troops have been brought up to Moscow, not only in the city, but in Moscow District and surrounding towns. And by issuing [these] decision[s], the group has exposed itself as no more than a right-wing junta. I appeared before the people and soldiers and I said that actions of the committee were unconstitutional, illegal, and have no force on Russian territory."[33] Remarkably, the man that most observers considered Gorbachev's main political opponent ardently defended him during the coup attempt. Over the next few days, Bush stayed in regular contact with Yeltsin and came to gain a new respect for the Russian leader. While Yeltsin was voicing his condemnation of the coup in Russia, Bush continued to call for the restoration of the legitimate government. In a press conference on August 20, 1991, Bush, in a somber and resolute tone, declared that U.S. policy toward the Soviet Union (such as MFN status and grain credits) would be put on hold until there was a resolution of the crisis, and the constitutional government was restored. In his statement, Bush praised Yeltsin for "standing courageously against military force."[34] The intent of Bush's words was not to threaten the coup plotters but to keep the heat on. He knew that the United States did not need to get involved militarily, and he knew that the coup leaders controlled enough of the military to crush Yeltsin. Bush had to rely on international pressure and hope that Yeltsin, who organized a demonstration of more than 150,000 people, could generate enough public pressure to force the coup leaders to release Gorbachev. Bush was betting that the coup leaders had underestimated the power of the people in their calculations, that the Soviet people were committed to democracy, and that the reforms started by Gorbachev could not be easily reversed. He knew that, if the coup failed, the hard-liners' influence would be broken, and democracy would take a gigantic leap forward. Bush and the world watched over the next few days as Yeltsin put on a masterful performance. He had the Russian Supreme Soviet unanimously declare the coup attempt illegal. The other republics soon followed suit and the coup fell apart. Bush, on vacation and out riding in his boat, the *Fidelity,* was summoned to shore to receive a telephone call. Scowcroft had instructed the Signal (military) switchboard to periodically attempt to call Gorbachev and had finally gotten through. Bush rushed into his home at Kennebunkport to speak with Gorbachev (fig. 16):

Figure 16. George Bush receiving a call from Gorbachev after the failed coup attempt, Kennebunkport, Aug. 21, 1991. *Courtesy of the George Bush Presidential Library*

Bush: Oh my God, that's wonderful. Mikhail!
Gorbachev: My dearest George. I am so happy to hear your voice again.
Bush: My God, I'm glad to hear you. How are you doing?
Gorbachev: Mr. President, the adventurers have not succeeded.[35]

The two men talked like old friends excited to hear from the other. It also suggests why some felt that Bush had become too friendly with Gorbachev and had stayed with him even when it was becoming apparent that Yeltsin was gaining power. James Baker explains the Bush administration's outrage to such charges: "The press loved that argument. . . . But when you've got a reformer in power and things are going the way you want 'em to go, then you stick with that person. . . . What did we lose by hanging in there with Gorbachev and Shevardnadze? When Yeltsin came to power, he embraced us even more whole-heartedly. We didn't lose a damn thing. And we gained a lot."[36] Certainly, Bush did side with Gorbachev until the coup attempt, but during and after the coup attempt Bush switched his support to Yeltsin. Yeltsin's actions during the failed coup attempt made him a force to be reckoned with, and Gorbachev faced a very difficult political reality: central Soviet authority was declining at an accelerated rate, and the Communist Party was discredited. Telephone records show that calls between Bush and Yeltsin increased sharply beginning with the coup and continued to outpace calls between Bush and Gorbachev until the Soviet Union collapsed.[37] Bush's diary just a couple of months after the coup, the day before he was to meet with Gorbachev in Madrid, demonstrates just how quickly things changed:

Diary, October 26

It is clear to me that things are an awful lot different regarding Gorbachev and the Center than they were. He's growing weaker all the time. I am anxious to see what his mood is. He's still important in nuclear matters, but all the economic stuff—it looks to me like the republics have been more and more exerting themselves. It will be interesting to figure out his mood. I remember not so long ago how he couldn't stand Yeltsin. How he, up at Camp David [in June 1990], made clear he didn't think Yeltsin was going anywhere. But, now all that has changed. Reports recently that he might not be around long. The briefing book indicates this may be my last meeting with him of this nature. Time marches on.[38]

This shift in power was also evident in Bush's public comments. Every time that Bush mentioned Gorbachev, he now also mentioned Yeltsin—an obvious sign of the changing reality in the Soviet Union. This change had begun when Yeltsin won his popular election and became a properly elected leader. During the coup attempt, the world watched Yeltsin in charge, on top of a tank, directing the opposition, almost single-handedly defeating the coup. That is the image people remembered because Gorbachev was not to be seen, and even Bush was quick to mention to the press that Gorbachev's first telephone call had been to Yeltsin. Yeltsin was, along with the republics, on the rise. The failed coup had accelerated the demise of Gorbachev and, with him, the Soviet Union.

At the time of the coup attempt, the world did not really know what had happened to Gorbachev. In his memoirs, Gorbachev gives a detailed account supported by passages from his wife's diary of what was occurring in his dacha.[39] He was visited on the night before he was scheduled to leave for the signing ceremony of the new Union Treaty by several of the coup plotters, who informed Gorbachev of the creation of an emergency committee and demanded that he sign the decree on the declaration of a state of emergency. When he refused, they suggested that he turn control over to Vice President Yanayev because of "failing health" or resign completely. Gorbachev refused; the plotters stormed out of the dacha, leaving Gorbachev and his family confined to the premises and with all outside communications severed. Gorbachev would remain there for a total of seventy-three hours, as the emergency committee told the world that Gorbachev was experiencing "health problems." It would not be until August 21, with the realization by the coup plotters that they had failed to gain public support, that outside communications were restored to Gorbachev's dacha and he was free to leave. The coup had failed in large part because Gorbachev had succeeded in establishing better relations with the outside world; Muammar Gaddafi and Saddam Hussein were the only world leaders to express approval of the coup. Along with the democratic achievements of perestroika and Yeltsin's ability to rally public support, the condemnation by world leaders helped convince the coup leaders to end Gorbachev's captivity. Upon returning to Moscow, Gorbachev made a statement in which he said that he returned from captivity "to another country, and I myself am a different man now."[40] Gorbachev's statement was correct in many respects. He had hoped that the Union Treaty would help transform the Soviet Union into a viable democratic federation, but the coup attempt had delivered to the separatists and extreme radicals a compelling argument to support the breakup of the Soviet Union. In an ironic twist, the coup, which had been led by hard-liners attempting to keep the Soviet Union from transforming, led to its complete breakup. The coup produced, in the words of Gorbachev, a "landslide" and "a strong impulse for disintegration."[41] Gorbachev himself resigned his post of general secretary of the Communist Party and recommended that the Central Committee be dissolved because he felt betrayed by the party leadership and a large number of party functionaries who had not supported him during the coup attempt. All of the republics declared their independence in September and October 1991. The coup shattered the process of establishing new Union ties between sovereign states and had left the machinery of the state in disorder. Authorities within the republics implemented only those decisions of the Union ministries they considered advantageous for themselves and ignored the rest. To make matters even harder to control for Gorbachev was the fact that power was now divided between the Kremlin and the Russian White House. This, of course, is explained by Yeltsin's increased status; he continued issuing decrees that applied to the entire Union for several days after Gorbachev returned to power. It seemed only a matter of time before Yeltsin would use his power to take complete control of the Kremlin.

The breakup of the Soviet Union seemed to many to be a victory rather than a tragedy, and the debate quickly centered on what would emerge out of the old Soviet Union. Gorbachev urged a union of sovereign states, a confederative state that would carry out the functions delegated to it by the various republics. Yeltsin, however, wanted a commonwealth of fully independent countries. Gorbachev warned that any gains attained from sovereignty could not compensate for the losses incurred as a result of the complete breakup of the USSR. The final agreement came as a result of a secret meeting between Yeltsin, Leonid Kravchuck, the president of Ukraine, and Stanislav Shushkevich, the president of Belarus. They met at Minsk during the first days of December 1991. At the meeting, the three leaders decided to dissolve the USSR and establish the CIS, or Commonwealth of Independent States. The purpose of the meeting had been zealously guarded because the three leaders did not want Gorbachev to attempt to stop them. It was not until the three leaders had reached full agreement and called President Bush to ask for his support that they called Gorbachev to inform him of the situation. During their phone call to Gorbachev, they told him President Bush had already given his support to their agreement. Gorbachev angrily replied to Yeltsin, "What you have done behind my back with the consent of the U.S. president is a crying shame, a disgrace!"[42] According to Bush, he had been very careful not to accept or reject the agreement reached by the three leaders at Minsk: "To me, the provisions sounded as though they'd been designed specifically to gain U.S. support for what was being done, since they directly addressed the conditions for recognition we had laid out. I did not want to imply prematurely our approval or disapproval. 'I see,' I said simply."[43]

Since the transcript of that phone conversation remains classified, there is no way yet to know whose account to believe.[44] Gorbachev believed that Bush had given his approval to the Minsk agreement, and the subsequent actions by the Bush administration did nothing to suggest otherwise. In fact, even in Bush's account, he basically told Yeltsin that he would go along with the agreement if Yeltsin gained the support of the other republics: "I promised to read the accord as soon as he sent it to me and to respond quickly. I felt a little uncomfortable. 'We will work with you and others as this develops,' I said. 'Of course, we hope that this whole evolution is a peaceful process.' Sidestepping the question of American support for Yeltsin's implication, I added that we understood this must be sorted out by the participants, not by outside parties such as the United States. Yeltsin agreed, and confidently added that he was sure all of the other republics would join them soon."[45] Another reason that Gorbachev was willing to believe that Bush would go along with Yeltsin's plan was the way that he had acted since the coup attempt. Gorbachev knew that Bush had been shifting his support to Yeltsin and was under increasing domestic pressure to recognize the sovereignty of the republics. In fact, the key to Yeltsin's success in convincing the other republics to agree to the Minsk agreement was the situation in Ukraine, which had not agreed to join the new Union proposed by Gorbachev. Yeltsin, and many other presidents of republics, did not feel that the Treaty on the Union of Sovereign States would be viable without Ukraine. Without Ukraine, the two Slavic countries, Belarus and Russia, could be outvoted. Adding to Gorbachev's troubles was Bush's decision to recognize Ukraine. The information had leaked out after a meeting between Bush and some Ukrainian Americans; it infuriated Gorbachev, who called Bush to voice his displeasure. Bush, however, had made up his mind. His decision to recognize Ukrainian independence, a decision that came four days before the Ukrainians themselves voted on independence, was based, according to Brent Scowcroft, entirely on domestic politics.[46] Bush had complained to Gorbachev in October during a Middle East peace conference in Madrid that the coming year was going to be difficult for him because of the looming presidential election.[47] Bush's foreign policy decisions would increasingly be influenced by domestic policy concerns, and his decisions to recognize Ukrainian independence and to back Yeltsin seem, in retrospect, almost inevitable given the pressures that he faced at home and the disagreement within his own foreign policy apparatus.

U.S. policy disagreements came to a head in a long NSC meeting on September 5, 1991. It was a complex situation: the Baltics had been granted independence by the Soviet State Council, and republics throughout the Soviet Union were threatening to secede. It was still unclear what would happen. Dick Cheney called for an aggressive approach in which the United States would "lead and shape events": "The voluntary breakup of the Soviet Union is in our interest. If it's a voluntary association, it will happen. If democracy fails, we're better off if they're small."[48] Cheney, in essence, argued that the United States should actively encourage the breakup of the Soviet Union. He did not simply want to react to events—he wanted to use the leverage that he believed the Bush administration had to shape the outcome. He suggested establishing consulates in all the republics and providing humanitarian assistance. Cheney's basic premise rested on his belief that the United States would be dealing with fifteen or sixteen independent countries. Baker disagreed: "The *peaceful* breakup of the Soviet Union is in our interest. We don't want another Yugoslavia."[49] In particular, Baker wanted to avoid a Russian-Ukrainian clash and felt it was best not to exacerbate any disputes among the center, Russia, and Ukraine.[50] When Scowcroft and Baker added that aid programs from the West were based on the premise of a strong center and that the United States should try to prop up the center, Cheney dismissed it as "old thinking." He saw Ukraine as the key to whether or not a viable Union could be maintained and predicted that it would not join a new Union. The possibility of a weak center especially disturbed Colin Powell, who worried about the fate and command and control of nuclear weapons.[51] The meeting ended without any clear decision. Scowcroft explains that the Bush administration really could not decide which plan would be preferable: "We had a long debate about what our preferences were, and Baker was on one side of the arguments that you just made [that it would be preferable to have at least some form of the Soviet Union survive rather than face the possibility of chaos, because a strong central authority could at least maintain reliable control over the nuclear arsenal]; Cheney was on the other side saying we actively ought to split up the Soviet Union. And we debated and came to no firm conclusion. So we really didn't have a position. We just let nature take its course."[52] Bush knew, however, that he wanted the process, regardless of which one occurred, to be a peaceful one and one that did not rush to independence at the expense of true democratic reforms. In Ukraine, in what would be labeled by the press as his "chicken Kiev" speech, Bush warned against local despotism: "Freedom is not the same as independence. Americans will not support those who seek independence in order to replace a far-off tyranny with a local despotism. They will not aid those who promote a suicidal nationalism based upon ethnic hatred. We will support those who want to build democracy."[53] Many members of the press mistakenly thought that Bush's speech was meant to dissuade the republics that were seeking self-determination. Instead, rather than calling for the Soviet Union to remain intact, Bush was warning against the outbreak of violence that could result from an upsurge of intolerant nationalism. U.S. Ambassador to the Soviet Union Jack Matlock explains the reason for Bush's warning:

> There were several reasons. One was that the nationalists in several of the republics wanted independence for their own reasons, and the Communists in other republics, once they saw that the Communist Party was losing power, wanted independence in order to save themselves and stay in power. This happened in central Asia. You ended up with five dictators in central Asia in those five countries and keeping the old system primarily open; therefore, with all of their talk of opening up the economies, they were basically a totalitarian political system in the way that they controlled things. That is why I think Bush was right when he said don't confuse independence with freedom. In

other words, if you have freedom and you want independence, eventually you're going to get it. But, if you take independence under conditions before you get freedom, you could be deprived of freedom for a long time, and that's happening in a lot of the republics. In fact, in all of them, except the Baltic states, it's happening. Now, I think we understood that we couldn't do it for them. It's something they had to do for themselves.[54]

While the Bush administration had varying views on what course of action would be best for the Soviet Union, the overriding concern, notwithstanding Cheney, was that they wanted the Soviet Union to work out the internal problems on their own and in a way that ensured a peaceful process. This preoccupation with assuring a peaceful process led Baker and the State Department to come up with a set of "five principles" that were similar to the "four principles," which had been used as a guideline on German unification:

1.   peaceful self-determination consistent with democratic values and principles
2.   respect for existing borders, with any changes occurring peacefully and consensually
3.   respect for democracy and the rule of law, especially elections and referenda
4.   human rights, particularly minority rights
5.   respect for international law and obligations[55]

Baker intended to use the "five principles" to create a political structure to guide U.S. policy through the transition period of the Soviet Union. Later, a sixth principle would be added—central control over nuclear weapons and safeguards against internal or external proliferation. Despite these principles, the Bush administration never arrived at a rigid policy on the potential breakup of the Soviet Union. This was due to the sheer rapidity of the events and the fact that many in the administration still had views that differed from Baker's. Most agreed, however, that the United States did have some role to play in regard to external concerns and obligations. Knowing that he would need the support of the United States, Yeltsin obviously geared the Minsk agreement to meet the concerns publicly expressed by the Bush administration. The plan that he read over the telephone after secretly meeting with the presidents of Ukraine and Belarus guaranteed international obligations, including foreign aid debt, under agreements and treaties signed by the former Soviet Union and provided for unitary control of nuclear weapons and nonproliferation. It was reasonable for Yeltsin to assume that the Bush administration would likely agree to a plan that seemed to mesh with the six principles outlined in various official U.S. public statements. That is, of course, if he could follow through with his claim that the other republics would soon be in agreement. Yeltsin's prediction soon came true. The Minsk agreement was released while the republics' parliaments were reviewing the Treaty on the Union of Sovereign States drafted by the USSR State Council and supported by Gorbachev. Their attention quickly turned to the Minsk agreement with eleven republics approving it almost immediately and the Central Asian states joining in at a later date.[56] Despite the continued objections by Gorbachev, the Declaration of Adherence to the Commonwealth of Independent States was signed on December 21, 1991, at Alma-Ata, by all of the republics save the Baltic states and Georgia.[57]

On December 25, 1991, Gorbachev signed a decree relinquishing his duties as president of the USSR. The end of the Soviet Union was not a surprise; President Bush had already had his staff write a letter to Gorbachev to be sent on the day he resigned. He had also had them write a draft statement on the resignation that praised Gorbachev for his contributions in ending the Cold War. Bush received the final draft the day before Gorbachev's announcement.[58] In reality, Gorbachev's resignation was anticlimactic. Yeltsin had been methodically stripping Gorbachev of power since the coup, thus ensuring that the Soviet Union would cease to exist. The morning of Gorbachev's resignation Bush, who was spending Christmas day at Camp David with his family, received a final call from Gorbachev.[59] Despite the events that led to Gorbachev's fall and Bush's role in recognizing Yeltsin, Bush and Gorbachev remained close friends. In fact, Bush actively tried to keep relations between Gorbachev and Yeltsin as cordial as possible to ensure a peaceful transfer of power. As Bush's press secretary recalls, "Maybe one of the best examples was when Yeltsin replaced Gorbachev after the coup attempt. It was President Bush who got on the phone to Yeltsin and convinced him that in a peaceful turnover, he needed to be good to Gorbachev. And [he] told him to give him a car, give him a house, and treat him well. And Yeltsin didn't want to because he hated Gorbachev, and then Bush called Gorbachev and said the same thing—You want to demonstrate a peaceful transition; you got to be praising Yeltsin or at least don't be criticizing him in public. Don't be tearing him down and picking a fight. You two guys have got to show that you can change power peacefully."[60] Despite the relationship between Bush and Gorbachev, Bush, in the end, supported the collapse of the Soviet Union. Many western politicians of the Cold War Era had seen the breakup of the Soviet Union as the main goal of the Cold War. Bush was

Figure 17. Bush prepares to speak from the Oval Office on Christmas night, 1991, announcing that the Soviet Union had ceased to exist. *Courtesy of the George Bush Presidential Library*

of that generation but was also fearful that the disintegration of the Soviet Union could leave a dangerous and unpredictable geopolitical vacuum. In that final telephone conversation, Gorbachev assured Bush that he was leaving everything under reliable control. He was, of course, referring to the former Soviet Union's nuclear weapons, because the lack of central authority did open up the danger of the loss of physical control. The Soviet arsenal of nuclear weapons was concentrated in four republics: Russia, Kazakhstan, Ukraine, and Belarus; the United States was not entirely confident that all four of the republics could handle or secure the weapons or fissionable materials to their satisfaction. The Bush administration had finally, after much debate among the advisors, reached the conclusion that it would be preferable to see the nuclear weapons under the control of one entity that had both the experience and stability to control them.[61] Gorbachev agreed with this and, just before leaving office, turned over the "presidential briefcase," which contained the control system for nuclear arms, to Yeltsin, so it would be controlled by the Russian Federation.[62] Russia would also take the Soviet Union's place on the United Nations Security Council. Gorbachev assured Bush that he could celebrate Christmas without worry, and, in an address from the Oval Office later that night, Bush spoke to the nation to explain the historic change that had taken place (fig. 17).[63] He expressed gratitude to Gorbachev for his commitment to peace, giving Gorbachev's policies the credit for changing the USSR. But he also gave credit to U.S. policies, citing the nine U.S. presidents since the Cold War began as playing key roles in the collapse of the Soviet Union. Bush then offered a three-tiered recognition process. The United States would first fully recognize Russia and Yeltsin.[64] Then full diplomatic recognition would be extended to the republics that had taken proper steps to achieving stability. Finally, the United States would recognize the independence of the rest of the republics on a conditional basis. "Our enemies have become our partners," Bush told U.S. viewers—with that, the official seal was placed on the end of the Cold War.

One final vestige of the Cold War was wrapped up by START II (Strategic Arms Reduction Treaty). The breakup of the Soviet Union had convinced Bush to reduce the number of nuclear weapons on both sides even further than what had been agreed upon in START. Scowcroft suggested getting rid of all tactical nuclear weapons with the exception of air-delivered ones. Short-range nuclear weapons were becoming increasingly undesirable. For example, in Europe, with the unification of Germany, short-range nuclear missiles would detonate on German territory. They were also problematic for the navy, who had received complaints from countries that were reluctant to allow warships carrying nuclear weapons into their ports. Scowcroft also suggested de-MIRVing of the ICBM force, perhaps the most destabilizing nuclear weapons used by either side.[65] These suggestions developed into START II, which was signed just before President Bush left office in January 1993.

Postscript: Why Did Gorbachev Fail?

The basic goal of the Cold War was seen by many to be the breakup of the Soviet Union. It is therefore important to understand Gorbachev's failure, because the collapse of the Soviet Union mirrored the collapse of Gorbachev. An understanding of Gorbachev's failure thus provides an explanation of why the Soviet Union itself imploded. The first step is to look at the task that Gorbachev had to address immediately upon taking power—the failing Soviet economy. The Soviet economy was failing because of isolation from the world economy. The Soviet Union was a pariah within the international system, and a fundamental shift in foreign policy had to be made in order to end the Soviet Union's economic and political isolation. Embracing the international system, however, would directly contradict what had been a source of pride for the Soviet Union. As Soviet expert

Condoleezza Rice points out, "the Soviet Union had taken pride in being a pariah—neither an accomplice to nor a victim of global capitalism's exploitation of the world."[66] This was the basic understanding of Marxist-Leninist ideology that had been used by Soviet leaders. The central tenet of Marxist-Leninist ideology since Joseph Stalin's rule had been that the Soviet Union's long-term interests could not be reconciled with the interests of an "international economic and political order dominated by capitalist democracies."[67] According to this ideology, the Cold War and the separation that it required was the very foundation of the Soviet Union. Until the day when socialism finally triumphed, that division had to be maintained in order to provide insulation from an international economic system that could destroy the Soviet Union. Stalin had actually formulated this plan prior to World War II and felt that the Soviet Union should be self-sufficient until a "ring of socialist brother states" would come along to provide the resources and additional insulation and security to protect against capitalism. Once this happened, a truly alternative system would be in place to counter capitalist democracies. This helps explain the evidence presented by the Venona intercepts and why the Soviet Union would be waging an espionage war against a supposed ally.[68] Of course, Stalin achieved the spheres of influence that he needed in the aftermath of World War II and would use Eastern Europe's resources to build a stronger Soviet Union, one that could hope to outlast capitalism. But the socialist economies had a flaw that the capitalist democracies did not—the system could not be regulated by the market. Therefore, the Soviets had to build a structure to coordinate the socialist economies. This structure, found largely in the Council for Mutual Economic Assistance (CMEA), would further isolate them from the capitalist democracies of the West. The U.S. containment policy actually mirrored Stalin's original blueprint, providing further insulation. Unfortunately for the East, it also kept them from gaining access to changing technologies that would have benefited the Soviet military economy as well as civilian needs. This flaw was readily apparent in the 1970s as the Soviet Union increasingly relied on foreign technologies as well as imported grain. This did not dissuade the Soviet Union from its goal; it hoped to revitalize its system through détente by acquiring technological help from the West while affirming its superpower status. On the other hand, the West hoped to use détente to force the Soviets into a "web of interdependence" that would chip away at the insulation from the economic and political order dominated by capitalist democracies. The hopes of the West had dissipated by the end of the 1970s as they realized that the Soviet invasion of Afghanistan in 1979 and the Soviet buildup of conventional forces demonstrated that they were trying to turn détente into a victory rather than an accommodation. Pres. Jimmy Carter responded to this challenge by ordering a sharp increase in defense spending at the end of his term, and Pres. Ronald Reagan extended this increase to even higher levels.

After decades of economic stagnation, the Soviet Union could not match U.S. technological innovation and could not afford to continue trying to overwhelm with brute strength. This placed Gorbachev in a difficult position. He knew that the very foundation of Marxist-Leninist ideology was the precept of a "permanent revolution" in which the socialist states would have to outlast the capitalist democracies. He knew that although the Soviet system was not in immediate danger of collapsing, the reality was that the West could almost certainly last longer. He could either follow the pattern set by previous Soviet leaders and wait for the system to eventually collapse because of economic pressure, or he could seek to reform the system by ending Soviet isolation and reintegrating it into the international system, creating, in the words of Gorbachev, a "common European home." This, of course, would mean the end of the Cold War. His critics would charge that such a move would shake the very foundation of Marxist-Leninist ideology and the Communist Party. Gorbachev, however, was more concerned with practical and fundamental reforms. He was a genuine reformer whose goal, unlike his predecessors, was not to accumulate more power for himself and the Communist Party but to establish a government based on the consent of the governed. In theory and on paper, the Soviet state was a voluntary federation of sovereign republics, but in practice the Soviet Union operated as an imperial state. As Gorbachev himself recalls, perestroika was meant to end this totalitarian system: "Yes, there were political, economic, and social problems—and problems between nationalities. These were not, however, problems of our country as a whole but of the system that had been established. This administrative-bureaucratic system, this totalitarian system, could not respond adequately to the problems that had built up. Not only did it fail to contribute to their solution; it deepened and intensified them. As a result, by the 1980s our country had entered a stage of crisis. It was in order to overcome this crisis that perestroika was begun."[69] The realization in the 1980s that the Soviet Union could not win the arms race helped Gorbachev deal with the hard-liners. Yet he still could push only limited reforms for fear of being removed from office by the Central Committee if he began to be seen as too radical. In short, Gorbachev realized that the Soviet Union could not continue as it had. He knew that the change must occur internally but with the cooperation of the West. But Gorbachev wanted to reform the Soviet Union, not destroy it, as the hard-liners accused him of doing. He wanted to transform the empire into a federated or confederated state:

> Today the assertion can often be heard that the Union treaty that was to be signed in August 1991 would have meant the destruction of the Soviet Union anyway. No! The signing of the treaty would have been a real alternative to the breakup of the Union. It would have meant preservation of Union-wide citizenship, which was recognized as a separate point in the document. The citizen of any state belonging to the Union was simultaneously a citizen of the Union. That was Article 2 of the treaty. The new Union treaty would have meant preservation and development of a unified Unionwide market. Armed forces under a single command (not "joint command") would have been preserved. The state security of the Union as a whole and a unified foreign policy would have been assured. Preservation, renewal, and reform of the Union was my main political and, if you will, moral task in my position as president of the USSR. I consider it my greatest sorrow and misfortune that I did not succeed in preserving the country as a single whole. All my efforts were focused on trying to preserve that unity.[70]

But Gorbachev failed to preserve that unity. His failure was assured by the August coup and the damage that it did to his ability to lead. According to Boris Yeltsin's journal, "Instead of a gradual transition from the unitarian Soviet Union to a softer, freer confederation, we had a complete vacuum at the political center. The center—in the person of Gorbachev—was totally demoralized. The emerging national states had lost faith in him. Something had to be done."[71] The only real chance that the Soviet Union had of remaining intact was for Gorbachev and Yeltsin to cooperate, but their personal antagonism prevented this from happening. From the time of the coup attempt, Yeltsin began seizing the bureaucratic structures of the Soviet Union in an effort to destroy the Soviet state and, with it, Gorbachev. In the past, Russia had been ruled directly by the central ministries. A fully sovereign Russia needed the institutions of government controlled by Gorbachev in order to prevent political gridlock. Indeed, Yeltsin would not remain content to share Moscow with Gorbachev. Thus, it was Gorbachev, backed into a corner by the August coup and Yeltsin, who bore the primary responsibility for bringing about the end of communism as a system of rule in the USSR and the end of the Soviet Union itself. The United States, as Ambassador Matlock explains, could only play a supporting role:

Obviously, some of the things we pushed for to end the Cold War, such as opening up the country, bringing in democratic processes, supporting the election process, were things that made the eventual disintegration of the Soviet Union possible. . . . In that sense, by opening up the country, encouraging them to open up and so on, we created conditions which when they could not deal with these other pressures, the state collapsed. So I'm not saying that none of our policies had any relevance. I'm just saying that we didn't bring it about. We didn't have the power to bring it about. It was brought about internally. Some of these internal forces had been encouraged by the United States and the West in general, not so much by a direct action, although by that too, but by our very existence. After all, as long as we [the West] existed as free societies, as democratic societies, with economies that seemed to work, we were a threat to the Soviet system. And their task was to try to be more like us without admitting it. And we were really in favor of that. It turned out that they couldn't. Well, that was their problem.[72]

The end of the Cold War set in motion forces that attacked the very foundation of the socialist system. By encouraging democratization, human rights, and the free flow of information, the United States helped introduce outside pressure on a flawed system. But in the end, Gorbachev would be the one who tried to alter the existing system in an effort to save his country, not destroy it. The type of radical change that could have made the Soviet Union viable, however, was exactly the type of change that it had been designed to block.[73]

Chapter 6

The Prudent Cold Warrior

The Foreign Policy Legacy of George Bush

Assessing the impact of any recent president is a difficult task for historians. The very use of the word *legacy* suggests a sense of judgment that is unavoidably subjective. But now that a reasonable amount of time has passed since the ending of the Cold War, it is necessary to examine the presidential organizational and policymaking arrangements that shaped that end at a time when many of the men and women who influenced those decisions are still alive to be questioned by historians. Interviews with President Bush and his principal aides and advisors have been a central underpinning of this study. It is still impossible to provide a complete—if history is ever complete—view of the end of the Cold War because of the limited, though not inconsequential, amount of documents available for research. Documents have been declassified and released to the public in sporadic bursts, offering a continuously changing image of exactly what occurred. This study is based on many recently declassified documents that challenge some of the well-accepted views of the Cold War; however, there is no reason to be alarmed if some conclusions are challenged or even replaced. As Cold War historian John Lewis Gaddis reminds us, "Cold War historians should retain the capacity to be surprised."[1] Thus, it has been the purpose of this study to examine the foreign policy apparatus and the decision-making process of the Bush administration to provide an accurate portrayal of the Bush administration's role in ending the Cold War. It is meant to complement more comprehensive examinations of the end of the Cold War as well as focused studies on Reagan, Gorbachev, other Cold War actors, and indeed the many fine general studies of the Bush presidency.

Bush vs. Reagan

A sense of competition seems to exist between Reagan supporters and Bush supporters. It is as if credit given to the accomplishments of one man somehow distracts from the significance of the other one. Reagan supporters seem especially hesitant to give Bush any credit because they want Reagan to be seen as solely responsible for the end of the Cold War, a view simply not supported by the facts. No one man ended the Cold War: neither Ronald Reagan, Mikhail Gorbachev, George Bush, nor any other single leader had that type of impact. But by foreign policy successes and mistakes, all influenced when and how that end occurred. In order to gauge the true impact of these people, one must understand when and exactly how that end was realized. Although the exact date has been endlessly argued by Cold War historians, the general public typically associates the end of the Cold War with the fall of the Berlin Wall. The dramatic television images of Germans "dancing on the wall"—something George Bush refused to do—are memorable, but the building of the Berlin Wall did not mark the beginning of the Cold War, nor did the fall of the Berlin Wall mark its end.

So when did the Cold War end? Participants cannot agree on an exact time. Some members of the Reagan administration still insist that it was over by the time Reagan left office. Attorney General Edwin Meese, perhaps Reagan's most devoted admirer, hailed Reagan as "the man who ended the Cold War."[2] Secretary of State George Schultz implies much the same as he recounts the final months of the Reagan administration in his memoir: "It was as if the whole world had breathed a deep sigh of relief. An immense tension had gone out of the system. The world had changed. Margaret Thatcher had it right. In an interview with the *Washington Post* and *Newsweek* on November 17, during her last official visit to Washington during the Reagan administration, she said flatly, 'We're not in a Cold War now.' Despite this new reality, many in the United States seemed unable or unwilling to grasp this seminal fact. But to me, it was all over but the shouting."[3] The "shouting," as Schultz describes it, would entail the collapse of Communist control of Eastern Europe, the reunification of Germany, the disintegration of the Warsaw Pact, and the breakup of the Soviet Union. Claiming that the Cold War ended in 1988 and declaring Reagan the man who had single-handedly won the war shows, of course, very heavy bias by Reagan loyalists, whose own reputations and legacies are inextricably linked to that of Reagan's. Certainly Reagan's strategy of "peace through strength" or "negotiation from strength" had helped the Soviets to lose ground to the United States, as far as military and economic power was concerned. But the Soviet Union remained a formidable nuclear power and, in terms of raw numbers, still held an edge in conventional forces in Europe. In addition, as historian Joseph Smith argues, "with the rise to power of Mikhail Gorbachev in 1985, a Soviet leader once again assumed a prominent role in world affairs reminiscent of Khrushchev's during the 1950s."[4] Bruce Porter of the Olin Institute of Strategic Studies at Harvard University boldly predicted "within the next five to ten years, Russia will resolve many of the internal contradictions now plaguing it, and the world will witness the resurgence of its military and industrial power. . . . When it occurs, we will look back with chagrin at today's casual assumptions about Russian decline."[5] While perhaps beaten, the Soviet Union in January of 1989 certainly was not vanquished.

The few people that served in both the Reagan and Bush administrations, many of whom were interviewed for this book, tend to take a more moderate view of Reagan's accomplishments. Marlin Fitzwater, White House press secretary for both President Reagan and President Bush, felt that Reagan had won the Cold War by 1988 but that the Malta conference on December 2 and 3, 1990, was the pivotal point in changing the relationship with the Soviet Union and making plans for the post–Cold War world: "I would say that [the Malta conference] was the pivotal point at which the West first recognized that Communism was changing and may collapse. And we met with the purpose of trying to define how that could happen, what our role would be, and how we could help guide the future of whatever Russia emerged. . . . [The Malta conference] was the point at which we recognized as a country, as a president, that Communism was gone, or on its way. And we were making plans for the post–Cold War world."[6] According to this view, although Reagan had accelerated the demise of the Soviet Union, there were still many aspects of the Cold War that had to be addressed before it would completely end. To Fitzwater, Malta was the turning point. Other officials would point to other "turning points" as the date when the Cold War could conclusively be deemed at an end. Bush's Secretary of State James Baker argues that the Cold War ended on August 2, 1990: "Saddam Hussein invaded Kuwait, and Iraq was a big Soviet client state. And I flew back—I happened to be in Mongolia at the time—I flew back through Moscow. And Shevardnadze, without even clearing it with Gorbachev, joined with me in a statement condemning the invasion and calling for an arms embargo of Iraq.

Now that was historic. The first time ever, that the Soviet Union foreign minister and the Secretary of State of the United States would ever have a joint press conference condemning the action of a Soviet client state. . . . That's the day, at least to me, it was quite clear, if it wasn't clear the day the wall fell, it was certainly clear that day that the Cold War was over."[7] National Security Advisor Brent Scowcroft takes a different view, pointing to July 15, 1990, as the end: "The point at which I was willing to say the Cold War is over is when Gorbachev in July of 1990 . . . Kohl went over to visit him . . . and Gorbachev said it was alright if a united Germany could belong to NATO. To me that was the end of the Cold War."[8] Chairman of the Joint Chiefs of Staff Colin Powell was not willing to say that the Cold War was over until December 25, 1991: "The end of the Cold War, I guess for me as a finite date in time was Christmas 1991 when the Soviet Union ended."[9] President Bush was asked the same question, reviewed the responses of his advisors, and, while unwilling to single out a point as the definitive end of the Cold War, indicated an event that he felt was pivotal: "I cannot specify a direct point when it was safe to say the Cold War had ended. There was a very important meeting in the White House when Gorbachev, to the surprise of his own colleagues, said that the German people had the right to determine their own future by deciding on unification and by deciding to remain in NATO if they wanted to do that."[10] That Cabinet Room discussion on the first full day of the Washington Summit, May 31, 1990, provides yet another possible date for the end of the Cold War. How can there be so much disagreement concerning an end date to the Cold War? How can historians set a date if the very men that lived through the events and made the decisions that shaped the end are in open disagreement? The answer to that question must be linked to the origins of the Cold War. After all, the Cold War could not end until the original issues that set in place the foundation of the Cold War had been resolved.

An examination of the beginning of the Cold War demonstrates that the acrimony between Reagan supporters and Bush supporters has been misguided. The Cold War began in 1945 with the division of Europe, and the policy of containment, formulated by George Kennan, had been meant to address that division.[11] But the Cold War's sudden expansion into Asia in 1949–50 demonstrated that World War II had "left not just a single power vacuum in that part of the world, as in Europe, but several."[12] The expansion of the Cold War to Asia meant that the United States began to look at the Cold War in more global terms. Korea and Vietnam would be the sites for much of the "hot" parts of the Cold War, with soldiers being brought home in body bags. The second phase of the Cold War moved beyond the division of Europe and went from the practical, concrete problem seen by Kennan into a more ideological one, pitting communism against capitalism, totalitarianism against democracy.[13] The Cold War became much more than just the division of Europe, and Kennan's policy of containment began to be used in ways that he had not foreseen. That second phase of the Cold War, the one built on ideology, was the war that Ronald Reagan fought; a war fought with rhetoric—a moral crusade to defeat the Evil Empire and stop the approaching Armageddon. While that might seem like a stretch, it is exactly how Ronald Reagan felt. It was the undercurrent of almost all of his speeches concerning the Soviet Union during his first term in office and, indeed, the undercurrent of his anti-communist speeches on behalf of the Screen Actors Guild early in his career. He became more conciliatory during his second term as it became apparent that the United States was winning the Cold War, and by 1988, the second phase of the Cold War was all but won.

But the original phase of the Cold War—the one Kennan had addressed— had not been resolved. The division of Europe still existed; two armed camps still were entrenched, exerting their power over their spheres of influence and forcing the other to be ready for an onslaught that would never come. More concerned with ideology and rhetoric, nuclear weapons and Armageddon, Reagan could not see that the division of Europe had to end before the Cold War would be completely finished. In fact, as U.S. Ambassador to the Soviet Union Jack Matlock recalls, Reagan saw the division of Europe as a symptom, not the cause, of the Cold War.[14] For the twenty years prior to the Reagan administration, the conflict between the United States and the Soviet Union had been funneled into arms control negotiations—a place where both sides could safely flex their might and use hot rhetoric to demonstrate that the Cold War was a battle between superpowers. Both sides wanted to show that their country, thus their ideology, was superior. When Brent Scowcroft was given the opportunity to be Bush's national security advisor, he felt that he had "inherited a movement in which the fundamentals had not gone nearly as far as the rhetoric."[15] He saw an opportunity to fundamentally change how the Cold War was being fought—to move it from an ideological battle fought with rhetoric to a pragmatic agenda resolved through diplomacy: "I wanted to change that [focus on arms control] a little and to focus on Eastern Europe. There was ferment in Eastern Europe, especially Poland. And I wanted to take advantage of that ferment to try and get the Soviet army out of Eastern Europe, or at least reduce their presence to allow the Eastern Europeans to develop in a progressive way."[16] And that is exactly what the Bush administration accomplished. They both encouraged and helped manage the end of the division of Europe in a way that would help it end with minimal turmoil and minimal bloodshed. Thus, the original phase of the Cold War, and with it the Cold War itself, ended when the division of Europe ended. More precisely, it ended when the center of Europe, where the Soviet and U.S. troops had met in 1945 to symbolize victory, was unified. The reunification of Germany ended the original phase of the Cold War. The official conclusion took place on September 12, 1990, when France, the United Kingdom, the United States, the Soviet Union, and East and West Germany signed an agreement that ended Allied occupation rights and united Germany, thus fully restoring its sovereignty.[17] The practical end, however, took place on July 15, 1990, when Gorbachev finally agreed to a unified Germany in NATO, thus clearing the final hurdle for reunification. That reunification, along with the dissolution of the Warsaw Pact, the withdrawal of Soviet troops from Eastern Europe, and NATO's shift toward a greater political and less military role, ended the division of Europe and fulfilled the underlying precept of Kennan's policy of containment.

The argument that two distinct dimensions to the Cold War existed is the only credible argument that explains the differences in President Reagan's and President Bush's foreign policy initiatives. Take, for example, the words of Marlin Fitzwater: "When Reagan came in . . . we were in the heat of the Cold War, and Reagan was *the* Cold Warrior. He knew how to fight communism. He had a strong ideology, a strong belief in America, and so he was a perfect president to take them on and say 'America's going to win this war.' And when President Bush came in, he had the international background and the diplomatic experience to then negotiate the new realities of an East-West relationship."[18] Fitzwater identified Reagan's fight, and his strength, as being based on ideology. Reagan was "*the* Cold Warrior" because he "knew how to fight communism"—with ideology. This ideology was manifested in rhetoric. Fitzwater identifies Reagan as the perfect president to take them on and "*say* [emphasis added] America's going to win this war." When Fitzwater refers to Bush, he praises him for his international background and diplomatic experience. Bush was the right president to "*negotiate* [emphasis added] the new realities of an East-West relationship." In that same interview, Fitzwater indirectly refers to Bush's ability to "*navigate* [emphasis added] the waters of European change." The difference in terminology could not be more striking. Reagan is going to "fight communism," "take them on," and "say America's going to win." Bush is going to use his "diplomatic experience" to "negotiate" and "navigate."

The two presidents were addressing the Cold War in two distinct ways. That is because they were fighting two different levels of the Cold War, partly because of their two markedly different backgrounds and partly because of the circumstances in which they found themselves: "The point is that the world changed there and it changed just about the time we changed presidents, so you can't really judge President Bush, his views on ending the Cold War, against Reagan's because the Cold War was different when he became president."[19]

It is difficult to compare the effectiveness of the foreign policy approach of each man because they had such different goals and such different concepts of the war that they were fighting. Reagan put his belief in words, words such as *freedom* and *democracy*. He felt that espousing those words was a goal in itself. If he could get people, Americans and Soviets, to believe in those words, successful policies would naturally follow. In essence, he used ideology as both a guide for policymaking and as a tool to justify policy once it was made. In his memoir, Reagan explains the essence of what the Cold War meant to him: "Democracy triumphed in the Cold War because it was a battle of values—between one system that gave preeminence to the state and another that gave preeminence to the individual and freedom."[20] To Reagan, the Cold War was a battle of ideology and values that had been won once it was demonstrated that democracy was superior. Indeed, Jack F. Matlock Jr., who served on Reagan's National Security Council staff from 1983 to 86 and as U.S. ambassador to the Soviet Union under both Reagan and Bush, confirms that Reagan viewed the Cold War as a war of ideology: totalitarianism versus freedom.[21] Matlock distinguishes between the ideological phase of the Cold War and the diplomatic phase, pointing to Gorbachev's speech before the United Nations in December 1988 as the point at which the Cold War philosophically came to an end:

> I distinguish between the ideological end to the Cold War and, as I say, all of the cleanup diplomacy, which was important. It's sort of like something happening as the end of a crisis, but you don't know if there's going to be a relapse if you're speaking in medical terms. So it had to be confirmed, but it was confirmed over the next two years. . . . So I think that, in general, we no longer had totally antagonistic goals. After all, the Cold War was conceived as a zero-sum game—any gain for one was [a loss for] the other—and then suddenly we were looking at how we can disengage, how can we serve the interests of everybody. . . . That's why I say I think it ended ideologically. That's not

to deny that there was a lot of diplomacy to be done to clear up the remnants of the Cold War, the results.[22]

According to this view, when President Bush took office, the United States needed a skillful diplomat who excelled at personal diplomacy and could help "wrap things up" peacefully—what Matlock refers to as "cleanup diplomacy." Although the Cold War's back had been broken in terms of ideology, the responsibility for cleaning up the remnants of the Cold War would fall on Bush. It was a role that Bush, who was wary of excessive rhetoric and preferred pragmatic (he would say "prudent") diplomatic solutions, was well suited to perform. Bush said as much in his speech announcing his candidacy for president: "I am a practical man; I like what's real. I'm not much for the airy and abstract; I like what works. I am not a mystic, and I do not yearn to lead a crusade; my ambitions are perhaps less dramatic, but they are no less profound."[23] Brent Scowcroft certainly sees a distinction between how Reagan and Bush fought the Cold War: "The Carter administration . . . well, they had a tough time. But in a way it was sort of a disaster because everything was going wrong for us and it was the end of Vietnam and Watergate, and the Soviet Union was talking about the correlation of forces and the world was changing in their favor and so on. So what we needed was Reagan to restore American spirits and to have us stand up and stand up tall. But it took Bush to bring it to an end."[24] Scowcroft certainly felt that Bush ended the Cold War: "The Cold War . . . well, you know the Reagan administration tends to think they ended the Cold War. I think the Cold War was not at all ended when Bush came into office. Eastern Europe was still divided just like it was before. The Soviet army was still manning barricades and so on. No, it happened under President Bush, and it happened the way it did in considerable part because of his great skill at diplomacy about eliciting cooperation from people, both friends and opponents."[25] Notice what Scowcroft points to as the reason the Cold War had not ended—Eastern Europe was still divided: "I thought that . . . the Cold War was really about Eastern Europe. And, with the unification of Germany and its membership in NATO, that really finished the Cold War."[26] President Bush agrees with Scowcroft's assessment: "Clearly, the Cold War could not have been called dead as long as Eastern Europe was not free."[27] The division of Europe that Kennan had addressed with his policy of containment had to end before the Cold War could be over. However, the division of Europe could not end, at least peacefully, until the Soviet Union allowed for that division to end.

Bush vs. Gorbachev

Gorbachev and the "new thinkers" who gained power in the Soviet Union in 1985 provided the initial conditions needed for the end of the Cold War. But he did not intend to end the division of Europe; he was more interested in internal change. Changes in foreign policy were merely designed to help perestroika (economic restructuring) succeed. Gorbachev looked favorably on world developments that he felt promoted perestroika and never considered that they might lead to the emergence of anti-communist and anti-Soviet governments: "If we can bring people back into the socialist system instead of alienating them, we can give socialism a second wind."[28] This optimistic remark in July 1989 demonstrated that the purpose of his policies was not to promote separation or grant independence. Instead, they were intended to "inspire much-needed reform and modernization."[29] His belief that socialism would be strengthened depended on his ability to revitalize the Soviet Union. Gorbachev's domestic reforms, however, could not revive an economy beleaguered by mismanagement and inefficiency.

With falling agricultural and industrial production, inflation, and increased foreign debt and trade deficits, criticism of Gorbachev's reform efforts led to demands for local autonomy by many of the more than one hundred different nationalities within the Soviet Union. Gorbachev's reforming activities and his denunciation of Brezhnev's "years of stagnation" did not merely impact the Soviet Union. The rising expectations sparked by glasnost (open debate on government policies) and perestroika led to movements in the satellite states for the same type of fundamental reforms and, thereby, challenged the power and authority of the local Communist bosses. This progression of change from "below" followed the path that Gorbachev was taking from "above." As Jack Matlock recalls, Gorbachev's initial foreign policy approach was that of a dogmatic defender of traditional nationalistic, exclusive, and intolerant Soviet attitudes.[30] But within just a few years he had rejected the class struggle ideology and embraced universal human values. Gorbachev knew that a less confrontational foreign policy would allow him to lower defense spending, thus freeing up needed resources for internal economic reform. Also, Soviet leaders had used the Cold War to justify internal repression. Gorbachev knew that the needed reforms might be blocked by hard-liners as long as the Cold War continued. In addition, continuing a confrontational security policy would make it imperative that the coercive control of Eastern Europe be maintained—something Gorbachev increasingly began to view as incompatible with his policies of democratization and economic reform within the Soviet Union.[31] Reducing the Soviet sphere of influence would have the added benefit of reducing the cost of economic subsidies to Eastern Europe, which had long been a burden to Soviet resources. For example, by ending the Soviet sale of oil and natural gas to Eastern Europe at prices far below world market, a key source of hard currency for the Soviet Union could become available.

Gorbachev's change in foreign policy was also done to help his country overcome "the hostility, and permanent tension with the outside world that the Bolshevik Revolution had engendered."[32] Gorbachev knew that, in order for his efforts to succeed, he was going to need better relations with the West. This change in relations started during Reagan's second term and was nearly complete by the time Bush assumed the presidency. Gorbachev recognized that between his last visit to the United States while Reagan was still in office and the first visit under President Bush, "the 'enemy image,' used to fuel the Cold War confrontation for decades, had lost much of its appeal."[33] Gorbachev's ideological pronouncements were more than a shift in rhetoric; they led to the reorientation of Soviet foreign policy to conform to them.[34] That is why Gorbachev, unlike previous Soviet leaders, consistently used force not as a first but as a last resort.[35] That is why, in the end, he was willing to agree to arms reductions based on equality rather than along proportional lines, which would have maintained Soviet superiority. That is why he took a non-interventionist policy toward Eastern Europe and allowed those countries to leave the Soviet sphere of influence and why he allowed a unified Germany in NATO and opposed aggression by a former Soviet client state in the Persian Gulf. As Matlock concludes, "[Gorbachev] did not originate the specific program that eventually ended the Cold War and eliminated the East-West divide. But he came to understand that the Soviet Union could benefit from joining the rest of the world, and he made an essential contribution when he found and adopted an ideological justification for making peace with the world."[36] Thus, Bush dealt with a Soviet leader with no clear strategic vision but one that eagerly wanted his internal reforms to succeed. The task for Bush was to find common interests that could move forward the U.S. objective of ending the division of Europe and aid Gorbachev in his task of preserving and developing the democratic transformations that were occurring within the Soviet Union.

Conclusion

Foreign relations are a major concern of every presidency. This was especially true in the presidency of George Bush, during which the Cold War ended; the Soviet Union collapsed; the former Soviet bloc countries began the transition to democracy and market economics; Germany was reunited; and the United States led the alliance that liberated Kuwait from Iraqi control. In no other area does the president play a more central role than in foreign affairs. This is especially true when, as in the case of Bush, both houses of Congress are controlled by the opposing party. The concept of George Bush as an excellent president with regards to foreign policy and a poor president in regards to domestic policy seems to have been universally accepted. It is worth noting that out of all of the Bush administration officials interviewed for this study, when asked to list the achievements of the Bush administration, not one cited a domestic policy achievement. All focused on accomplishments in foreign affairs. When asked the same question, President Bush's response also focused exclusively on foreign affairs: "That the Cold War ended without a shot being fired was a major accomplishment, but so, too, was standing against Iraq's aggression in the Gulf. I hope historians will say that the unification of Germany, the liberation of Eastern Europe and the Baltic States, the implosion of the Soviet Union, and, yes, NAFTA, which we initiated before leaving office, were all significant accomplishments."[37] The members of the press were quick to see this disparity and focused on it throughout the Bush presidency. At the end of 1990, *Time* magazine named its "Man of the Year." The award was supposed to go to the person who, for better or for worse, had made the most impact on news that year. Their selection was unusual in that they named "the two George Bushes" as "Men of the Year."[38] They claimed that George Bush had seemed like two presidents: one displaying a commanding vision of a new world order, the other showing little vision for his country. In short, they were making a distinction between a remarkably successful "International George Bush" and a rudderless "Domestic George Bush." This perception was not confined to 1990, nor was it limited to *Time* magazine. In fact, this is the image that most of the general public, and many trained observers and historians, have of George Bush's entire presidency. Economist Robert Reich mockingly labeled Bush the "best secretary of state we've ever had."[39] Economist John Kenneth Galbraith added that, in his opinion, "[Bush] becomes slightly depressed when he has to come home and deal with economic or other dreary subjects of that sort."[40] Bush did have some limited success on domestic policy, such as passage of a clean air bill, legislation to help disabled Americans, an improved immigration bill, and efforts to bail out the savings-and-loans. But then-Senator Al Gore seems to have summed up the prevailing opinion when he labeled Bush a "do nothing president on domestic problems."[41] Democrats stressed the theme that Bush had no domestic agenda and had more interest in foreign policy than in America. One running joke by the Democrats said that "To get assistance to Americans, we'll have to give them foreign addresses!"[42] Internally, the Bush administration faced the reality: "The President is not *personally* associated with a known, serious, *coherent* domestic agenda. This is not for lack of domestic activity. The President is seen in a limitless set of domestic drop-bys, report-receipts, bill-signings, initiative announcements, listening sessions, photo-ops, etc. But there is a distinction between this imagery and the perception of coherent substantive engagement with serious problem-solving. The latter is what is perceived with respect to foreign policy—and, ironically, its very success sets a somewhat higher standard for domestic performance."[43] Even Marlin Fitzwater's suggested solution of focusing on "Domestic Storm" was a clear example that the Bush administration's foreign policy successes overshadowed any possible domestic achievements.[44] It is not unusual for a president who was in office during a war—indeed Bush had to deal with both the Cold War and the Persian Gulf War—to be remembered primarily in conjunction with that war. But Bush is one of the few who is remembered only in relation to the wars that he fought. If not for the victories in two wars, the assumption is that Bush would have been a rather forgettable president or remembered only as the man entrusted with the Reagan legacy. Such a hypothesis attempts to separate Bush from his historical context and judge him apart from the events that confronted his presidency. Such an effort would be foolish. The success of a president depends largely on the crises that confront him. How he deals with the situation in which he has been placed determines how he should be remembered. George Bush was president at a time when the United States needed a capable foreign policy leader, and his accomplishments must be seen as the culmination of his long career in foreign affairs and national security policy. Bush's tenure as U.S. ambassador to the United Nations, envoy to China, director of the Central Intelligence Agency, and vice president of the United States uniquely prepared him to be an excellent foreign policy president. Even apart from the shadow of Reagan, Bush was highly qualified to assume the presidency when it was apparent that the Cold War was coming to a conclusion. And it was logical in 1992, with the end of the Cold War and with the public perception that foreign policy expertise was not needed as much as domestic policy experience, that George Bush would lose the presidency. That does not mean to discount the campaign mistakes made by Bush in what even Bush supporters such as John Sununu refer to as "the worst run presidential campaign in history": "George Bush's people listened to the newspapers that foreign policy wasn't important and so they never advertised his foreign policy successes and they believed everybody who said he had no domestic agenda so they never advertised his great successes domestically."[45] The irony in that election was that Bush's foreign policy successes did overshadow other aspects of his presidency and helped define George Bush's domestic agenda as nonexistent. The Bush campaign was not successful in combating that view, which led not only to Bush's loss to Bill Clinton but to a public perception that continues to linger.

It is within the context of historical events that Bush should be judged. That does not mean that Bush should be hailed as having masterminded the end of the Cold War. Indeed, Bush received substantial criticism at the beginning of his administration for inaction, and many of the decisions made in 1989 in particular were reactionary in nature. But just as Bush did not chart a clear course of action, U.S. foreign policy from 1947 to 1950 was not based upon a clearly delineated policy of containment. Both Truman, with the help of men such as Kennan and Marshall, and Bush, with Scowcroft and Baker, decided upon the major elements of a U.S. response to the Soviet Union in a piecemeal and staggered manner.[46] The events in 1989 in particular were so unpredictable that any precisely laid out plan would have to be continually altered. According to Brent Scowcroft, Bush, with his strong background in foreign affairs, excelled in this sort of ad hoc policymaking: "He was not a great strategist, but he had wonderful instincts and he wanted to move out and get things done. And so when you'd give him an idea, if it was a good one, he was ready to charge off on it, and did frequently."[47] In fact, one of Bush's strengths, as Scowcroft recalls, was his ability to recognize and then guide the effects of the historic events that occurred during his presidency: "President Bush recognized historic change was taking place. He didn't create the change. But what he did is manage it in a way that these really cataclysmic changes in the world structure took place without a shot being fired."[48] Bush led a transition, a transition from the Cold War to a post–Cold War world. He recognized practical diplomatic problems and addressed them with practical diplomatic solutions. Marlin Fitzwater argues that Bush should get credit for that transition: "[Bush should get credit] for transitioning, for understanding the relationships of the country, for having a geo-political view of the world that allowed him to work cooperatively with Gorbachev and with Kohl and with Mitterand in France and with John Major in Great Britain in a very cooperative way in shaping that year or two where Germany was reunited and the Soviet Union was trying to sort itself out."[49] And he was responsible for it ending it peacefully. The Cold War did not have to end peacefully. Gen. Colin Powell, who served under both Bush and Reagan, explains Bush's foreign policy legacy: "[Bush] is the one who guided the Cold War to its end, and he did it with great skill. The unification of Germany, the collapse of the Soviet Union without us gloating about it was very wisely done by the president, certain magnanimity in the manner in which he dealt with Gorbachev and then Yeltsin, and I think he played a key role at the end."[50] It was Bush's adroit management—diplomatic and political—that allowed for a peaceful transition. The Bush presidency had many faults—especially with the domestic agenda and the inattention to the ceremonial aspect of the presidency—but its one great strength allowed for the division of Europe to finally be resolved and for the Cold War to end "with a whimper, not a bang."[51]

Postscript: In Search of the "New World Order"

In the summer of 1992, in the final months of Bush's failed reelection campaign, an article appeared in *Foreign Affairs* asking an important question: "What does a superpower do in a world no longer dominated by superpower conflict?"[52] The Bush administration had clearly considered that question, but the collapse of the Soviet Union occurred just as the election year began, which left Bush little time to orchestrate a grand scheme for a "new world order."[53] Even though Bush had presided over the end of the Cold War, his reelection defeat to Bill Clinton denied him the chance to firmly establish the direction that U.S. foreign policy would take in the post–Cold War landscape. Instead, it would be left up to the new generational perspective of the Clinton administration and then, ironically, to the administration of Bush's eldest son to search for an answer.

The "peace dividend" from the end of the Cold War would ensure that the last decade of the twentieth century was a prosperous one for the United States, thus providing an illusionary promise of continued U.S. dominance. To those who looked with euphoria toward post–Cold War possibilities, the United States "seemed more immune than ever from the perils of the outside world and more capable of fulfilling its mission to lead the world toward freedom, peace, and prosperity."[54] According to this argument, a lone superpower has no rivals; it does not need to compete and can merely react to world events, secure in the fact that it will remain in the dominant position. The economic boom of the mid-1990s allowed Clinton, whose election campaign clearly demonstrated a preference for domestic policy, to postpone the development of a grand strategy for the post–Cold War era. Lacking the foreign policy experience of Bush, Clinton "was more of a participant than the dominant voice" in foreign policy meetings, and when a meeting ended, "it was often unclear what if any decisions had been reached."[55] This disorderly process led to "more drift than direction" in foreign policy matters.[56] Consequently, Clinton continued many of the policies of the Bush administration, moving beyond containment by encouraging the development of free markets and democracies, including pushing Bush's North American Free Trade Agreement (NAFTA) through Congress, repeatedly renewing China's most-favored-nation privileges, and extending billions of dollars in aid packages to the former Soviet Union. It was not until his second administration that a more confident Clinton began to craft his own foreign policy approach, becoming more hawkish and demonstrating a higher degree of activism. To this end Clinton shook up his foreign policy team, selecting Sandy Berger as his national security advisor and Madeline Albright as his new secretary of state. Resurrecting "Cold War certitudes," Albright spoke of the United States as the lone superpower: "If we use force, it is because we are America. We are the indispensable nation."[57] Clinton would indeed use force in Bosnia, Kosovo, Somalia, and the Sudan, among other places. In these instances Clinton displayed a preference for the multilateral action and use of international organizations that had characterized Bush's "new world order" approach. But Clinton found peacekeeping and nation building far more difficult in a multipower post–Cold War world. Other problems became more intense as arms sales accelerated throughout the 1990s and the specter of biological and chemical terrorism became increasingly more difficult to predict. Terrorism attacks continued to increase throughout the 1990s.[58] For foreign policy leaders who had been hard-wired for the bipolar world of Cold War strategy, the new complexities and realities of a multipolar world proved difficult to grasp.

In 2001, George W. Bush returned many familiar faces to foreign policy, including Dick Cheney, Colin Powell, and Condoleezza Rice. Each had played important roles in the elder Bush's administration, yet none had been as vital to the foreign policy apparatus as they would be this time around. Bush, Scowcroft, and Baker served as the senior decision makers of the earlier administration, directing foreign policy with a top-down approach. Lacking the experience and foreign policy expertise of his father, George W. Bush would rely more on his advisors, particularly Rice, who began tutoring him on foreign policy during his successful campaign for the presidency. Criticizing Clinton's failure to form an "articulated 'national interest,'" Rice rejected "assertive multilateralism" and preferred to concentrate on traditional big power relationships, particularly with Russia and China, to reassert U.S. self-interests.[59]

Yet there was still no clear foreign policy doctrine for the new Bush administration, and its unilateral approach would be implemented in much the same case-by-case, "crisis-by-crisis" basis that Rice had chided the Clinton administration over during the 2000 election. By the end of the first year of the new administration, the terrorist attacks on September 11, 2001, would set the priority of re-exerting U.S. hegemony abroad and lead to the Bush doctrine, which called for military preemption against emergent threats. Bush's reductive rhetoric would echo Ronald Reagan's moralistic view of good versus evil, as would his muscular responses to any such threats by the evildoers. Bush's response to the terrorists would lead him to military action in Afghanistan later that year and, by 2003, to an invasion of Iraq and the removal of Saddam Hussein. The situation in Iraq was considerably more complex than the relatively clear-cut mission in Afghanistan, which was to hunt down the Al-Qaeda leadership. In Iraq, the Persian Gulf War so successfully orchestrated by Bush's father had not led to the ouster of Saddam Hussein or "his capacity for mischief making."[60] Economic sanctions by the United Nations continued throughout the 1990s, as did Saddam Hussein's defiance of them and his obstruction of UN weapons inspectors. His actions had led President Clinton to launch missile attacks on Baghdad in 1993, 1996, and 1998. Clinton had clearly been concerned that the degrading of Iraq's conventional weapons during the Persian Gulf War and the ensuing years of sanctions might push Saddam toward a greater reliance on unconventional weapons such as biological, chemical, and even nuclear weapons.[61] In the wake of the chaos of the September 11 attacks, the Bush administration worried about the same thing, especially fearing that Iraq would become a base for terrorism. Both Clinton and Bush had pondered how to react to terrorists that acted on behalf of no state but rather in support of a militant anti-Americanism infused with religious zeal. Clinton confessed in 2000 to then president-elect Bush that his failure to capture Osama bin Laden and head off the emerging threat of terrorism was his "biggest disappointment."[62]

By 2003, the Bush administration had concluded that regime change in Iraq would help further the goal of weakening the terrorist threat and launched Operation Iraqi Freedom. Unlike his father, George W. Bush did not work to garner the same level of consensus among a broad coalition, preferring to act in a more unilateral manner. Despite disagreement within the world community concerning the validity of the invasion, Saddam Hussein was quickly ousted from power, and the Bush administration was left to begin the more difficult task of creating a provisional government and reconstructing the economy and security of the conquered nation.

When Pres. George H. W. Bush used the term "new world order," he envisioned a post–Cold War world that would replace the bipolar Cold War stalemate with a greater use of international organizations in order to uphold widely accepted norms of international behavior. He provided a glimpse of the "new world order" in the Persian Gulf War. Now his son was using the same arena, Iraq, to illustrate the rising importance of national self-interest and unilateral action. Although this was markedly different from the elder Bush's foreign policy outlook, it was not a viewpoint that originated with George W. Bush but rather one that was rooted in U.S. experience prior to the start of the Cold War.[63] As George H. W. Bush's secretary of state, Dick Cheney, said a few years before becoming George W. Bush's vice president, "[Capturing Saddam] would have turned what had up to that time been a very successful U.S.-led coalition effort to roll back aggression into a situation where the heavy hand of the U.S. occupies an Arab nation and starts taking down governments. . . . If we crossed over that line and begun to try to dictate who's going to govern Iraq, if we can take down the president of Iraq—hell!—we can take down anybody. . . . It's always going to be a messy situation over there."[64] With the end of the Cold War, the future became less certain, but what became increasingly more likely was that there were not going to be any easy answers, no grand strategy, no further counting "on power and legitimacy to preserve traditional stability," no reliance on "globalization to generate progress."[65] In that sense, the process started during the presidency of George H. W. Bush was complete, and a now undefined "new world order" was at hand. The only post–Cold War certitude was the existence of revived debates about America's world role.

Timeline of Events

George Bush and the End of the Cold War

1981

January 20   Bush is sworn in for the first of two terms as vice president. Early in the Reagan administration Bush will begin to assume an important role in the development of foreign policy as he takes an increasing number of foreign trips on behalf of President Reagan, representing him in talks with world leaders.

1982

November 15   Bush attends Brezhnev funeral in Moscow; sends cable to Reagan with first impressions of the new Soviet leader, Yuri Andropov: "He conveyed strength, but not in a bellicose way. He dished it out, but did not flinch as I mentioned Poland, Afghanistan, and Human Rights. . . . It is of course too early to predict how things will evolve in Moscow, but for some reason I feel up-beat, opportunity may well lie ahead, though much of the rhetoric was predictable and accusatory."

1983

March 8   During remarks at the Annual Convention of the National Association of Evangelicals in Orlando, Florida, Reagan refers to the Soviet Union as the "Evil Empire."

March 23	Reagan announces his proposal for a Space Defense Initiative (SDI) in a national address to the nation on defense and national security.
September 1	Soviet attack on Korean airliner KAL 007. In remarks to reporters the following day, Reagan refers to the incident as "a barbaric act committed by the Soviet regime."

1984

February 14	Bush attends Andropov funeral in Moscow; sends cable to Reagan after meeting with the new Soviet leader, Konstantin Chernenko: "Despite reports that he might be ill and lacks the intellect and authority of Andropov, Chernenko seemed in command of the situation. . . . He asked me to tell you that we can have better relations. . . . I told him that we, too, were ready for dialogue and progress. . . . Chernenko is no pushover but he does seem open and treated us graciously. He gave the clear impression that there is somebody at home in the Kremlin with whom we can do business."

1985

March 13	Bush attends Chernenko funeral in Moscow; sends cable to Reagan with first impressions of the new Soviet leader Mikhail Gorbachev: "Gorbachev will package the Soviet line for Western consumption better than any (I repeat any) of his predecessors. . . . The big question will be—will this 'new look man' merely be a more effective spokesman for tired, failed policies or will he have enough self assurance to 'start anew'—a term he himself used in expressing hope for U.S.-Soviet relations. I don't know the answer to this question but I strongly urge that we try to find out."
November 19–20	Geneva summit (Reagan-Gorbachev): It was the first summit meeting of the two men, and, although no formal agreements were reached, it represented a renewed dialogue and the first step in an improved relationship between the two countries.

1986

October 11–12	Reykjavik summit (Reagan-Gorbachev): In this second meeting of the two leaders, Gorbachev and Reagan appeared to be on the verge of eliminating most, possi-

bly all, nuclear weapons; however, Reagan's refusal to abandon SDI caused the meeting to end abruptly without an accord. Still, in retrospect, the meeting was an important breakthrough in strategic arms control and helped establish the dialogue that led to the INF treaty (1987), which dealt with the elimination of intermediate-range nuclear forces.

November 25   Iran-Contra scandal breaks.

1987

June 12   In a speech at the Brandenburg Gate, Reagan says, "Mr. Gorbachev, tear down this wall!" Despite this rhetoric, the Reagan administration continues to see the division of Germany as a stabilizing force.

December 8–10   Washington summit (Reagan-Gorbachev): Bush tells Gorbachev not to be concerned about the "empty cannons of rhetoric" that he would hear from Bush during the 1988 presidential campaign. INF treaty signed.

1988

May 29–June 2   Moscow summit (Reagan-Gorbachev): No new agreements reached, but Reagan helps build support within the Soviet Union for Gorbachev's reforms by declaring that the Soviet Union was no longer an "evil empire": "That was another time, another era." According to Ambassador Jack Matlock, "If Reagan believed the country was overcoming its past, then Gorbachev had to be doing something right, most Soviet citizens reasoned."

November 6   A confident presidential candidate Bush asks long-time friend James Baker to be his secretary of state two days *before* the election.

November 8   Bush defeats Michael Dukakis in the presidential election.

November 10   All presidential appointees were asked to submit their resignations "in order to give the President-elect Bush maximum flexibility in the staffing of his administration." This affirmed what James Baker had already told his aides: "This is *not* a friendly takeover."

November 20   President-elect Bush asks Brent Scowcroft to be his national security advisor. In selecting Scowcroft, Bush wanted to send a message that "the NSC's function was to be critical in the decision making process."

| December 7 | Governors Island (in New York Harbor) summit (Reagan-Gorbachev-President-elect Bush): Final official meeting between Reagan and Gorbachev. Bush avoids specifics and pledges "general continuity" with Reagan's policies toward the Soviet Union. |

1989

January 20	George H. W. Bush is inaugurated as the 41st president. Bush would soon initiate a foreign policy review that would be referred to by critics as "the pause."
March 14	The formal report from the strategic review on the Soviet Union (NSR-3) was presented to Bush; it was a big disappointment. The "big picture" document did not provide the kind of specific initiatives that were needed, and Bush simply was not satisfied with the approach suggested by the review, which was quickly labeled "status quo plus." Instead of using the disappointing review, Scowcroft ordered the NSC to work "instead with a 'think piece' on Gorbachev's policies and intentions, drafted by an NSC team headed by Condoleezza Rice."
April 17	Bush gives speech in Hamtramck, Michigan, in which he lays out his plan for Eastern Europe: new U.S. trade and credits to countries experiencing economic and political reforms, thus establishing a link between help from the West and significant political and economic liberalization. The Bush team hoped that by offering economic rewards, they could keep reform going in Eastern Europe; they also hoped to eventually extend the link between aid and reform to the Soviet Union itself.
May 12	In a commencement address at Texas A&M University, Bush announces his strategy for future policy toward the Soviet Union. In what became known as "Beyond Containment," Bush challenged the Soviets to reduce their conventional forces, abandon the Brezhnev Doctrine, and allow self-determination for all of Eastern and Central Europe, in the process removing the Iron Curtain. (National Security Directive 23)
May 20–21	Bush and François Mitterrand meet at Kennebunkport. It was Bush's style of personal diplomacy at its very best,

	and it helped establish a deep level of trust and personal rapport between the two presidents.
May 21	In a commencement address at Boston University, Bush announces his strategy for Western Europe. Bush made clear in his speech that a strong NATO became more important, not less, with the changes occurring within the Soviet Union. François Mitterrand followed Bush's speech with one of his own, and, afterwards, the two leaders gave a joint press conference.
May 24	In a commencement address at the Coast Guard Academy, Bush focuses on defense strategy and arms control. Bush emphasized his commitment to maintaining an effective nuclear deterrent but promised to seek arms reductions that would allow stability with the lowest number of weapons that the administration felt was prudent. Any advance in arms control, however, would have to be prefaced by a Soviet move away from an offensive military strategy.
May 29–30	Bush attends NATO summit in Brussels; presents his CFE (Conventional Forces in Europe) proposal to widespread acclaim.
May 31	Bush makes address in the Rheingoldhalle in Mainz, Germany, in which he links the end of the Cold War to an end of the division of Europe: "Let Europe be whole and free."
June 4	Armed units of the People's Liberation Army pour into Tiananmen Square in Beijing, brutally dispersing thousands of student demonstrators with bullets and tanks, leaving hundreds dead and thousands wounded.
July 2	Brent Scowcroft and Lawrence Eagleburger conduct a secret trip to Beijing to meet with Deng Xiaoping following the suppression of demonstrators at Tiananmen Square.
July 9–13	Bush visits Poland and Hungary to show that he was backing the political and economic reform efforts in Eastern Europe.
July 15–16	Bush attends G-7 summit in Paris in hopes of convincing them to share the burden of helping Eastern Europe's economic distress.
October 1	Colin Powell assumes the position of chairman of the

	Joint Chiefs of Staff; the first chairman to begin his tenure with the added benefit of Goldwater-Nichols authority.
November 9	Fall of Berlin Wall: East German government announces that border crossings will be allowed. Bush offers tepid response during an impromptu news conference in Oval Office in which he refers to the fall of the Berlin Wall as "a good development." He is roundly criticized by the press for not "Dancing on the Berlin Wall." What the press did not know was that Bush had received a cable from Gorbachev urging him not to "overreact" to the "chaotic situation" lest there be "unforeseen consequences."
November 24	Bush and Margaret Thatcher meet at Camp David. Thatcher expresses a "lack of sympathy for and even distrust of [German] reunification." Instead, Thatcher encourages Bush to focus on democracy for Eastern Europe rather than reunification. Bush disagrees.
December 2–3	Malta summit (Bush-Gorbachev): Gorbachev tells Bush that he did not consider him an enemy anymore and actually wanted the United States to maintain a presence in Europe. The meeting was important because it built trust between the two sides, the two leaders, and, according to Baker, demonstrated that the U.S.-Soviet relationship had moved "from confrontation to cooperation."
December 20	Bush administration commences military operation in Panama to capture Manuel Noriega.
1990	
February 13	"Two-plus-Four" agreed upon by the United States, the Soviet Union, Great Britain, and France at meeting in Ottawa.
February 24–25	Bush and Helmut Kohl meet at Camp David. Kohl suggests that Soviet acceptance of a unified Germany in NATO might "end up as a matter of cash."
May 4	Bush gives commencement address at Oklahoma State University in which he announces his plans for the future of NATO.
May 4	In a speech during the first ministerial meeting of Two-plus-Four in Bonn, Germany, Shevardnadze lays down

	a tough Soviet position that there could be no NATO membership for a unified Germany.
May 31–June 2	Washington summit (Bush-Gorbachev): In a stunning reversal of the Soviet position, Gorbachev concedes that NATO membership was a matter for the Germans to decide. The two men then traveled to Camp David for more relaxed discussions.
July 5–6	Bush attends NATO summit in London where he unveils his plan for NATO to become more of a political alliance, thus clearing the way for Soviet acceptance of a unified Germany as a NATO member.
July 14	Gorbachev and Kohl meet in the Caucasus. In exchange for a monetary offer from Kohl to boost the Soviet economy, Gorbachev agrees to German unification within NATO without conditions or reservations.
August 2	Iraq invades Kuwait. As Secretary of State Baker sums up, "Practically overnight, we went from trying to work with Saddam to likening him to Hitler."
August 3	During an impromptu meeting in the lobby of Vnukovo II Airport outside Moscow, Baker and Shevardnadze issue a joint condemnation of Iraq. Baker would later refer to this day as "the day the Cold War ended."
August 8	Bush authorizes the deployment of U.S. troops to protect Saudi Arabia (Operation Desert Shield).
September 9	During a meeting in Helsinki, Finland, Bush and Gorbachev issue a joint declaration on Iraq. It mirrors the Baker-Shevardnadze joint condemnation of August 3. A small, but in no way insignificant, example of the increasing mood of cooperation also occurred when Bush and Gorbachev agreed to start using first names to address one another in small private meetings.
September 12	Two-plus-Four ministerial meeting in Moscow: Soviets agree on a final price for their consent to the reunification of Germany.
October 3	The Federal Republic of Germany absorbs the German Democratic Republic; Germany is unified.
November 19	Bush signs Conventional Armed Forces Treaty, which reduced the size of NATO and Warsaw Pact forces in Europe.
November 29	The United Nations, with Soviet support, authorizes

	"all necessary means" to compel Iraqi compliance with UN resolutions on Kuwait (UNSC Resolution 678).
December 20	Shevardnadze, already under intense criticism for his decision to join the United States in support of the Gulf War, resigns, delivering a scathing speech in which he warned "against the onset of dictatorship."

1991

January 12	Congress votes largely along party lines to give President Bush the authority to wage war under the terms laid out in UN Security Council Resolution 678. Bush later admitted that "even had Congress not passed the resolution I would have acted and ordered our troops into combat."
January 15	Deadline under UNSC Resolution 678 for Iraqi withdrawal of Kuwait.
January 16	Operation Desert Storm begins.
February 23	Bush orders the use of ground forces against Iraqi troops in Kuwait.
February 27	Bush announces end of Persian Gulf War: "Kuwait is liberated. Iraq's army is defeated."
July 22–28	Gen. Colin Powell visits the Soviet Union and notices a "deep, deep uncertainty and discomfort among the senior ranks of the Soviet military leaders"; tours Soviet military facilities that were "essentially bankrupting the country"; meets with a "beaten down" Gorbachev.
July 31	Moscow summit (Bush-Gorbachev): Bush meets with a "pragmatic" Gorbachev who was "resigned to the fact that he would not get funds"; START (Strategic Arms Reduction Treaty) signed, which called for reductions in intercontinental ballistic missiles.
August 1	Bush visits Ukraine and gives what would be labeled by the press as his "chicken Kiev" speech in which he warns against "suicidal nationalism." Arguing that "freedom is not the same as independence," Bush promises to support "those who want to build democracy."
August 18–21	Coup attempt against Gorbachev; Bush and Yeltsin work together to put pressure on the coup plotters to release Gorbachev; Bush praises Yeltsin for "standing courageously against military force." Upon being released Gorbachev places a telephone call to Bush in which he

exclaims, "My dearest George. I am so happy to hear your voice again." Despite the continuing friendship between Bush and Gorbachev, calls between Bush and Yeltsin increase sharply and continue to outpace calls between Bush and Gorbachev until the Soviet Union collapses.

September 2   Bush recognizes Estonia, Latvia, and Lithuania as newly independent countries; Bush was going to announce U.S. recognition on August 30 but postpones announcement at the request of Gorbachev to coordinate with Soviet recognition of Baltic independence.

October 29   Bush and Gorbachev have dinner together; Gorbachev asks for aid; Bush and Gorbachev spend much of the time discussing Yeltsin. In the week leading up to the meeting Bush writes in his diary that Gorbachev is "growing weaker all the time" and that this might be his "last meeting with [Gorbachev] of this nature. Time marches on."

October 30 –   Middle East Peace Conference in Madrid, Spain; the
November 1   United States and the Soviet Union co-host meeting, which was a breakthrough in Arab-Israeli diplomacy because representatives of Israel, Syria, Egypt, Jordan, and the Palestinians met in public. Began a series of meetings that led to the 1993 Oslo Accord, in which Israel and the Palestine Liberation Organization (PLO) agreed to recognize each other.

December 8   Secret meeting at Minsk between Yeltsin, Leonid Kravchuck, the president of Ukraine, and Stanislav Shushkevich, the president of Belarus. The three leaders decide to dissolve the Soviet Union and establish the CIS, or Commonwealth of Independent States. It was not until the three leaders had reached full agreement and called President Bush to ask for his support that they called Gorbachev to inform him of the situation. Gorbachev angrily replied to Yeltsin: "What you have done behind my back with the consent of the U.S. president is a crying shame, a disgrace!"

December 21   Despite the continued objections by Gorbachev, the Declaration of Adherence to the Commonwealth of Independent States was signed at Alma-Ata by all of the republics save the Baltic states and Georgia.

| December 25 | Gorbachev announces his resignation and telephones Bush; the Soviet Union ceases to exist. Bush makes a televised address from the Oval Office in which he tells U.S. viewers, "Our enemies have become our partners"; with that, the official seal was placed on the end of the Cold War. |

1992

| November 3 | Bush loses his reelection bid to Bill Clinton. Despite Bush's foreign policy success, the main issue in the election was the economy. In his diary, Bush sums up his emotions as "hurt, hurt, hurt. . . . I was absolutely convinced we would prove them wrong but I was wrong and they were right." |

1993

| January 3 | Bush and Yeltsin sign START II; the breakup of the Soviet Union had convinced Bush to reduce the number of nuclear weapons on both sides even further than what had been agreed upon in START. |
| January 20 | Bush's final day in office before returning to Houston. |

Notes

Preface

1. Winston Churchill gave his famous "Iron Curtain" speech on March 5, 1946, at Westminster College in Fulton, Missouri. Pres. Harry Truman appeared on the platform with Churchill. The two men had decided that the speech should be delivered as a warning to the world of the growing threat posed by the Soviet Union.
2. "Press Statement on Berlin Wall," Nov. 9, 1989, video footage from the Audio-Visual Archives, George Bush Presidential Library.
3. Jack F. Matlock Jr., interview by author, Boston, Jan. 6, 2001.
4. Marlin Fitzwater, telephone interview by author, May 9, 2000.
5. George Bush, letter to author, July 3, 2001.
6. Brent Scowcroft, telephone interview by author, May 23, 2000.
7. See "National Security Strategy Report," Mar. 20, 1990, folder "National Security," OA/ID 13152, Subject Files, Box 3, White House Press Office, Bush Presidential Records, George Bush Presidential Library.
8. Ibid.
9. Fitzwater, telephone interview by author, May 9, 2000.
10. Baker with DeFrank, *Politics of Diplomacy,* 558.

Chapter 1. The Primacy of the National Security Council

1. *Measuring Soviet GNP: Problems and Solutions,* 188.
2. Kennedy, *Rise and Fall of the Great Powers,* 436.
3. Letter, Jay Keyworth to Ronald Reagan, Dec. 17, 1985, folder "Strategic Defense Initiative (SDI)," box OA 94261, William Gresham Files, Reagan Presidential Records, Ronald Reagan Library.
4. Fitzwater, telephone interview by author, May 9, 2000.
5. Scowcroft, telephone interview by author, May 23, 2000.
6. As historian Paul Kennedy has observed, "Russia has always enjoyed its greatest military advantage vis-à-vis the West when the pace of weapons technology has slowed down enough to allow a standardization of equipment and thus of fighting units and tactics—whether that be the eighteenth-century infantry column or the mid-twentieth-century armored division." Kennedy, *Rise and Fall of the Great Powers,* 500.
7. Memo, Mike Schwartz to Jay Keyworth, July 18, 1984, folder "SDI: Strategic Defense Initiative (July–December 1984)," box OA 94709, Jay Keyworth Files, Reagan Presidential Records, Ronald Reagan Library; Flora Lewis, "Soviet SDI Fears," *New York Times,* Mar. 6, 1986, A27.
8. James A. Baker III, telephone interview by author, May 22, 2000.

9. Scowcroft, telephone interview by author, May 23, 2000.

10. Ibid.

11. Baker, telephone interview by author, May 22, 2000.

12. Beschloss and Talbott, *At the Highest Levels,* 26.

13. Memorandum, John Sununu to Kenneth Duberstein, Jan. 6, 1989, folder "Transition—Miscellaneous (1989) [1]," OA/ID 01806, John Sununu, Issues File Box 88, White House Office of Chief of Staff, Bush Presidential Records, George Bush Presidential Library.

14. Greene, *Presidency of George Bush,* 49.

15. Bush's appointment of Richard Darman as director of the Office of Management and Budget is another example of a Reagan critic joining the Bush administration.

16. The National Security Council has four statutory members: the president, vice president, secretary of state, and secretary of defense. The director of Central Intelligence, the chairman of the Joint Chiefs of Staff, and the national security advisor also attend NSC meetings and serve as statutory advisors.

17. Baker with DeFrank, *Politics of Diplomacy,* 26.

18. Ibid.

19. Richard Allen (Jan. 1981–Jan. 1982), William Clark (Feb. 1982–Oct. 1983), Robert McFarlane (Oct. 1983–Dec. 1985), John Poindexter (Dec. 1985–Nov. 1986), Frank Carlucci (Dec. 1986–Nov. 1987), Colin Powell (Nov. 1987–Jan. 1989); John Barry and Evan Thomas, "Colin Powell: Behind the Myth," *Newsweek,* Mar. 5, 2001, 36.

20. The National Security Council was established by the National Security Act of 1947 and amended by the National Security Act Amendments of 1949. Later in 1949, as part of the Reorganization Plan, the council was placed in the Executive Office of the President.

21. "History of the National Security Council, 1947–1997," official National Security Council website, www.whitehouse.gov/WH/EOP/NSC/html/NSChistory.html.

22. Colin Powell, telephone interview by author, Aug. 7, 2000.

23. Woodward, *Commanders,* 51.

24. Bush and Scowcroft, *A World Transformed,* 33.

25. Scowcroft, telephone interview by author, May 23, 2000.

26. Bush and Scowcroft, *A World Transformed,* 19.

27. Andrew Rosenthal, "Scowcroft and Gates: A Team Rivals Baker," *New York Times,* Feb. 21, 1991, A14, folder "National Security Advisor (Scowcroft) 1991," OA/ID CF 00468, John Sununu, White House Office File Box 94, White House Office of Chief of Staff, Bush Presidential Records, George Bush Presidential Library.

28. Baker with DeFrank, *Politics of Diplomacy,* 32.

29. Ibid., 20.

30. Michael Kramer and Christopher Ogden, "I Want to Be the President's Man," *Time,* Feb. 13, 1989, 31.

31. "President's News Conference," Mar. 10, 1989, http://bushlibrary.tamu.edu/research/public_papers.php?id=156&year=1989&month=3

32. Dick Cheney, telephone interview with John Robert Greene, Mar. 7, 1997. Taped recording on closed reserve in the Audio-Visual Archives, George Bush Presidential Library.

33. Baker with DeFrank, *Politics of Diplomacy,* 70.

34. The Defense Reorganization Act of 1986 is commonly referred to as the Goldwater-Nichols Act because it had been sponsored by Sen. Barry Goldwater and Congressman Bill Nichols.

35. Powell with Persico, *My American Journey*, 411.

36. Ibid., 388.

37. Powell, telephone interview by author, Aug. 7, 2000.

38. Ibid.

39. Russell Watson with Richard Sandza, "Cleaning Up the Mess," Newsweek, Oct. 12, 1987, p. 9.

40. William Webster, interview with John Robert Greene, July 8, 1997. Taped recording on closed reserve in the Audio-Visual Archives, George Bush Presidential Library.

41. Ibid.

42. Quoted in an interview with *Newsweek* editors, Oct. 12, 1987, p. 29–35.

43. Broder and Woodward, *Man Who Would Be President*, 96.

44. An example of this occurred when the Tower nomination failed in the Senate. Quayle made a blistering speech in Indianapolis that accused Senate Democrats of using "McCarthy-like tactics" to defeat John Tower. Although Bush privately agreed with that statement, he could not publicly condemn the actions of Senate Democrats because he still had several nominations that needed to be confirmed in the Senate.

45. Greene, *Presidency of George Bush*, 46.

46. Ibid., 153.

47. Bush and Scowcroft, *A World Transformed*, 24.

48. John Sununu, interview with John Robert Greene, July 8, 1997. Taped recording on closed reserve in the Audio-Visual Archives, George Bush Presidential Library.

49. Fitzwater, *Call the Briefing!*, 144.

50. Scowcroft, telephone interview by author, May 23, 2000.

51. Ibid.

52. Powell, telephone interview by author, Aug. 7, 2000.

53. Notice to the press, Jan. 23, 1989, folder "Cabinet Affairs (1989) [2]," OA/ID 01806, John Sununu, White House Office File Box 90, White House Office of Chief of Staff, Bush Presidential Records, George Bush Presidential Library.

54. Press Release, "Excerpts of Remarks for Vice President George bush Announcement Speech, Houston, Texas," Oct. 12, 1987, folder "Debate Material [2 of 2]," OA/ID 144322, David Bates Files, Vice President George Bush Series, Bush Vice-Presidential Records, George Bush Presidential Library.

55. Oberdorfer, *From the Cold War to a New Era*, 333.

56. Beschloss and Talbott, *At the Highest Levels*, 28.

57. Ibid., 34.

58. Matlock, *Reagan and Gorbachev*, 315.

59. Matlock, interview by author, Boston, Jan. 6, 2001.

60. Baker, telephone interview by author, May 22, 2000.

61. Baker with DeFrank, *Politics of Diplomacy*, 70.

62. Scowcroft, telephone interview by author, May 23, 2000.

63. Baker with DeFrank, *Politics of Diplomacy*, 68.

64. Ibid.

65. Ibid., 69.

66. Bush and Scowcroft, *A World Transformed*, 40.
67. Rice's memo would eventually evolve into National Security Directive 23, which was finally signed by Bush on September 22, 1989.
68. Bush and Scowcroft, *A World Transformed*, 40.
69. Fitzwater, telephone interview by author, May 9, 2000.
70. Lou Cannon, "Reagan Is Concerned about Bush's Indecision," *Washington Post*, May 6, 1989, A21.
71. Beschloss and Talbott, *At the Highest Levels*, 49.
72. Ibid., 50.
73. Bush and Scowcroft, *A World Transformed*, 47.
74. Ibid., 51.
75. "Remarks by the President to Citizens of Hamtramck," Apr. 17, 1989, Subject File: Foreign Policy Speeches, 4/89–2/90, Box 13, Bush Presidential Records, George Bush Presidential Library. Video footage provided by the George Bush Presidential Library.
76. Bush and Scowcroft, *A World Transformed*, 52.
77. Fitzwater, telephone interview by author, May 9, 2000.
78. "National Security Directive 23: United States Relations with the Soviet Union," Bush Presidential Records, George Bush Presidential Library.
79. "Remarks by the President at Texas A&M University," May 12, 1989, Subject File: Foreign Policy Speeches, 4/89–2/90, Box 13, Bush Presidential Records, George Bush Presidential Library. Video footage provided by the George Bush Presidential Library.
80. Bush and Scowcroft, *A World Transformed*, 54.
81. "Remarks by the President at Boston University Commencement Ceremony," May 21, 1989, Subject File: Foreign Policy Speeches, 4/89–2/90, Box 13, Bush Presidential Records, George Bush Presidential Library. Video footage provided by the George Bush Presidential Library.
82. Ibid.
83. "Remarks by the President at the Coast Guard Academy Graduation Ceremony," May 24, 1989, Subject File: Foreign Policy Speeches, 4/89–2/90, Box 13, Bush Presidential Records, George Bush Presidential Library. Video footage provided by the George Bush Presidential Library.
84. Talking Points on the Soviet Union, June 26, 1989, folder "National Security," OA/ID 13152, Subject File Box 3, White House Press Office, Bush Presidential Records, George Bush Presidential Library.
85. Bush and Scowcroft, *A World Transformed*, 55–56.
86. "The History of the National Security Council, 1947–1997," official NSC website.

Chapter 2. Bush and Gorbachev

1. Powell, telephone interview by author, Aug. 7, 2000.
2. Ibid.
3. Ibid.
4. Memcon, "The President's Private Meeting with Gorbachev," Dec. 7, 1988, folder, "Governor's Island," system file 8890931, Executive Secretariat, NSC: Records, Ronald Reagan Library.
5. Ibid.
6. Oberdorfer, *From the Cold War to a New Era*, 321–22.

7. Scowcroft, telephone interview by author, May 23, 2000.

8. Zelikow and Rice, *Germany Unified,* 26.

9. Ibid., 28.

10. Scowcroft, telephone interview by author, May 23, 2000.

11. Bush and Scowcroft, *A World Transformed,* 57.

12. Baker with DeFrank, *Politics of Diplomacy,* 85.

13. Bush and Scowcroft, *A World Transformed,* 58.

14. Ibid., 60.

15. Baker with DeFrank, *Politics of Diplomacy,* 94.

16. A full description of the Conventional Parity Initiative can be found in President Bush's "Proposals for a Free and Peaceful Europe," Current Policy No. 1179, published by the United States Department of State, Bureau of Public Affairs, Washington, D.C.

17. Beschloss and Talbott, *At the Highest Levels,* 79.

18. *London Guardian,* May 31, 1989.

19. "Remarks by the President at Rheingoldhalle," May 31, 1989, Subject File: Foreign Policy Speeches, 4/89–2/90, Box 13, Bush Presidential Records, George Bush Presidential Library. Video footage provided by the George Bush Presidential Library.

20. Ibid.

21. Ibid.

22. Spence, *Search for Modern China,* 696–704.

23. Baker with DeFrank, *Politics of Diplomacy,* 97–98.

24. Press statement, White House Office of the Press Secretary (Kennebunkport, Maine), "Statement by the President," June 3, 1989, folder "China," Box 4, OA/ID 12905, Marlin Fitzwater files, White House Press Office, Subject File: Alpha File, Bush Presidential Records, George Bush Presidential Library.

25. Bush, *All the Best,* 428–31.

26. Ibid, 343.

27. The pattern set by Bush with his reaction to Tiananmen Square has been followed since, as presidents and Congress voice objections to the PRC's actions on issues ranging from Chinese exploitation of Tibet to charges that China was selling nuclear technology to countries such as Iran and Pakistan. Despite these "empty cannons of rhetoric," China has retained its MFN status and remains a lucrative trading partner with the United States.

28. Press statement, Dec. 18, 1989, folder "China," Box 4, OA/ID 12905, Marlin Fitzwater files, White House Press Office, Subject File: Alpha File, Bush Presidential Records, George Bush Presidential Library.

29. Undated meeting notes in Fitzwater's handwriting, folder "China," Box 4, OA/ID 12905, Marlin Fitzwater files, White House Press Office, Subject File: Alpha File, Bush Presidential Records, George Bush Presidential Library.

30. Bush and Scowcroft, *A World Transformed,* 89.

31. Undated meeting notes in Fitzwater's handwriting, folder "China," Box 4, OA/ID 12905, Marlin Fitzwater files, White House Press Office, Subject File: Alpha File, Bush Presidential Records, George Bush Presidential Library.

32. Lévesque, *Enigma of 1989,* 117.

33. Ibid., 118n (Translated from *Pravda,* July 7, 1989).

34. Bush and Scowcroft, *A World Transformed,* 113.

35. "Remarks by the President at Joint Session of Parliament, the Sejm, Warsaw,

Poland," July 10, 1989, Subject File: Foreign Policy Speeches, 4/89–2/90, Box 13, Bush Presidential Records, George Bush Presidential Library

36. Bush and Scowcroft, *A World Transformed,* 117.

37. Lévesque, *Enigma of 1989,* 123.

38. Scowcroft, telephone interview by author, May 23, 2000.

39. Bush and Scowcroft, *A World Transformed,* 131.

40. Bush, *All the Best,* 433.

41. Scowcroft, telephone interview by author, May 23, 2000.

42. Beschloss and Talbott, *At the Highest Levels,* 108.

43. Baker, telephone interview by author, May 22, 2000.

44. Zelikow and Rice, *Germany Unified,* 101.

45. Beschloss and Talbott, *At the Highest Levels,* 132.

46. Fitzwater, *Call the Briefing!,* 261–62.

47. "Press Statement on Berlin Wall," Nov. 9, 1989, video footage provided by the George Bush Presidential Library.

48. Ibid.

49. Ibid.

50. Fitzwater, *Call the Briefing!,* 262–63.

51. Bush and Scowcroft, *A World Transformed,* 149.

52. George Bush, letter to author, July 3, 2001.

53. Fitzwater, telephone interview by author, May 9, 2000.

54. Baker, telephone interview by author, May 22, 2000.

55. Bush and Scowcroft, *A World Transformed,* 150.

56. Baker, telephone interview by author, May 22, 2000.

57. Scowcroft, telephone interview by author, May 23, 2000.

58. "National Security Council Meeting, November 30, 1989—List of Participants," folder "Malta Summit—December 2–3, 1989," National Security Council, Condoleezza Rice Files, Bush Presidential Records, George Bush Presidential Library.

59. Beschloss and Talbott, *At the Highest Levels,* 150.

60. "Foreign Media Reaction to Malta Summit," Dec. 3, 1989, Heather Wilson Files, Bush Presidential Records, George Bush Presidential Library.

61. Beschloss and Talbott, *At the Highest Levels,* 153–54.

62. "Foreign Media Reaction to Malta Summit."

63. "Letter from Richard Nixon to President Bush regarding comments on upcoming Malta summit," Nov. 16, 1989, folder "Malta Summit Paper (Preparation) December 1989 [3]," National Security Council, Condoleezza Rice Files, Bush Presidential Records, George Bush Presidential Library. Also quoted in Baker, *Politics of Diplomacy,* 170.

64. Bush and Scowcroft, *A World Transformed,* 155.

65. "Remarks by the President upon Departure to Malta and Brussels," the Rose Garden, Nov. 30, 1989, Susan Koch Files, Bush Presidential Records, George Bush Presidential Library. Video footage provided by the George Bush Presidential Library.

66. Bush and Scowcroft, *A World Transformed,* 162.

67. "Memo to Scowcroft concerning departure and arrival statements for Malta with attached statements for President's use," Susan Koch Files, Bush Presidential Records, George Bush Presidential Library.

68. Fitzwater, *Call the Briefing!,* 259.

69. Bush and Scowcroft, *A World Transformed*, 163.
70. Fitzwater, telephone interview by author, May 9, 2000.
71. Baker with DeFrank, *Politics of Diplomacy*, 171.
72. "Statements by and Question and Answer Session with President Bush and Chairman Gorbachev Aboard the Maxim Gorky, Marsaxlokk Harbor, Malta," Dec. 3, 1989, folder "Cabinet Affairs," Cooper Evans Files, Box 3 of 6, Bush Presidential Records, George Bush Presidential Library. Video footage provided by the George Bush Presidential Library.
73. Fitzwater, telephone interview by author, May 9, 2000.
74. Scowcroft, telephone interview by author, May 23, 2000.
75. Baker, telephone interview by author, May 22, 2000.
76. Ibid.
77. "Interview of Secretary of State Baker by CNN Headline News, Interview of Brent Scowcroft by ABC Good Morning America, Interview of Chief of Staff John Sununu by CBS Morning News," NATO Headquarters, Brussels, Belgium, Dec. 4, 1989, folder "Cabinet Affairs," Cooper Evans Files, Box 3 of 6, Bush Presidential Records, George Bush Presidential Library. Video footage provided by the George Bush Presidential Library.
78. George Bush, letter to author, July 3, 2001.
79. Bush and Scowcroft, *A World Transformed*, 180.

Chapter 3. Personal Diplomacy

1. *Vice President Bush Visits North Africa and Europe: Address at the Hofburg, Vienna, September 21, 1983*, Department of State Bulletin 83, no. 2080, Nov. 1983 (Washington, D.C.: GPO, 1983), 19–21.
2. "Remarks on East-West Relations at the Brandenburg Gate in West Berlin, June 12, 1987," *Public Papers of the President of the United States: Ronald Reagan, 1980–1989*, 1987, Book I—January 1 to July 3, 635.
3. Zelikow and Rice, *Germany Unified*, 96.
4. Thatcher, *Downing Street Years*, 792.
5. Zelikow and Rice, *Germany Unified*, 26.
6. McAdams, *Germany Divided*, 208n.
7. Ash, *In Europe's Name*, 343.
8. "Memorandum of Telephone Conversation between Helmut Kohl and George Bush, November 10, 1989," Telcons and Memcons—Bush/Kohl, Bush Presidential Records, George Bush Presidential Library.
9. Ibid.
10. "Statement by Press Secretary Fitzwater on the President's Telephone Conversation with West German Chancellor Helmut Kohl, November 10, 1989," *Public Papers of the President of the United States: George Bush, 1989–1992*, 1989, vol. 2 (Washington, D.C.: GPO, 1990), 1498.
11. Zelikow and Rice, *Germany Unified*, 105.
12. "Unofficial translation of Gorbachev letter to President Bush," folder "Gorbachev," 9000 APNSA Chrons, National Security Council, Brent Scowcroft Files, Bush Presidential Records, George Bush Presidential Library.
13. Bush and Scowcroft, *A World Transformed*, 149–50.
14. Records of calls between Bush and foreign leaders found in "Presidential Telcons Notebook (July–December 1989)," National Security Council Files,

Bush Presidential Records, George Bush Presidential Library. Records of letters between Bush and Gorbachev found in "Presidential Memcons Notebook (January–December 1989)," National Security Council Files, Bush Presidential Records, George Bush Presidential Library.

15. Laird, *Soviets, Germany, and the New Europe,* 79–80.
16. Thatcher, *Downing Street Years,* 810.
17. Ibid., 360.
18. Quoted in Evans, *Thatcher and Thatcherism,* 104.
19. Thatcher, *Downing Street Years,* 791.
20. Ibid., 793.
21. "Speech by Brent Scowcroft, Assistant to President Bush for National Security Affairs, Wehrkunde Conference, February 3, 1990," transcript in Freedman, ed., *Europe Transformed,* 452–57.
22. Merkl, *German Unification,* 315n.
23. Stokes, *Walls Came Tumbling Down,* 183.
24. "Speech by Chancellor Kohl to the Bundestag on Intra-German Relations, November 28, 1989," in Freedman, ed., *Europe Transformed,* 372–76.
25. "Soviet Spokesman G. Gerasimov on Soviet Reaction to Kohl's Ten Points, November 29, 1989," in Freedman, ed., *Europe Transformed,* 377.
26. Shumaker, *Gorbachev and the German Question,* 135.
27. Baker with DeFrank, *Politics of Diplomacy,* 196–98.
28. For example, the agreements of Brest-Litovsk in 1918, Rapallo in 1922, and the Molotov-Ribbentrop Accord in 1939.
29. Genscher, *Rebuilding a House Divided,* 339–40.
30. Baker, telephone interview by author, May 22, 2000.
31. Excerpt of letter from Bush to Kohl can be found in Bush and Scowcroft, *A World Transformed,* 240–41.
32. "Memorandum of Telephone Conversation between Bush and Kohl, February 13, 1990," Telcons and Memcons—Bush/Kohl, Bush Presidential Records, George Bush Presidential Library.
33. Ibid.
34. Beschloss and Talbott, *At the Highest Levels,* 190.
35. Zelikow and Rice, *Germany Unified,* 196.
36. Bush and Scowcroft, *A World Transformed,* 245.
37. Ibid., 253.
38. Ibid., 253.
39. Original list in memorandum from Zelikow through Blackwill to Scowcroft and Gates on Mar. 12, 1990, "The Two Plus Four Agenda," National Security Council Files, George Bush Presidential Library. A summary of this memorandum can be found in Zelikow and Rice, *Germany Unified,* 227.
40. A record of these telephone calls can be found in the "Presidential Telcons Notebook (January–June 1990)," National Security Council Files, Bush Presidential Records, George Bush Presidential Library.
41. "Results of the Parliamentary Elections in East Germany, March 18, 1990," in Jarausch and Gransow, eds., *Uniting Germany,* 128.
42. "Memorandum of Telephone Conversation between Bush and Kohl, March 20, 1990," Telcons and Memcons—Bush/Kohl, Bush Presidential Records, George Bush Presidential Library.
43. Baker with DeFrank, *Politics of Diplomacy,* 232.

44. Zelikow and Rice, *Germany Unified*, 246.
45. "Remarks at the Oklahoma State University Commencement Ceremony in Stillwater, May 4, 1990," *Public Papers of the President of the United States: George Bush, 1989–1993*, 1990 Book I—January 1 to June 30, 1990, 627.
46. Ibid.
47. Excerpt in Fritsch-Bournazel, *Europe and German Unification*, 66–67.
48. Summary of proposals found in Bush and Scowcroft, *A World Transformed*, 293.
49. Detailed information concerning the Washington summit can be found in White House Press Office, Fitzwater's Files, Subject File: USSR-US/USSR Summit 5/30/90–6/03/90, Bush Presidential Records, George Bush Presidential Library.
50. "Texts of Remarks by the President During Toast Honoring Soviet President Mikhail Gorbachev, the White House, Washington, D.C.," May 31, 1990, White House Press Office, Fitzwater's Files, Subject File: USSR-US/USSR Summit, 5/30/90–6/03/90 [1], Bush Presidential Records, George Bush Presidential Library.
51. Bush and Scowcroft, *A World Transformed*, 282.
52. Ibid.
53. Ibid., 282–83.
54. "Press Conference by the President and President Mikhail Gorbachev, the East Room," June 3, 1990, White House Press Office, Fitzwater's Files, Subject File: USSR-US/USSR Summit: 5/30/90–6/03/90, Bush Presidential Records, George Bush Presidential Library. Video footage provided by the George Bush Presidential Library.
55. Beschloss and Talbott, *At the Highest Levels*, 230.
56. Baker with DeFrank, *Politics of Diplomacy*, 255.
57. Bush and Scowcroft, *A World Transformed*, 295.
58. "Kohl on His Caucasus Meeting with Gorbachev, July 17, 1990," in Jarausch and Gransow, eds., *Uniting Germany*, 175–78.
59. Thatcher, *Downing Street Years*, 792.
60. "Treaty on the Final Settlement with Respect to Germany, September 12, 1990," in Jarausch and Gransow, eds., *Uniting Germany*, 204–208.
61. Cheney, telephone interview with Greene, Mar. 7, 1997.
62. Baker, telephone interview by author, May 22, 2000.
63. Ibid.
64. Scowcroft, telephone interview by author, May 23, 2000.
65. Ibid.

Chapter 4. A Glimpse of the Post–Cold War World

1. Brent Scowcroft, interview with John Robert Greene, June 11, 1997. Transcript on closed reserve at the Bush Presidential Library.
2. "National Security Decision Directive Number 99: United States Security Strategy for the Near East and South Asia," July 12, 1983, folder "Working Files Iraq—Pre 8/12/90," National Security Council, Richard Haass Files, Bush Presidential Records, George Bush Presidential Library.
3. Bush and Scowcroft, *A World Transformed*, 306.
4. National Security Directive 26, 10/02/1989, Subject: U.S. Policy Toward the Persian Gulf, Bush Presidential Records, George Bush Presidential Library.

5. U.S. exports to Iraq in 1989 were $1.2 billion (mostly agricultural commodities) and imports from Iraq in 1989 were $2.4 billion (mostly crude petroleum). See "Facsimile from Alixe Glen to Marlin Fitzwater," Aug. 2, 1990, folder "Iraq 1990," White House Press Office, Fitzwater Files, Subject File: Alpha File, Box 17, Bush Presidential Records, George Bush Presidential Library.
6. See for example, "Memorandum of Telephone Conversation between the President and King Hussein of Jordan," July 31, 1990, folder "Working Files Iraq—Pre 8/12/90," National Security Council, Richard Haass Files, Bush Presidential Records, George Bush Presidential Library.
7. Baker with DeFrank, *Politics of Diplomacy,* 331.
8. "Statement by the Deputy Press Secretary," Aug. 2, 1990, folder "Kuwait-Iraq/ Middle East," National Security Council, Roman Popadiuit Files, Bush Presidential Records, George Bush Presidential Library.
9. "NSC Meeting on the Persian Gulf," Aug. 3, 1990, folder "Kuwait-Iraq/Middle East Folder," National Security Council, Roman Popadiuit Files, Bush Presidential Records, George Bush Presidential Library.
10. Ibid.
11. Ibid.
12. See "Presidential Calls During Iraq-Kuwait Crisis," undated, folder "Kuwait-Iraq/Middle East Folder," National Security Council, Roman Popadiuit Files, Bush Presidential Records, George Bush Presidential Library; and "George Bush Library Withdrawal Sheets for Memcons and Telcons," folder "Working Files Iraq—Pre 8/12/90," National Security Council, Richard Haass Files, Bush Presidential Records, George Bush Presidential Library.
13. See for example "Minutes of NSC Meeting on Iraqi Invasion of Kuwait," Aug. 5, 1990, and "Minutes of NSC Meeting on Iraqi Invasion of Kuwait," Aug. 6, 1990, folder "Kuwait-Iraq/Middle East," National Security Council, Roman Popadiuit Files, Bush Presidential Records, George Bush Presidential Library.
14. "Minutes of NSC Meeting on Iraqi Invasion of Kuwait," Aug. 6, 1990, folder "Kuwait-Iraq/Middle East," National Security Council, Roman Popadiuit Files, Bush Presidential Records, George Bush Presidential Library.
15. National Security Directive 45, 08/20/1990, Subject: U.S. Policy in Response to the Iraqi Invasion of Kuwait, Bush Presidential Records, George Bush Presidential Library.
16. See United Nations Security Council Resolution 660 (Aug. 2, 1990), 661 (Aug. 6, 1990), 662 (Aug. 9, 1990), 664 (Aug. 18, 1990), and 665 (Aug. 25, 1990), Security Council Resolutions—1990, Department of Public Relations, the United Nations.
17. Baker, telephone interview by author, May 22, 2000.
18. "Soviet Union–United States Joint Statement on the Persian Gulf Crisis, September 9, 1990," *Public Papers of the President of the United States: George Bush, 1989–1993,* 1990, 1204–13.
19. See folder "Gorbachev Correspondence," National Security Council, Nicholas Burns Files, Bush Presidential Records, George Bush Presidential Library.
20. "Cable #30468/Matlock," Aug. 30, 1990, James A. Baker III Institute for Public Policy, www.bakerinstitute.org/vrtour/gulf_war_col_tour/GWC_images/gulfwar_006_full.jpg
21. Baker with DeFrank, *Politics of Diplomacy,* 2–3.
22. Ibid., 305.

23. Ibid., 306.
24. See "Memorandum for the President from James A. Baker III, Subject: Gulf Trip," Nov. 6, 1990, and "Memorandum for the President from James A. Baker III, Subject: Cairo Meetings," Nov. 7, 1990, folder "Working Files Iraq—November 1990," National Security Council, Richard Haass Files, Bush Presidential Records, George Bush Presidential Library.
25. "Memorandum for the President from James A. Baker III, Subject: Cairo Meetings," Nov. 7, 1990.
26. The Chinese made it clear that they would only vote yes if the United States agreed to a presidential visit to China and the lifting of the economic sanctions that were imposed after Tiananmen Square. It was a bribe Baker was not willing to make.
27. Baker with DeFrank, *Politics of Diplomacy*, 310.
28. "Memorandum for the President from James A. Baker III, Subject: My day in Moscow," Nov. 8, 1990, folder "Working Files Iraq—November 1990," National Security Council, Richard Haass Files, Bush Presidential Records, George Bush Presidential Library.
29. Ibid.
30. "Memorandum for the President from James A. Baker III, Subject: London Meetings," Nov. 10, 1990, folder "Working Files Iraq—November 1990," National Security Council, Richard Haass Files, Bush Presidential Records, George Bush Presidential Library.
31. Ibid.
32. Baker with DeFrank, *Politics of Diplomacy*, 318.
33. Ibid., 322.
34. See United Nations Security Council Resolution 678 (Nov. 29, 1990), Security Council Resolutions—1990, Department of Public Relations, the United Nations.
35. Freedman and Karsh, *Gulf Conflict*, 211.
36. Quotes based on handwritten notes taken by James Baker, "Bipartisan Leadership Meeting, White House," Nov. 14, 1990, James A. Baker III Institute for Public Policy, www.bakerinstitute.org/vrtour/gulf_war_col_tour/GWC _images/gulfwar_015_full.jpg
37. Baker with DeFrank, *Politics of Diplomacy*, 338.
38. Quoted in Bush and Scowcroft, *A World Transformed*, 445. For an expanded record of Senator Kennedy's remarks see "War Means Death and Destruction," U.S. Senate, Jan. 10, 1991, 102d Congress (1991–92), Congressional Record Text.
39. Quoted in Bush and Scowcroft, *A World Transformed*, 445. For an expanded record of the debate see for example "Authorizing Use of U.S. Armed Forces Pursuant to UN Security Council Resolution," U.S. Senate, Jan. 12, 1991, and "Authorization for Use of Military Force Against Iraq Resolution," U.S. Senate, Jan. 11, 1991, 102d Congress (1991–92), Congressional Record Text.
40. United Nations Security Council Resolution 678.
41. Bush and Scowcroft, *A World Transformed*, 446.
42. George Bush, interview with David Frost, Public Broadcast System (PBS) (first broadcast January 2, 1991).
43. George Bush, interview with David Frost, *One on One with David Frost: George Bush: A President's Story*, Arts and Entertainment Network (A&E) (first broadcast June, 1998).

44. R. W. Apple Jr., quoted in Barilleaux and Rozell, *Power and Prudence,* 25.

45. Freedman and Karsh, *Gulf Conflict,* 358.

46. Baker with DeFrank, *Politics of Diplomacy,* 289.

47. For details on foreign commitments see "Fact Sheet: Desert Shield," Feb. 13, 1991, folder "Iraq 1991 [2]," OA/ID 12918, Subject File, Alpha File, Box 17, Fitzwater Files, Bush Presidential Records, George Bush Presidential Library.

48. Baker with DeFrank, *Politics of Diplomacy,* 295.

49. Scowcroft, interview with Greene, June 11, 1997.

50. "Responding to Saddam's Pre-January 15 Initiatives, Deputies Committee Top Secret Working Paper," Dec. 31, 1990, folder "Working Files Iraq—January 1991," National Security Council, Richard Haass Files, Bush Presidential Records, George Bush Presidential Library. Also see "Participants: Deputy Committee Meetings on Gulf Crisis," undated, folder "Minutes for DC Meetings on Gulf," National Security Council, Richard Haas Files, Bush Presidential Records, George Bush Presidential Library.

51. "Responding to Saddam's Pre-January 15 Initiatives, Deputies Committee Top Secret Working Paper," Dec. 31, 1990, folder "Working Files Iraq—January 1991," National Security Council, Richard Haass Files, Bush Presidential Records, George Bush Presidential Library.

52. Ibid.

53. Ibid.

54. See NODIS: *Flash cable from American Embassy, Baghdad to Secretary of State: Iraqi Response to U.S. Offer of Meeting Dates,* undated, folder "Working Files Iraq—January 1991," National Security Council, Richard Haass Files, Bush Presidential Records, George Bush Presidential Library.

55. See "NODIS: Flash cable from American Embassy, Baghdad to Secretary of State: Iraqi Response to U.S. Offer of Meeting Dates," undated, folder "Working Files Iraq—January 1991," National Security Council, Richard Haass Files, Bush Presidential Records, George Bush Presidential Library.

56. See for example "Rose Garden Remarks by the President Following Meeting with Coalition Ambassadors," undated, folder "Working Files Iraq—December 1990," National Security Council, Richard Haas Files, Bush Presidential Records, Bush Presidential Records, George Bush Presidential Library.

57. "Memorandum of Telephone Conversation between President Bush and President Mitterand of France," Jan. 3, 1991, folder "Working Files Iraq—January 1991," National Security Council, Richard Haass Files, Bush Presidential Records, George Bush Presidential Library.

58. Ibid.

59. Baker with DeFrank, *Politics of Diplomacy,* 346.

60. Scowcroft, interview with Greene, June 11, 1997.

61. Cheney, telephone interview with Greene, Mar. 7, 1997.

62. Ibid.

63. Ibid.

64. Bush and Scowcroft, *A World Transformed,* 354.

65. Baker with DeFrank, *Politics of Diplomacy,* 409.

66. Bush and Scowcroft, *A World Transformed,* 381.

67. Dick Cheney, interview on PBS Frontline/BBC, undated, http://www.pbs .org/wgbh/pages/frontline/gulf/oral/cheney/1.html

68. Baker with DeFrank, *Politics of Diplomacy,* 409.

69. United Nations Security Council Resolution 678.

70. Undated call sheet, folder "Working Files Iraq—January 1991," National Security Council, Richard Haass Files, Bush Presidential Records, George Bush Presidential Library.

71. See for example "Memorandum of Telephone Conversation between President Bush and President Mubarak of Egypt," Jan. 21, 1991, and "Memorandum of Telephone Conversation between President Bush and President Mitterand of France," Jan. 20, 1991, folder "Working Files Iraq—January 1991," National Security Council, Richard Haass Files, Bush Presidential Records, George Bush Presidential Library.

72. "Memorandum of Telephone Conversation between President Bush and President Mitterand of France."

73. "President's Letter to Prime Minister Shamir RE UN Security Council Resolution 672," Oct. 18, 1990, folder "Working Files Iraq—October 1990," National Security Council, Richard Haass Files, Bush Presidential Records, George Bush Presidential Library. See also United Nations Security Council Resolution 672 (Oct. 12, 1990), Security Council Resolutions—1990, Department of Public Relations, the United Nations.

74. White House Situation Room Report, "Public Affairs Strategy for the Kuwait/Iraq Crisis," Aug. 1990, folder "Kuwait-Iraq/Middle East," National Security Council, Roman Popadiuit Files, Bush Presidential Records, George Bush Presidential Library.

75. "Memorandum of Conversation of One-on-One Meeting between the President and Israeli Prime Minister Shamir," Dec. 11, 1990, folder "Working Files Iraq—December 1990," National Security Council, Richard Haass Files, Bush Presidential Records, George Bush Presidential Library.

76. Ibid. Portions of Shamir's response are redacted, but a recounting of the conversation can be found in Bush and Scowcroft, *A World Transformed*, 425.

77. Bush and Scowcroft, *A World Transformed*, 454.

78. Ibid., 456.

79. Ibid.

80. Ibid.

81. Baker with DeFrank, *Politics of Diplomacy*, 396.

82. Ibid, 397.

83. "Gorbachev Call to Bush," Feb. 21, 1991, folder "Working Files Iraq—February 1991," National Security Council, Richard Haass Files, Bush Presidential Records, George Bush Presidential Library.

84. Untitled letter from Bush to Gorbachev, Feb. 18, 1991, and untitled letter from Bush to Gorbachev, Feb. 19, 1991, folder "Working Files Iraq—February 1991," National Security Council, Richard Haass Files, Bush Presidential Records, George Bush Presidential Library.

85. "Flash to London, Paris, Ankara, Cairo, Riyadh, Taif, Damascus, Tel Aviv, Rome, Canberra," undated, folder "Working Files Iraq—February 1991," National Security Council, Richard Haass Files, Bush Presidential Records, George Bush Presidential Library.

86. See "Points for Calls on Gulf state of play," folder "Working Files Iraq—February 1991," National Security Council, Richard Haass Files, Bush Presidential Records, George Bush Presidential Library.

87. "Memorandum of Telephone Conversation between President Bush and Presi-

dent Mitterand," Feb. 19, 1991, folder "Working Files Iraq—February 1991," National Security Council, Richard Haass Files, Bush Presidential Records, George Bush Presidential Library.

88. "Gorbachev Call to Bush."
89. "Phone call to Gorbachev," Feb. 22, 1991, folder "Working Files Iraq—February 1991," National Security Council, Richard Haass Files, Bush Presidential Records, George Bush Presidential Library.
90. Ibid.
91. Ibid.
92. Baker with DeFrank, *Politics of Diplomacy,* 405–406.
93. Ibid, 406.
94. "Address to the Nation on the Suspension of Allied Offensive Combat Operations in the Persian Gulf, February 27, 1991," *Public Papers of the President of the United States: George Bush, 1989–1993,* 1991, Book I, 187–88. For an explanation of announcement strategy see "Memorandum from Marlin Fitzwater to Governor Sununu," Jan. 14, 1991, folder "Iraq 1991 [2]," OA/ID 12918, Subject File: Alpha File, Box 17, Fitzwater Files, Bush Presidential Records, George Bush Presidential Library.
95. See for example Greene, *The Presidency of George Bush,* 130–31.
96. "Memorandum for Correspondents," Aug. 27, 1992, folder "Desert Storm," OA/ID 12908, White House Press Office, Fitzwater Papers, Bush Presidential Records, George Bush Presidential Library.
97. For a more complete examination of the discontent see Atkinson, *Crusade,* 472–77.
98. Peter Applebome, *New York Times,* Jan. 16, 1992.
99. Atkinson, *Crusade,* 497.
100. Bush, interview with Frost, *One on One with David Frost: George Bush: A President's Story.*
101. Cheney, telephone interview with Greene, Mar. 7, 1997.
102. Scowcroft, interview with Greene, June 11, 1997.
103. Baker with DeFrank, *Politics of Diplomacy,* 511.
104. Bush and Scowcroft, *A World Transformed,* 548.
105. "Notes of luncheon meeting between George Bush and Mikhail Gorbachev," Oct. 29, 1991, National Security Council, Nicholas Burns Files, Bush Presidential Records, George Bush Presidential Library.
106. Lafeber, *America, Russia, and the Cold War,* 361.
107. Baker with DeFrank, *Politics of Diplomacy,* 512.
108. Baker, telephone interview by author, May 22, 2000.
109. William Schneider, "What Would Defeating Saddam Trigger?" *The Atlantic Online,* Nov. 26, 2002.

Chapter 5. "When You Lose Your Best Enemy"

1. Baker, telephone interview by author, May 22, 2000.
2. Robert Gates, interview on PBS Frontline/BBC, undated, http://www.pbs.org/wgbh/pages/frontline/gulf/oral/gates/1.html
3. Baker with DeFrank, *Politics of Diplomacy,* 282–83.
4. Powell, telephone interview by author, Aug. 7, 2000.

5. Jack F. Matlock Jr., speech at a luncheon for the Society for Historians of American Foreign Relations, Boston, Jan. 6, 2001.

6. Baker with DeFrank, *Politics of Diplomacy*, 294–95.

7. *Theme Paper: Perestroyka and U.S.-Soviet Economic Relations*, May 21, 1990, Department of State Freedom of Information Act Electronic Reading Room, http://foia.state.gov/

8. Ibid.

9. Matlock, *Autopsy on an Empire*, 293.

10. Gorbachev, *Memoirs*, 673.

11. *Theme Paper: European Security*, May 22, 1990, Department of State Freedom of Information Act Electronic Reading Room, http://foia.state.gov/

12. Matlock, *Autopsy on an Empire*, 422–23.

13. Chafetz, *Gorbachev, Reform, and the Brezhnev Doctrine*, 124.

14. Matlock, *Autopsy on an Empire*, 447. Polls conducted by Yuri Levada's All-Union Public Opinion Center.

15. Ibid.

16. Oberdorfer, *From the Cold War to a New Era*, 442–43.

17. Powell with Persico, *My American Journey*, 537.

18. Powell, telephone interview by author, Aug. 7, 2000.

19. Powell with Persico, *My American Journey*, 537.

20. Bush and Scowcroft, *A World Transformed*, 511.

21. Based on Telcon and Memcon records, Bush Presidential Library.

22. Matlock, interview by author, Boston, Jan. 6, 2001.

23. Ibid.

24. Ibid.

25. See handwritten note by Bob Gates, undated, folder "Gorbachev [2 of 2]," OA/ID 41504, Burns/Hewitt Files, Box 1, National Security Council, Bush Presidential Records, George Bush Presidential Library.

26. White House Situation Room Report, "TASS Overview of 'State of Emergency,'" Aug. 19, 1991, folder "USSR—Part 1 of 4: Moscow Coup Attempt (1991) [2]," OA/ID 41563, NSC, White House Situation Room Files Box 1, Bush Presidential Records, George Bush Presidential Library.

27. White House Situation Room Report, "Xinhua Reports Tanks on Moscow Streets," Aug. 19, 1991, folder "USSR—Part 1 of 4: Moscow Coup Attempt (1991) [2]," OA/ID 41563, NSC, White House Situation Room Files Box 1, Bush Presidential Records, George Bush Presidential Library.

28. Presidential Press Conference from Walker's Point, Kennebunkport, Maine, Aug. 19, 1991. Video footage provided by the George Bush Presidential Library.

29. Quoted in Bush and Scowcroft, *A World Transformed*, 524.

30. Ibid.

31. White House Situation Room Report, "Yanayev Denies State Coup, Comments on Gorbachev Status," Aug. 19, 1991, folder "USSR—Part 1 of 4: Moscow Coup Attempt (1991) [1]," OA/ID 41563, NSC, White House Situation Room Files Box 1, Bush Presidential Records, George Bush Presidential Library.

32. Reported by CNN on Aug. 22, 1991. Video footage provided by the Bush Presidential Library.

33. "Memorandum of telephone conversation between George Bush and Boris

Yeltsin," Aug. 20, 1991, National Security Council, Nicholas Burns/Ed Hewitt Files, Bush Presidential Records, George Bush Presidential Library. Also quoted in Bush and Scowcroft, *A World Transformed,* 527.

34. Press conference on Aug. 20, 1991. Video footage provided by the George Bush Presidential Library.
35. "Memorandum of telephone conversation between George Bush and Mikhail Gorbachev," Aug. 21, 1991, National Security Council, Nicholas Burns Files, Bush Presidential Records, George Bush Presidential Library. See also Bush and Scowcroft, *A World Transformed,* 531–32.
36. Baker, telephone interview by author, May 22, 2000.
37. Based on an analysis of the Telcon and Memcon records, George Bush Presidential Library.
38. Bush's Presidential Diary quoted in Bush and Scowcroft, *A World Transformed,* 548.
39. Gorbachev, *Memoirs,* 626–45.
40. Ibid., 642.
41. Ibid., 646.
42. Ibid., 659.
43. Bush and Scowcroft, *A World Transformed,* 555.
44. "Memorandum of telephone conversation between George Bush and Boris Yeltsin," Dec. 8, 1991, folder "USSR Chrons—Dec 1991 [2 of 3]," OA/ID 41504, National Security Council, Nicholas Burns/Ed Hewitt Files, Bush Presidential Records, George Bush Presidential Library.
45. Bush and Scowcroft, *A World Transformed,* 555–56.
46. "Draft Statement on Results of Ukrainian Referendum," Dec. 2, 1991, folder "USSR Chrons—Dec 1991 [2 of 3]," OA/ID 41504, National Security Council, Nicholas Burns/Ed Hewitt Files, Bush Presidential Records, George Bush Presidential Library; Scowcroft, telephone interview by author, May 23, 2000.
47. Gorbachev, *Memoirs,* 665.
48. Quoted in Bush and Scowcroft, *A World Transformed,* 541.
49. Ibid.
50. Baker with DeFrank, *Politics of Diplomacy,* 560.
51. Quoted in Bush and Scowcroft, *A World Transformed,* 542.
52. Scowcroft, telephone interview by author, May 23, 2000.
53. "Remarks to the Supreme Soviet of the Republic of the Ukraine in Kiev, Soviet Union, August 1, 1991," *Public Papers of the Presidents of the United States: George Bush,* 1991, Book II—July 1 to December 31, 1991, 1007.
54. Matlock., interview by author, Boston, Jan. 6, 2001.
55. Baker with DeFrank, *Politics of Diplomacy,* 525.
56. For information on Republic Leaders see "Republic Leaders 12/23/91," Dec. 24, 1991, folder "Commonwealth," OA/ID 41503, National Security Council, Nicholas Burns Files, Box 3, Bush Presidential Records, George Bush Presidential Library.
57. "Talking Points: Guidance on Commonwealth Agreement," undated, folder "Commonwealth," OA/ID 41503, National Security Council, Nicholas Burns Files, Box 3, Bush Presidential Records, George Bush Presidential Library.
58. "Draft Statement of Resignation of President Gorbachev," Dec. 24, 1991, National Security Council, Nicholas Burns Files, Bush Presidential Records, George Bush Presidential Library.

59. "Memorandum of telephone conversation between George Bush and Mikhail Gorbachev," Dec. 25, 1991, National Security Council, Nicholas Burns Files, Bush Presidential Records, George Bush Presidential Library.

60. Fitzwater, telephone interview by author, May 9, 2000.

61. See "Draft Joint Statement on Secretary Baker's Visit to Ukraine," undated, folder "USSR Chrons—Dec 1991 [2 of 3]," OA/ID 41504, National Security Council, Nicholas Burns /Ed Hewitt Files, Box 1, Bush Presidential Records, George Bush Presidential Library.

62. Gorbachev, *Memoirs,* 671

63. Address from the Oval Office, Dec. 25, 1991. Video footage provided by the George Bush Presidential Library.

64. See "Camp David Declaration on New Relations by President Bush and President Yeltsin," Feb. 1, 1992, folder "Russia," OA/ID 01498, National Security Council, Nicholas Burns Files, Box 3, Bush Presidential Records, George Bush Presidential Library.

65. This would mean that intercontinental ballistic missiles would no longer have multiple warheads that could be targeted separately.

66. Zelikow and Rice, *Germany Unified,* 7.

67. Ibid.

68. See Haynes and Klehr, *VENONA.*

69. Gorbachev, *On My Country,* 84.

70. Ibid., 158.

71. Yeltsin, *Struggle for Russia,* 105–106.

72. Matlock, interview by author, Boston, Jan. 6, 2001.

73. Matlock, *Autopsy on an Empire,* 650.

Chapter 6. The Prudent Cold Warrior

1. Gaddis, *We Now Know,* 294.

2. Meese, *With Reagan,* 163.

3. Schultz, *Turmoil and Triumph,* 1131.

4. Smith, *The Cold War,* 149.

5. See Porter's quote on handwritten note by Bob Gates, undated, folder "Gorbachev [2 of 2]," OA/ID 41504, Burns/Hewitt Files, Box 1, National Security Council, Bush Presidential Records, George Bush Presidential Library.

6. Fitzwater, telephone interview by author, May 9, 2000.

7. Baker, telephone interview by author, May 22, 2000.

8. Scowcroft, telephone interview by author, May 23, 2000.

9. Powell, telephone interview by author, Aug. 7, 2000.

10. George Bush, letter to author, July 3, 2001.

11. Simply stated, the idea behind the policy of containment was to contain the Soviet Union and communism from spreading further in Europe until it decayed from within and brought the Soviets to the bargaining table.

12. Gaddis, *We Now Know,* 54.

13. Russell, *George F. Kennan's Strategic Thought,* 10.

14. Matlock, speech given at a luncheon for the Society of Historians of American Foreign Relations, Boston, Jan. 6, 2001.

15. Scowcroft, interview with Greene, June 11, 1997.

16. Scowcroft, telephone interview by author, May 23, 2000.

17. Hill, *Cold War Chronology*, 327.
18. Fitzwater, telephone interview by author, May 9, 2000.
19. Ibid.
20. Reagan, *An American Life*, 715.
21. Matlock, speech given at a luncheon for the Society of Historians of American Foreign Relations, Boston, Jan. 6, 2001.
22. Matlock, interview by author, Boston, Jan 6, 2001.
23. "Excepts of Remarks for Vice President George Bush Announcement Speech, Houston Texas," Oct. 12, 1987, folder "Debate Material [2 of 2]," OA/ID 14322, David Bates Files, Assistant to the Vice President and Deputy Chief of Staff, Box 1, Bush Vice-Presidential Records, George Bush Presidential Library.
24. Scowcroft, telephone interview by author, May 23, 2000.
25. Ibid.
26. Ibid.
27. George Bush, letter to author, July 3, 2001.
28. Quoted in Stokes, *Walls Came Tumbling Down*, 75.
29. Smith, *The Cold War*, 142.
30. Matlock, speech given at a luncheon for the Society of Historians of American Foreign Relations, Boston, Jan. 6, 2001.
31. Painter, *Cold War*, 104.
32. Matlock, *Autopsy on An Empire*, 658.
33. Gorbachev, *Memoirs*, 536.
34. For an excellent explanation of the shift in Soviet foreign policy, see Zelikow and Rice, *Germany Unified*, 15–18.
35. Unlike his non-interventionist policy towards Eastern Europe, Gorbachev was prepared to use armed force to maintain the Soviet Union itself, but, again, only as a last resort.
36. Matlock, *Autopsy On An Empire*, 658.
37. George Bush, letter to author, July 3, 2001.
38. George J. Church, "Men of the Year: A Tale of Two Bushes," Time, Jan. 7, 1991, 18–33.
39. Quoted in "Bush—*Time* Man of the Year," CNN, Dec. 30, 1990. Video footage provided by the George Bush Presidential Library.
40. Quoted in ibid.
41. Quoted in ibid.
42. Marlin Fitzwater, memorandum, "A Few Observations About 'The Domestic Agenda,'" Aug. 22, 1991, folder "Domestic Agenda [2]," OA/ID 12908, White House Press Office, Alpha File, Subject File, Box 7, Marlin Fitzwater Papers, Bush Presidential Records, George Bush Presidential Library.
43. Ibid.
44. Ibid.
45. Sununu, interview with Greene, July 8, 1997.
46. For a detailed description of foreign policymaking between 1947 and 1950, see Miscamble, *George F. Kennan*.
47. Scowcroft, telephone interview by author, May 23, 2000.
48. Ibid.
49. Fitzwater, telephone interview by author, May 9, 2000.
50. Powell, telephone interview by author, Aug. 7, 2000.
51. Baker with DeFrank, *Politics of Diplomacy*, 558.

52. Norman J. Orenstein, "Foreign Policy and the 1992 Election," *Foreign Affairs*, 71, no. 3 (summer 1992): 1.

53. "New world order" was a term Bush used in an address to a joint session of Congress in March 1991.

54. Hook and Spanier, *American Foreign Policy*, 301.

55. Brzezinski, *Second Chance*, 87.

56. James M. Lindsay, "The Superpower Blues," review of *Second Chance* by Zbigniew Brzezinski. *Washington Post Book World*, Mar. 25, 2007.

57. Albright quoted in Patterson et al., *American Foreign Relations*, 320.

58. There were at least nine significant terrorist actions against the United States during the 1990s including a bomb attack on the World Trade Center (1993), an assassination attempt against former president George H. W. Bush (1993), a bomb attack on U.S. military personnel in Saudi Arabia (1996), Al-Qaeda attacks on U.S. embassies in Kenya and Tanzania (1998), and the bomb attack against the USS *Cole* (2000).

59. Condoleezza Rice, "Promoting the National Interest," *Foreign Affairs* 79 (Jan.–Feb. 2000): 45–62.

60. Brands, *United States in the World*, 400.

61. Clinton, *My Life*, 833.

62. Ibid., 935.

63. See Gaddis, *Surprise, Security*.

64. Cheney, telephone interview with Greene, Mar. 7, 1997.

65. Brzezinski, *Second Chance*, 179.

Bibliography

Archival Collections

Baker, James A., III, Institute for Public Policy, Houston, Texas. http://www
.bakerinstitute.org

Bush, George, Presidential Library, College Station, Texas. http://bushlibrary
.tamu.edu. Bush Presidential Records; Bush Vice-Presidential Records; Audio-
Visual Archives.

Central Intelligence Agency. http://www.foia.ucia.gov. Electronic Document Release Center.

National Archives and Records Administration. http://www.nara.gov/nara. Records
Management and Research Room.

Reagan, Ronald, Presidential Library, Simi Valley, California. http://www.reagan
.utexas.edu. Reagan Presidential Records; Personal Collection of Ronald Reagan.

United Nations, Department of Public Relations. http://www.un.org/documents/
. Security Council Resolutions.

U.S. Department of State. http://foia.state.gov. Freedom of Information Act Electronic Reading Room.

U.S. National Security Council. http://www.whitehouse.gov/nsc

Wilson, Woodrow, International Center for Scholars. http://cwihp.si.edu. Cold
War International History Project.

Books, Articles, and Unpublished Documents

Ash, Timothy Garton. *In Europe's Name: Germany and the Divided Continent*. New
York: Vintage Books, 1993.

Atkinson, Rick. *Crusade: The Untold Story of the Persian Gulf War*. Boston:
Houghton Mifflin, 1993.

Baker, James A., III, with Thomas M. DeFrank. *The Politics of Diplomacy: Revolution, War & Peace, 1989–1992*. New York: Putnam's Sons, 1995.

Baker, James A., III, with Steve Fiffer. *"Work Hard, Study . . . and Keep Out of
Politics!": Adventures and Lessons from an Unexpected Public Life*. New York:
Putnam's Sons, 2006.

Barilleaux, Ryan J. *The Post-Modern Presidency: The Office after Ronald Reagan*.
New York: Praeger, 1988.

Barilleaux, Ryan J., and Mark J. Rozell. *Power and Prudence: The Presidency of George
H. W. Bush*. College Station: Texas A&M University Press, 2004.

Barry, John, and Evan Thomas. "Colin Powell: Behind the Myth." *Newsweek*, March
5, 2001, 36.

Bell, Coral. *The Reagan Paradox: American Foreign Policy in the 1980s*. New Bruns-
wick, N.J.: Rutgers University Press, 1989.

Beschloss, Michael R., and Strobe Talbott. *At the Highest Levels: The Inside Story of the End of the Cold War.* Boston: Little, Brown, 1993.

Bialer, Seweryn, and Michael Mandelbaum, eds. *Gorbachev's Russia and American Foreign Policy.* Boulder, Colo.: Westview, 1988.

Brands, H. W. *The United States in the World.* Vol. 2. Boston: Houghton Mifflin, 1994.

Broder, David S., and Bob Woodward. *The Man Who Would Be President: Dan Quayle.* New York: Simon & Schuster, 1992.

Brzezinski, Zbigniew. *Second Chance: Three American Presidents and the Crisis of American Superpower.* New York: Basic Books, 2007.

Bush, Barbara. *Barbara Bush: A Memoir.* New York: Scribner's Sons, 1994.

Bush, George. *All the Best, George Bush: My Life in Letters and Other Writings.* New York: Scribner, 1999.

————. Interview with David Frost, A&E, June 1998.

————. Interview with David Frost, PBS, January 2, 1991.

————. *Looking Forward.* Garden City, N.Y.: Doubleday, 1987.

————. *Public Papers of the Presidents: George Bush, 1989–1993,* 8 vols. Washington, D.C.: GPO, 1993.

Bush, George, and Brent Scowcroft. *A World Transformed.* New York: Knopf, 1998.

Buzzanco, Robert. "What Happened to the New Left? Toward a Radical Reading of American Foreign Relations." *Diplomatic History* 23, no. 4 (fall 1999): 575–607.

Campbell, Colin S. J., and Bert A. Rockman, eds. *The Bush Presidency: First Appraisals.* Chatham, N.J.: Chatham House, 1991.

Cannon, Lou. *Reagan.* New York: Putnam's Sons, 1982.

Chafetz, Glenn R. *Gorbachev, Reform, and the Brezhnev Doctrine: Soviet Policy toward Eastern Europe, 1985–1990.* Westport, Conn.: Praeger, 1993.

Church, George J. "Men of the Year: A Tale of Two Bushes." *Time,* January 7, 1991, 18–33.

Clinton, Bill. *My Life.* New York: Knopf, 2004.

Cohen, Warren I. *The Cambridge History of American Foreign Relations, IV: America in the Age of Soviet Power 1945–1991.* New York: Cambridge University Press, 1993.

Crockatt, Richard. *The Fifty Years War: The United States and the Soviet Union in World Politics, 1941–1991.* London: Routledge, 1995.

Cronin, James E. *The World the Cold War Made: Order, Chaos, and the Return of History.* New York: Routledge, 1996.

Degregorio, William A. *The Complete Book of U.S. Presidents.* New York: Wings Books, 1993.

Duffy, Michael, and Dan Goodgame. *Marching in Place: The Status Quo Presidency of George Bush.* New York: Simon & Shuster, 1992.

Dumbrell, John. *American Foreign Policy: Carter to Clinton.* New York: St. Martin's, 1997.

Duncan, Philip D. *Candidates '88.* Washington, D.C.: Congressional Quarterly, 1988.

Erickson, Paul D. *Reagan Speaks: The Making of an American Myth.* New York: New York University Press, 1985.

Evans, Eric J. *Thatcher and Thatcherism.* London: Routledge, 1997.

Fischer, Beth A. *The Reagan Reversal: Foreign Policy and the End of the Cold War.* Columbia: University of Missouri Press, 1997.

Fitzwater, Marlin. *Call the Briefing! Bush and Reagan, Sam and Helen: A Decade with Presidents and the Press.* New York: Times Books, 1995.

Freedman, Lawrence, ed. *Europe Transformed: Documents on the End of the Cold War.* New York: St. Martin's, 1990.

Freedman, Lawrence, and Efraim Karsh. *The Gulf Conflict, 1990–1991: Diplomacy and War in the New World Order.* Princeton, N.J.: Princeton University Press, 1992.

Fritsch-Bournazel, Renata. *Europe and German Unification.* New York: St. Martin's, 1992.

Gaddis, John Lewis. "International Relations Theory and the End of the Cold War." *International Security* 17 (winter 1992–93): 5–58.

———. "On Moral Equivalency and Cold War History." *Ethics and International Affairs* 10 (1996): 131–48.

———. *Surprise, Security, and the American Experience: The Joanna Jackson Goldman Memorial Lectures on American Civilization and Government.* Cambridge: Harvard University Press, 2004.

———. "The Tragedy of Cold War History." *Diplomatic History* 17, no. 1 (winter 1993): 1–16.

———. *The United States and the End of the Cold War: Implications, Reconsiderations, Provocations.* New York: Oxford University Press, 1992.

———. *We Now Know: Rethinking Cold War History.* Oxford: Clarendon, 1997.

Gaddis, John Lewis, and Paul Nitze. "NSC 68 and the Soviet Threat Reconsidered." *International Security* 4, no. 4 (spring 1980): 164–76.

Garthoff, Raymond L. *The Great Transition: American-Soviet Relations and the End of the Cold War.* Washington, D.C.: Brookings Institution, 1994.

Gates, Robert M. *From the Shadows: The Ultimate Insider's Story of Five Presidents and How They Won the Cold War.* New York: Simon & Shuster, 1996.

———. Interview on *Frontline*, PBS/BBC, undated. http://www.pbs.org/wgbh/pages/frontline/gulf/oral/gates/1.html

Gedmin, Jeffrey. *The Hidden Hand: Gorbachev and the Collapse of East Germany.* Washington, D.C.: AEI Press, 1992.

Genscher, Hans-Dietrich. *Rebuilding a House Divided: A Memoir by the Architect of Germany's Reunification.* Translated by Thomas Thornton. New York: Broadway Books, 1998.

Gilpin, Robert. "American Policy in the Post-Reagan Era." *Daedalus* 116 (summer 1987): 33–67.

Gimlin, Hoyt, ed. *President Bush: The Challenge Ahead.* Washington D.C.: Congressional Quarterly, 1989.

Goldman, Peter, and Tom Mathews. *The Quest for the Presidency, 1988.* New York: Simon & Schuster, 1989.

Gorbachev, Mikhail. *Memoirs: Mikhail Gorbachev.* New York: Doubleday, 1995.

———. *On My Country and the World.* Translated by George Shriver. New York: Columbia University Press, 2000.

———. *Perestroika and Soviet-American Relations.* Madison, Conn.: Sphinx, 1990.

Green, Fitzhugh. *George Bush: An Intimate Portrait.* New York: Hippocrene, 1989.

Greene, John Robert. *The Presidency of George Bush.* Lawrence: University Press of Kansas, 2000.

Greenstein, Fred I., ed. *Leadership in the Modern Presidency.* Cambridge: Harvard University Press, 1988.

Hannaford, Peter. *The Reagans: A Political Portrait.* New York: Coward-McCann, 1983.

Hannaford, Peter, ed. *Recollections of Reagan: A Portrait of Ronald Reagan.* New York: William Morrow, 1997.

Haynes, John Earl, and Harvey Klehr. *VENONA: Decoding Soviet Espionage in America.* New Haven, Conn.: Yale University Press, 1999.

Hertsgaard, Mark. "A Press Critic Charges: Journalists Played Dead for Reagan—Will They Roll Over Again for Bush?" *Washington Journalism Review* 11 (January–February 1989): 30–33.

Hill, Kenneth L. *Cold War Chronology: Soviet-American Relations, 1945–1991.* Washington, D.C.: Congressional Quarterly, 1993.

Hixon, Walter. *George F. Kennan: Cold War Iconoclast.* New York: Columbia University Press, 1989.

Hoffman, Elizabeth Cobbs. "Diplomatic History and the Meaning of Life: Toward a Global American History." *Diplomatic History* 21, no. 4 (fall 1997): 499–518.

Hogan, Michael J., ed. *The End of the Cold War: Its Meanings and Implications.* Cambridge, England: Cambridge University Press, 1992.

———, ed. *Paths to Power: The Historiography of American Foreign Relations to 1941.* Cambridge, England: Cambridge University Press, 2000.

———, ed. *America in the World: The Historiography of American Foreign Relations since 1941.* Cambridge, England: Cambridge University Press, 1995.

Hogan, Michael J., and Thomas G. Paterson, eds. *Explaining the History of American Foreign Relations.* Cambridge, England: Cambridge University Press, 1991.

Holm, Hans Henrik. *Whose World Order?: Uneven Globalization and the End of the Cold War.* Boulder, Colo.: Westview, 1995.

Hook, Steven W., and John Spanier, *American Foreign Policy since World War II.* 17th ed. Washington, D.C.: CQ Press, 2007.

Hosking, Geoffrey. *The Awakening of the Soviet Union.* Cambridge: Harvard University Press, 1990.

Hough, Jerry. *Russia and the West: Gorbachev and the Politics of Reform.* 2d ed. New York: Simon & Schuster, 1990.

Hyland, William G. *The Cold War Is Over.* New York: Random House, 1990.

Inderfurth, Karl F., and Loch K. Johnson, eds. *Decisions of the Highest Order: Perspectives on the National Security Council.* Pacific Grove, Calif.: Brooks/Cole, 1988.

Isaacs, Jeremy. *Cold War: An Illustrated History, 1945–1991.* Boston: Little, Brown, 1998.

Jarausch, Konrad H., and Volker Gransow, eds. *Uniting Germany: Documents and Debates, 1944–1993.* Translated by Allison Brown and Belinda Cooper. Providence, R.I.: Berghahn, 1994.

Kennan, George F. *At a Century's Ending: Reflections 1982–1995.* Norton, 1997.

———. *The Cloud of Danger: Current Realities of American Foreign Policy.* Boston: Little, Brown, 1977.

———. *Memoirs: 1925–1950.* Boston: Little, Brown, 1967.

Kennan, George F., and John Lukacs. *George F. Kennan and the Origins of Containment, 1944–1946: The Kennan-Lukacs Correspondence.* Columbia: University of Missouri Press, 1997.

Kennedy, Paul. *The Rise and Fall of the Great Powers: Economic Change and Military Conflict from 1500 to 2000.* New York: Random House, 1987.

Kolb, Charles. *White House Daze: The Unmaking of Domestic Policy in the Bush Years.* New York: Free Press, 1994.

Kugler, Richard L. *Commitment to Purpose: How Alliance Partnership Won the Cold War.* Santa Monica, Calif.: RAND, 1993.

Lafeber, Walter. *America, Russia, and the Cold War, 1945–2002.* Updated 9th ed. New York: McGraw-Hill, 2002.

Laird, Robbin F. *The Soviets, Germany, and the New Europe.* Boulder, Colo.: Westview, 1991.

Lebow, Richard Ned. *We All Lost the Cold War.* Princeton, N.J.: Princeton University Press, 1994.

Ledeen, Michael A. *Freedom Betrayed: How America Led a Global Democratic Revolution, Won the Cold War, and Walked Away.* Washington, D.C.: AEI Press, 1996.

Levering, Ralph B. *The Cold War: A Post–Cold War History.* Arlington Heights, Ill.: Harlan Davidson, 1994.

Lévesque, Jacques. *The Enigma of 1989: The USSR and the Liberation of Europe.* Translated by Keith Martin. Berkeley: University of California Press, 1997.

Levy, Peter B. *Encyclopedia of the Reagan-Bush Years.* Westport, Conn.: Greenwood, 1996.

Lindsay, James M. "The Superpower Blues," review of *Second Chance: Three Presidents and the Crisis of American Superpower* by Zbigniew Brzezinski. *Washington Post Book World,* March 25, 2007. http://washingtonpost.com

Lippmann, Walter. *The Cold War: A Study in U.S. Policy.* New York: Harper & Row, 1947.

Lundestad, Geir, ed. *The Fall of Great Powers: Peace, Stability, and Legitimacy.* New York: Oxford University Press, 1994.

Lynch, Allen. *The Cold War Is Over—Again.* Boulder, Colo.: Westview, 1992.

McAdams, A. James. *Germany Divided: From the Wall to Reunification.* Princeton, N.J.: Princeton University Press, 1993.

McMalla, Robert B. *Uncertain Perceptions: U.S. Cold War Crisis Decision Making.* Ann Arbor: University of Michigan Press, 1992.

McNamara, Robert S. *Out of the Cold: New Thinking for American Foreign Policy in the 21st Century.* New York: Simon & Schuster, 1989.

Mandelbaum, Michael, and Strobe Talbott. *Reagan and Gorbachev.* New York, Vintage, 1987.

Matlock, Jack F., Jr. *Autopsy on an Empire: The American Ambassador's Account of the Collapse of the Soviet Union.* New York: Random House, 1995.

———. *Reagan and Gorbachev: How the Cold War Ended.* New York: Random House, 2004.

———. Speech at a luncheon for the Society for Historians of American Foreign Relations, Boston, January 6, 2001.

Mauro, Tony. "Harvard's Memo to Bush; It's Not Too Late to Save the Presidential Press Conference." *Washington Journalism Review* 11 (January–February 1989): 36–37.

May, Ernest R. *American Cold War Strategy: Interpreting NSC-68.* Boston: St. Martin's, 1993.

Measuring Soviet GNP: Problems and Solutions: A Conference. Washington, D.C.: Central Intelligence Agency, Directorate of Intelligence, 1990.

Medhurst, Martin J., Robert L. Ivie, Philip Wander, and Robert L. Scott. *Cold War Rhetoric: Strategy, Metaphor, and Ideology.* East Lansing: Michigan State University Press, 1997.

Meese, Edwin. *With Reagan: The Inside Story.* Washington, D.C.: Regenery Gateway, 1992.

Merkl, Peter H. *German Unification in the European Context.* University Park: Pennsylvania State University Press, 1993.

Mervin, David. *George Bush and the Guardianship Presidency.* New York: St. Martin's, 1996.

Miscamble, Wilson D. *George F. Kennan and the Making of American Foreign Policy, 1947–1950.* Princeton, N.J.: Princeton University Press, 1992.

Morley, Morris H., ed. *Crisis and Confrontation: Ronald Reagan's Foreign Policy.* Totowa, N.J.: Rowman & Littlefield, 1988.

Muir, William Ker, Jr. *The Bully Pulpit: The Presidential Leadership of Ronald Reagan.* San Francisco: Institute for Contemporary Studies Press, 1992.

Nash, Garry B., and Ronald Schultz, eds. *Retracing the Past: Readings in the History of the American People.* Vol. 2. 4th ed. New York: Longman, 2000.

Neville, John F. *The Press, the Rosenbergs, and the Cold War.* Westport, Conn.: Praeger, 1995.

Ninkovich, Frank A. *Germany and the United States: The Transformation of the German Question since 1945.* New York: Twayne, 1995.

Nitze, Paul H., with Ann M. Smith and Steven L. Rearden. *From Hiroshima to Glasnost: At the Center of Decision: A Memoir.* New York: Grove Weidenfeld, 1989.

Oberdorfer, Don. *From the Cold War to a New Era: The United States and the Soviet Union, 1983–1991.* Baltimore: Johns Hopkins University Press, 1998.

Orenstein, Norman J. "Foreign Policy and the 1992 Election." *Foreign Affairs* 71, no. 3 (summer 1992): 1–16.

Oye, Kenneth A., Robert J. Lieber, and Donald Rothchild, eds. *Eagle Resurgent! The Reagan Era in American Foreign Policy.* Boston: Little, Brown, 1987.

Painter, David S. *The Cold War: An International History.* London: Routledge, 1999.

Parmet, Herbert S. *George Bush: The Life of a Lone Star Yankee.* New York: Scribner, 1997.

Patterson, Thomas G., J. Garry Clifford, Shane J. Maddock, Deborah Kisatsky, and Kenneth J. Hagan. *American Foreign Relations: A History.* Vol. 2. Brief ed. Boston: Houghton Mifflin, 2006.

Pittman, Avril. *From Ostpolitik to Reunification: West German–Soviet Political Relations since 1974.* Cambridge, England: Cambridge University Press, 1992.

Powell, Colin L., with Joseph E. Persico. *My American Journey.* New York: Random House, 1995.

"Proposals for a Free and Peaceful Europe," Current Policy No. 1179. Washington, D.C.: U.S. Department of State, Bureau of Public Affairs, 1989.

Reagan, Ronald. *An American Life.* New York: Simon & Schuster, 1990.

———. *Public Papers of the Presidents: Ronald Reagan, 1980–1989, 8 vols.* Washington, D.C.: Government Printing Office, 1989.

———. *The Reagan Diaries.* Edited by Douglass Brinkley. New York: HarperCollins, 2007.

Rice, Condoleezza. "Promoting the National Interest." *Foreign Affairs* 79 (January–February 2000): 45–62.

Ritter, Kurt, and David Henry. *Ronald Reagan: The Great Communicator.* New York: Greenwood, 1992.

Rose, Richard. *The Postmodern President: George Bush Meets the World.* Chatham, N.J.: Chatham House, 1991.

Rozell, Mark J. *The Press and the Bush Presidency.* Westport, Conn.: Praeger, 1996.

Runkel, David R. *Campaign for President: The Managers Look at '88.* Dover, Mass.: Auburn House, 1989.

Russell, Richard L. *George F. Kennan's Strategic Thought: The Making of an American Political Realist.* Westport, Conn.: Praeger, 1999.

Schieffer, Bob, and Gary Paul Gates. *The Acting President.* New York: Dutton, 1989.

Schneider, William. "What Would Defeating Saddam Trigger?" *The Atlantic Online,* November 26, 2002.

Schultz, George P. *Turmoil and Triumph: My Years as Secretary of State.* New York: Scribner's Sons, 1993.

Schwartz, Richard Alan. *The Cold War Reference Guide: A General History and Annotated Chronology, with Selected Biographies.* Jefferson, N.C.: McFarland, 1997.

Shumaker, David H. *Gorbachev and the German Question: Soviet–West German Relations, 1985–1990.* Westport, Conn.: Praeger, 1995.

Smith, Joseph, *The Cold War: Second Edition, 1945–1991.* Malden, Mass.: Blackwell, 1998.

Spence, Jonathan D. *The Search for Modern China.* 2d ed. New York: Norton, 1999.

Staar, Richard F., ed. *East-Central Europe and the USSR.* New York: St. Martin's, 1991.

Stempel, Guido H., III, and John W. Windhauser, eds. *The Media in the 1984 and 1988 Presidential Campaigns.* New York: Greenwood, 1991.

Stephanson, Anders. *Kennan and the Art of Foreign Policy.* Cambridge: Harvard University Press, 1989.

Strober, Deborah Hart, and Gerald S. Strober. *Reagan: The Man and His Presidency.* Boston: Houghton Mifflin, 1998.

Stokes, Gale. *The Walls Came Tumbling Down: The Collapse of Communism in Eastern Europe.* New York: Oxford University Press, 1993.

Stuckey, Mary E. *Playing the Game: The Presidential Rhetoric of Ronald Reagan.* New York: Praeger, 1990.

———. *The President as Interpreter-in-chief.* Chatham, N.J.: Chatham House, 1991.

Summy, Ralph, and Michael E. Salla, eds. *Why the Cold War Ended: A Range of Interpretations.* Westport, Conn.: Greenwood, 1995.

Szabo, Stephen F. *The Diplomacy of German Unification.* New York: St. Martin's, 1992.

Talbott, Strobe. *The Russians and Reagan.* New York: Vintage, 1984.

Thatcher, Margaret. *The Downing Street Years.* New York: HarperCollins, 1993.

Theme Paper: European Security, May 22, 1990, Department of State Freedom of Information Act Electronic Reading Room. http://foia.state.gov

Theme Paper: Perestroyka and U.S.-Soviet Economic Relations, May 21, 1990, Department of State Freedom of Information Act Electronic Reading Room. http://foia.state.gov

Thompson, Kenneth W., ed. *Foreign Policy in the Reagan Presidency: Nine Intimate Perspectives.* Lanham, Md.: University Press of America, 1993.

Tiefer, Charles. *The Semi-sovereign Presidency: The Bush Administration's Strategy for Governing without Congress.* Boulder, Colo.: Westview, 1994.

Tolz, Vera, compiled by, and Melanie Newton, ed. *The USSR in 1989: A Record of Events*. Boulder, Colo.: Westview, 1990.

Vogelle, William B. *Stepping Back: Nuclear Arms Control and the End of the Cold War*. Westport, Conn.: Praeger, 1994.

Walker, Martin. *The Cold War: A History*. New York: Henry Holt, 1993.

Watt, D. Cameron. "Intelligence and the Historian." *Diplomatic History* 14 (spring 1990): 199–204.

Weiler, Michael, and W. Barnett Pierce, eds. *Reagan and Public Discourse in America*. Tuscaloosa: University of Alabama Press, 1992.

Weinberger, Casper. *Fighting for Peace: Seven Critical Years in the Pentagon*. New York: Warner Books, 1990.

Whelan, Joseph G. *The Moscow Summit, 1988: Reagan and Gorbachev in Negotiation*. Boulder, Colo.: Westview, 1990.

Wilson, Theodore A. *The First Summit: Roosevelt and Churchill at Placenta Bay, 1941*. Lawrence: University Press of Kansas, 1991.

Wohlforth, William C., ed. *Witnesses to the End of the Cold War*. Baltimore: Johns Hopkins University Press, 1996.

Woodward, Bob. *The Commanders*. New York: Simon & Shuster, 1991.

X [Kennan, George F.]. "The Sources of Soviet Conduct." *Foreign Affairs* 25, no. 4 (July 1947): 566–82.

Yeltsin, Boris. *The Struggle for Russia*. Translated by Catherine A. Fitzpatrick. New York: Times Books, 1994.

Young, John W. *The Longman Companion to America, Russia and the Cold War 1941–1998*. London: Longman, 1999.

Zelikow, Philip, and Condoleezza Rice. *Germany Unified and Europe Transformed: A Study in Statecraft*. Cambridge: Harvard University Press, 1995.

Index

Photographs are indicated with *f*.

NSC meetings, 13; NSC review period, 18; Reagan's Cold War approach, xi; Reagan *vs.* Bush roles, 121–22, 128–29; Strategic Defense Initiative in summit meetings, 3

Ford administration, 7, 9, 10

Foreign Affairs, 129

Four Powers conference, 55–56, 60

France: and German reunification, 56, 57, 59, 60, 66; Persian Gulf War, 80. *See also* Mitterand, François

G-7 summits, 30, 38, 72

Gaddafi, Muammar, 104

Gaddis, John Lewis, 116

Galbraith, John Kenneth, 126

Gates, Robert, 7–8, 14*f*, 15, 32, 92

Geneva summit, 134

Genscher, Hans-Dietrich, 55, 60–61, 62, 72

Gephardt, Dick, 81

German Democratic Republic (GDR). *See* East Germany; German reunification

German reunification: Bush-Kohl meeting, 62–65; in Bush's Eastern Europe speeches, 18–20, 33–34; as Cold War endpoint, 119, 121; constitutional options, 65; Gorbachev's final policy position, 68–69, 70, 72–73; internal opinion, 54, 57–58; international perspectives, 54–55, 56–57, 59–60; Kohl-Gorbachev meeting, 60–61; Kohl's proposal, 58–59; NATO role development, 65–68; personal diplomacy importance, 73–74; timeline of events, 138–39; in Washington summit, 67–69, 70

Glaspie, April, 76

GNP statistics, Soviet Union, 2

Goldwater-Nichols Act, 10, 145*n*34

Gorbachev, Mikhail: authority problems, 91, 94–95, 99–104; Berlin wall collapse, 45–46, 50, 55; Brezhnev Doctrine rejection, 36–37, 41; Bush's first impression, 134; Bush's Moscow visit, 96–97; Cheney's prediction, 10; China visit, 34–35; coup attempt, 99–104; economic policy, 93–94; failure factors summarized, 111–15; German reunification, 60–61, 62, 68–69, 72–73, 119; Governor's Island meeting with Bush, 27–29; at Madrid meeting, 91; Malta conference, 39–40, 46–52;

Minsk agreement, 105–106; and nationalism movement, 40–41; NSC review period, 15–17; Persian Gulf War, 78, 79–80, 82, 85, 87 88; reform goals, 113–14, 124–25; resignation, 109–11; Strategic Defense Initiative, 3; timeline of events, 134–42; UN speech, 27; uranium/plutonium announcement, 18; Washington summit, 68–72; West Germany visit, 38. *See also* Soviet Union *entries*

Gore, Al, 126

Governor's Island meeting, 27–29

Graves, Howard, 79

Great Britain: and German reunification, 54–57, 66; Persian Gulf War, 80, 85; Soviet Union coup attempt, 99; Soviet Union economic aid, 98. *See also* Thatcher, Margaret

Greene, Robert, 90

Hamtramck, Michigan, Eastern Europe speech, 19–20

Heath, Edward, 53

Helinski Final Act, 58, 68–69, 70

Hungary, 34, 37, 38, 41

Hurd, Douglas, 55, 60, 62

Hu Yaobang, 34

Interdepartmental Groups (IGs), 6

International Monetary Fund, 72

Iran-Iraq War, 75–76

Iraq, 75–76, 131, 152*n*5

Iron Curtain speech, 143*n*1

Israel, 78, 85–87, 90–91

Jakes, Milos, 37

Japan, 82

Jaruzelski, General, 37–38

Johnson, Lyndon B., 84

Joint Chiefs of Staff, 10–11. *See also* Powell, Colin

Jordan, 76, 90–91

Kazakhstan, 110

Kennan, George, 18, 119–20

Kennedy, Edward, 81

Kennedy, Paul, 143*n*6

Kerry, John, 81

Kohl, Helmut: Berlin Wall collapse, 54; coup attempt in Soviet Union, 99; Four Powers proposal, 56; Gorbachev meeting, 61; NATO summit, 31. *See also* German reunification

Philippines, 47
Poindexter, John, 144n19
Poland, 19, 36–38, 58
Porter, Bruce, 118
post-Cold War policy directions, 129–32
Powell, Colin: background, 10–11; in
   G. W. Bush administration, 130; on
   Bush's policymaking style, 13–14; on
   Cold War endpoint, 119; on Gor-
   bachev and Bush, 27, 28; Persian Gulf
   War, 89, 92–93; as Reagan's NSC
   advisor, 5, 6, 144n19; Soviet Union
   dissolution, 107; Soviet Union visit,
   95–96
press conferences: Baker-Shevardnadze,
   78, 118–19; Berlin Wall collapse, ix,
   42–45, 55; coup attempt in Soviet
   Union, 99–100, 101; with Gorbachev,
   50, 70; Malta conference, 50; with
   Mitterand, 23–24
Primakov, Yevgeny, 87
Pugo, Boris, 99

Qian Qichen, 79
Quayle, Dan, 12, 71f, 145n44

Reagan, Ronald (and administration):
   Berlin Wall speech, 53; and Bush
   administration, 18, 29; Cold War approach summarized, x–xi, 120, 121–22;
   in Cold War endpoint perspectives,
   117–18; German reunification speech,
   53; Governor's Island meeting with
   Gorbachev, 27–29; Iran-Iraq War,
   75–76; media relations, 1–2; military
   spending, 113; and Mitterand, 23; NSC
   operations, 5–6, 144n19; timeline of
   events, 133–36
Reich, Robert, 126
Resolution 672, United Nations, 85
Resolution 678, United Nations, 78–80,
   81, 84
Reykjavik summit, 134–35
Rice, Condoleezza, 17, 112, 130–31
Ridgway, Rozanne, 29
Romania, 37, 51–52
Russian Federation, 110–11

Saddam Hussein, 104, 131. See also Iraq;
   Persian Gulf War
Saleh, Ali Abdullah, 80
sanctions: China, 35, 147n27, 153n26;
   Israel, 85

Saudi Arabia, 76, 77, 79, 82, 85, 93
Schabowski, Günter, 42
Schultz, George, 117
Schwarzkopf, Norman, 89
Scowcroft, Brent: arms control policies,
   3–4, 7, 25, 31; background/working
   style, 6–8; Berlin Wall collapse, 43,
   46; on Bush's policymaking approach,
   13, 128; China mission, 35; on Cold
   War endpoint, x–xi, 119, 123; Eastern Europe policy focus, 20, 29–30,
   120–21; Europeanization opposition,
   57; Four Powers conference, 55–56;
   German reunification, 73, 74; Malta
   conference, 39–40, 48, 51; on NSC review report, 16; Open Skies proposal,
   22; Persian Gulf War, 76–77, 82, 84,
   87, 90; photographs, 8f, 14f, 71f; Soviet
   Union dissolution, 101, 106, 107, 111;
   on speech writing conflicts, 19; Two-
   plus-Four proposal, 60
Scud missile attacks, on Israel, 86–87
SDI (Strategic Defense Initiative),
   2–3
Senior Interdepartmental Groups
   (SIGs), 6
Shamir, Yitzhak, 85, 86, 87
Shevardnadze, Eduard: Camp David
   meeting, 71f; CFE agreement, 62;
   German reunification, 60, 69, 72; on
   NSC review period, 14; Persian Gulf
   War, 78, 79; resignation, 95
short-range nuclear forces (SNF), 31, 33,
   38, 111
Shushkevich, Stanislav, 105
SIGs (Senior Interdepartmental
   Groups), 6
Slava, 47
Smith, Joseph, 118
SNF (short-range nuclear forces), 31, 33,
   38, 111
Solidarity, 19, 36–37
Soviet Union: Bush's visit, 96–97; in
   commencement speeches, 21–26;
   economic conditions, 93–94, 111–12;
   and German reunification, 58, 59–61,
   62, 65–69, 73–74, 119; internal unrest,
   94–95; Middle East Peace Conference, 90–91; Persian Gulf War, 78–80,
   82, 87–89, 92–93, 118–19; Powell's
   visit and assessment, 95–96; timeline
   of events, 133–42. See also Gorbachev,
   Mikhail; Warsaw Pact

Soviet Union, dissolution process: breakup process, 104–109; coup activity, 99–104; factors summarized, 111–15; leader transition, 109–11
Special Situation Group (SSG), 6
speech writing responsibilities, conflicts, 19
SSG (Special Situation Group), 6
staff and advisors, 4–5, 6–14
Stahl, Lesley, 44
Stalin, Joseph, 112
Staodubstev, Valery, 99
START II, 111, 142
State Department: German reunification, 60; Persian Gulf War, 92; during Reagan administration, 5–6; Soviet Union dissolution, 108; Soviet Union economy, 93. *See also* Baker, James
Strategic Arms Reduction Treaty, 111
Strategic Defense Initiative (SDI), 2–3
Sununu, John, 12–13, 14*f*, 43, 51, 127
Syria, 90–91

Talbott, Strobe, 4
technological advances, 3
Teltschik, Horst, 55, 60
terrorist attacks, 130, 131, 161*n8*
Texas A&M University, Soviet Union speech, 21–22
Thatcher, Margaret: Bush relationship, 56; on end of Cold War, 117; German reunification, 54, 56–57, 66, 72, 138; Gorbachev meeting, 40–41; NATO summit, 32; NSC review period, 18; Persian Gulf War, 80; Soviet Union economic aid, 98
Tiananmen Square massacre, 34–36, 153*n26*
Tibet, 147*n27*
Time magazine, 9, 126
tin-cup diplomacy, Persian Gulf War, 81–82
Tizyakov, A. I., 99
Tower, John, 6, 9, 145*n44*
Tower Board, 6
trade agreements: Iraq, 75–76, 152*n5*; U.S.-Soviet Union, 69–70. *See also* economic aid *entries*

transition period, staff changes, 4–5. *See also* National Security Council (NSC)
Truman, Harry, 143*n1*
Turkey, 79
Two-plus-Four proposal/talks, 60–61, 62, 73

Ukraine, 40, 106–107, 110
Union Treaty, 99, 104, 114
United Kingdom. *See* Great Britain
United Nations: Gorbachev's speech, 27, 30; Iraq sanctions, 131; Persian Gulf War, 77–80, 85

vice-presidential period: German reunification speech, 53; Gorbachev meeting, 27–29; loyalty character, 2; Moscow funeral attendance, 133, 134; timeline of events, 133–36
Vietnam legacy, Persian Gulf War, 83–85

Warsaw Pact: in commencement speeches, 24; and German reunification, 58, 59, 61–62, 121; internal conflicts, 37; in NATO summit discussions, 31; Ottawa meeting, 61–62
Washington Post, 18, 117
Washington summits, 68–72, 135
weapons of mass destruction, 76, 131
Webster, William, 11–12
Western Europe, in Boston University speech, 18, 23–24
West Germany: Gorbachev visit, 38; NATO summit, 31; Persian Gulf War, 82. *See also* German reunification; Kohl, Helmut
Wolfowitz, Paul, 87

Yanayev, Gennady, 99, 100, 101, 103–104
Yazov, Dmitri, 99
Yeltsin, Boris: during coup attempt, 100–101, 102–103; leadership transition, 109–10; Minsk agreement, 105–106, 108–109; popularity rise, 94–95; power consolidation, 109, 114
Yemen, 79, 80